Uncertain Worlds

Uncertain Worlds

World-Systems Analysis in Changing Times

Immanuel Wallerstein
Charles Lemert
Carlos Antonio Aguirre Rojas

with translations by George Ciccariello
and José A. Mota Lopes

Paradigm Publishers
Boulder • London

Copyright © 2013 Paradigm Publishers

Published in the United States by Paradigm Publishers, 5589 Arapahoe Avenue, Boulder, CO 80303 USA.

Paradigm Publishers is the trade name of Birkenkamp & Company, LLC, Dean Birkenkamp, President and Publisher.

Library of Congress Cataloging-in-Publication Data

Wallerstein, Immanuel Maurice, 1930–
  Uncertain worlds : world-systems analysis in changing times / b Immanuel Wallerstein, Carolos Antonio Aguirre Rojas, and Charles Lemert ; with translations by George Ciccariello.
     p. cm.
  Includes index.
  ISBN 978-1-59451-979-6 (paperback : alk. paper)
  1. Social history. 2. Social change. 3. Social systems. 4. Economic history. 5. Wallerstein, Immanuel Maurice, 1930– I. Aguirre Rojas, Carlos Antonio. II. Lemert, Charles C., 1937– III. Title.
  HN13.W3495 2012
  303.4—dc23

                                                                2012005996

Printed and bound in the United States of America on acid-free paper that meets the standards of the American National Standard for Permanence of Paper for Printed Library Materials.

Designed and Typeset by Straight Creek Bookmakers.

17 16 15 14 13   1 2 3 4 5

Contents

Introduction

Immanuel Wallerstein and the Critical "World-Systems Analysis" Perspective

Carlos Antonio Aguirre Rojas

"How is it possible to maintain a position of resistance when one is becoming an established theory?"

Immanuel Wallerstein, "The Itinerary of World-Systems Analysis, or How to Resist Becoming a Theory," 2002

Immanuel Wallerstein is today, without a doubt, one of the best-known social scientists in the world. As he is an acute observer of the most contemporary events, the author of an already classic and fundamental work on the history of capitalism, an active promoter of a total restructuring of the social sciences, and an implacable critic of the most common explanations for the phenomena and processes of the "long twentieth century," his figure and his work have been disseminated and projected the length and breadth of the five continents on our ever smaller and more interconnected planet. Through the numerous translations of his texts into the most diverse of languages, or through varying sorts of conferences, colloquia, symposiums, and university forums

Originally published in Immanuel Wallerstein, *La crisis estructural del capitalismo* (Mexico City: Contrahistorias, 2005), 5–56.

among historians, sociologists, economists, and political scientists, as well as philosophers, epistemologists, anthropologists, and specialists in international relations, the work and contributions of Immanuel Wallerstein have come to represent one of the most indispensable theoretical reference points for the everyday work of practically all present-day social scientists.

At the same time, and given that Wallerstein also deals with the analysis and critical diagnosis of the events and processes of our most immediate present, his work has also been circulated among political activists and members of the most diverse range of social movements the world over, a fact that explains, for example, why he has been invited several times as a distinguished panelist to the World Social Forum in Porto Alegre, Brazil.

Alongside these planetary echoes of his most important essays and books, there has also been an equally global dissemination of his personality, sometimes in the role of distinguished lecturer at that global summit of *altermundialist* movements, other times in the role of the director of the distinguished and well-reputed Fernand Braudel Center at the State University of New York, Binghamton, but equally as the president of the International Sociological Association or as a sharp critic of the present-day McCarthyism in the United States, who speaks from within the very bowels of that North American nation.

As a result, it is hardly surprising that the fortnightly commentaries that he writes about current events have already been translated into twenty-seven languages or that the Center for Research, Information, and Documentation, located in the city of San Cristóbal de las Casas in Chiapas, Mexico, has been named the Immanuel Wallerstein Center.[1] Nor should it surprise us that his books form part of the essential bibliography for innumerable history, economics, sociology, philosophy, anthropology, and political science courses in universities the world over, or that he has received *honoris causa* doctorates from universities in France and Peru, as well as Mexico and Portugal.

In this way, and alongside this planetary dissemination of Wallerstein's work, we have also seen the global projection of his most important creation, that is, the critical analytical perspective that Wallerstein himself calls "world-systems analysis." Across a rich lifetime and a complex intellectual itinerary—which led him from the analysis of African realities and the disciplinary field of sociology to the study of the past and present of global capitalism and toward a unidisciplinary horizon of new historical social sciences[2]—Immanuel Wallerstein has been constructing precisely those distinct pieces and the different fields that today constitute this same critical perspective for the analysis of world-systems, a perspective that, as the organizing axis of the entirety of Wallerstein's work over the past three decades, has equally become an indispensable reference point and an ever-present element in the most important contemporary debates in the social sciences.

So, criticized by some and distorted and caricatured by others, but also recovered and defended by many contemporary critical social scientists, the perspective of world-systems analysis has also been popularized and circulated enormously, contributing to the projection of Wallerstein himself, who has been without a doubt its principal creator, theorist, and promoter.

This all leads us to ask ourselves what explains the extraordinarily broad dissemination of this world-systems perspective and, with it, the totality of Immanuel Wallerstein's work. What are its most original moments? What central themes does it deal with? How is it useful as a critical tool for understanding the contemporary world? Why has it achieved such a vast and profound impact over the past three decades? In an effort to respond to these questions, it is worth attempting to reconstruct the whole map of the central thematic axes that constitute the world-systems analysis perspective, as well as the essential hypotheses and proposals postulated within each of these axes, which as a whole will provide the keys not only to the work and the precise contribution of Immanuel Wallerstein but also, and above all, to the enormous projection and global dissemination mentioned above.

A GENERAL MAP OF THE WORLD-SYSTEMS ANALYSIS PERSPECTIVE

"I still believe that world-systems analysis is in the first place a protest against the present forms of the social sciences, and this includes the environment of their mode of theorizing."
Immanuel Wallerstein, "The Itinerary of World-Systems Analysis, or How to Resist Becoming a Theory," 2002

If we observe as a whole all the work written up to the present by Immanuel Wallerstein, as well as the all the lines along which he has developed his world-systems perspective,[3] we will realize that this work and this perspective unfold fundamentally along four major thematic axes, which connect to one another in various ways to provide us with the complete architecture of the conceptual and theoretical edifice of world-systems analysis.

These are four axes that—sometimes superimposed on one another and at other times intersecting transversally—also contain the main keys to grasping the originality of world-systems analysis and its exceptional dissemination throughout the most diverse of academic and intellectual environments the world over. Upon carefully traversing Wallerstein's work it becomes clear that its first axis is the *historical-critical axis,* which seeks to explain in a novel way the entire history of capitalism and modernity within which we still find ourselves today, and which, having begun their historical existence in the crucial and decisive "long sixteenth century" once postulated by Fernand Braudel, have unfolded in an uninterrupted manner since then until the very beginnings of the chronological twenty-first century. This historical-critical axis of a global history of modern capitalism—from the sixteenth century until today—not only serves as the original matrix of the entire world-systems analysis perspective but is also already partially formulated in what is without a doubt Wallerstein's best-known and most widely translated book worldwide: *The Modern World-System.* Of this work, four volumes have already seen publication, covering the critical history of the long sixteenth, the long seventeenth, and the long eighteenth centuries[4]; its fourth volume—consisting of the analysis and global characterization of the long nineteenth century—was published in 2011.

A second axis constituting this perspective—one that simultaneously prolongs and concretizes the argument of the first axis—is the *critical analysis* of the principal events and processes of the long twentieth century, that is, of those realities and tendencies closest and most familiar to us, insofar as these correspond to the specific contexts of characters, events, and evolutionary processes that we have lived and observed and in which we have been involved, whether personally or through the generations of our parents and grandparents alongside which we have lived directly. This is a critical diagnosis of the historical long twentieth century that, while supporting a rupture with the deeply rooted but absurd myth of history as a "science of the past," gives us the keys for understanding the essential processes of our own historical century. That is to say, this century, which began approximately around 1870, will not finish its historical cycle for several years or even decades yet.

Along these same lines—and in what would appear to be successive movements toward a more close-up analysis—the third axis tackles a double problematic, covering both the *study of immediate history* as well as the audacious exercise of *defining possible prospective scenarios* of the future evolution of the capitalist world-system. This is because, since 1968 and the subsequent foundation of this analytical perspective in 1974, Immanuel Wallerstein has accompanied the events that he has lived with critical explanations that—while introducing a powerful "historical density" into the interpretation of those immediate facts, a density derived, naturally, from Wallerstein's own work with regard to the previously mentioned critical axes—always resituate those very events through a clear global and comparativist perspective, that is, from a geographically planetary perspective that is relentlessly attentive to similarities, differences, causalities, and common recurrences among those facts under analysis. At the same time, Wallerstein has also constantly engaged in projecting the historical tendencies of the global evolution of the capitalist world-system that he has studied into the future, with the intention of prefiguring—and it is worth emphasizing that he has done so with a notable degree of success[5]—the possible prospective scenarios of this same evolution of global capitalism.

Finally, a fourth organizing axis of Wallerstein's work and the world-systems perspective is *critical epistemological reflection* with respect to our habitual modes of learning about the social realities that we investigate and, more generally, the very configurati.on of the present structure of knowledges constituted by this same and still predominant capitalist modernity. This critique of the present-day social sciences and of the currently dominant structure of knowledge, in contrast to the three previous axes, cannot be located within the same movement of successive approximations—from the most distant history of capitalism to its most living present; rather, it cuts transversally across these three axes in order to make explicit and radically critique the unrecognized presuppositions of their own construction, with the intent of showing their epistemological limits and stimulating the construction of radically new and profoundly unidisciplinary "historical social sciences."[6]

These four organizing axes of the world-systems perspective have been supported, in the course of their construction and successive edification, principally by two matrices of contemporary critical thought: in the first place, the most important intellectual legacy in the contemporary social sciences—that is, during approximately the past 150 years—and in the second place, the most relevant work on the global level within historical studies of the entire chronological twentieth century. Here we refer, on the one hand, to the matrix represented by the critical thinking of Karl Marx and some of his disciples and later epigones and, on the other hand, to the matrix of the heritage constituted by the work of Fernand Braudel and, as a result, some of the principal contributions of the French Annales School.[7]

Beyond the complex "genealogical tree" of intellectual affiliations that have fed into the intellectual journey of Immanuel Wallerstein and, with it, the world-systems analysis perspective—affiliations that include such outstanding thinkers as Frantz Fanon, Ilya Prigogine, Marc Bloch, Raúl Prebisch, and Paul Sweezy, among many others—it seems clear that the two matrices of thought upon which Wallerstein's perspective fundamentally depends are, as we have said, the Marxist and the Braudelian.[8] Therefore, Marx's categorical apparatus is present and active throughout Wallerstein's analysis and work, as he speaks of a historical capitalism, one based on the logic of capital accumulation and permanently marked by the dynamic of class struggle, all the while emphasizing clear processes of ideological alienation and capitalist states that obey the interests of the dominant classes at each moment.

If Wallerstein interprets many of the traditional debates and Marxist theses in an original and unorthodox manner, he always does so from the horizon of assuming the general conceptual and fundamental theoretical apparatus elaborated by Marx himself a century and a half ago as the general framework of his analysis. At the same time, as he himself has declared on various occasions, Wallerstein's work has drawn in very important ways upon several of the most important Marxist works and debates on economic history and critical sociology from the 1960s onward, debates and works with respect to which Wallerstein would take positions, thereby recuperating certain authors and elements and rejecting others, precisely from the distinguishing criterion of his world-systems analysis perspective.

On the other hand, Wallerstein's enormous debt to Fernand Braudel is also clear: from Braudel he adopted the theory of different historical times, especially the focus on long historical duration, as well as some central concepts, such as the world-economy, and some specific theses, like the particular relation between monopolies and free competition within the global dynamics of capitalism. At the same time, recovering the Braudelian idea of *global* history—which is otherwise aligned with the Marxian demand to analyze all problems "from the point of view of the totality"—and his call for *critical* history—another obvious space in which Braudel coincides with Marx—Wallerstein also feeds equally upon research in the field of economic history developed by some thinkers from the Annales current, a spectrum that extends from the brilliant works of Marc Bloch to the contributions of Braudel himself and a few of his direct disciples.

This is the double matrix underlying the work of Immanuel Wallerstein, without an understanding of which it is not possible to grasp the richness and originality of the world-systems perspective. We could even affirm that for an adequate and accurate understanding of this perspective, it is also necessary to have a minimum knowledge of the complex contribution of Marx and some later Marxist positions, as well as the work of Braudel and important contributions by some of the Annalist authors mentioned above. Working from this general map of world-systems analysis, and from these two fundamental matrices upon which its structure rests, we can now reexamine in closer detail what constitutes the particularly original contributions of this approach, those that have given it not only its peculiar heuristic strength but also its vast capacity for global dissemination and circulation.

THE HISTORICAL-CRITICAL AXIS ON THE
GLOBAL HISTORY OF CAPITALISM

"My preoccupation with method led me to consider as central the question of the 'unit of analysis,' and this is why we speak of 'world-systems analysis.'"
Immanuel Wallerstein, "Hold the Tiller Firm:
On Method and the Unit of Analysis," 1994

If we look more closely at the first organizing axis of the world-systems perspective—the *historical-critical axis*—we see that Immanuel Wallerstein has formulated in this field what we could consider his most ambitious and long-winded task, one that remains unfinished and has up to the present emerged through the four volumes we know as *The Modern World-System*. And a possible fifth and even sixth volume would have as their objectives a discussion of the long twentieth century and perhaps a prospective exercise regarding immediate-future scenarios of the capitalist world-system.

These four plus volumes hope to provide a global history of the capitalist world-system—from its origins to the present—one that differs vastly from the boring traditional and descriptive histories of the sixteenth through twentieth centuries with which we are all familiar. Against such histories, Wallerstein's work seeks to provide an entirely new theoretical model for global discussions and for comprehensive and critical explanation of the complete itinerary of capitalist history during the past five or six centuries. That is, it provides an interpretive and theoretical history of capitalism, or a historical theory and interpretation of the evolution of modern capitalist society, which as a result inscribes the name of Immanuel Wallerstein on that very short list of thinkers of the past fifty years who have dared to think about capitalism as a global problem in its integral unity and most general dimensions—a list that begins with Karl Marx and includes only a few others, like Max Weber, Werner Sombart, Norbert Elias, Karl Polanyi, and Fernand Braudel.

If this effort to grasp modern capitalism—from its global history and from the theoretical reconstruction of its essential structures—draws Wallerstein into the orbit of these important thinkers, his specific moment of originality can be asserted, on the other hand, with regard to three principal theses that constitute the singularity of focus of world-systems analysis, with respect to this same theme of the theoretical-historical explanation of modern capitalism. These three theses, or methodological proposals, include, in the first place, the *unit of analysis* relevant to the analysis and investigation of distinct phenomena, events, and processes that have unfolded within this long history of capitalism. In the second place, we can refer to the *internal hierarchical structure* through which capitalism itself is configured. Finally, in the third place, we can refer to the distinct *dynamics and transformative curves* that provide the rhythm of the historical life and continuity of the capitalist system.

As a result, one of the most original and controversial proposals of world-systems analysis refers to defining the specific unit of analysis that we should use to frame our research. Here, in open disagreement with practically all prior social scientists, Immanuel Wallerstein affirms that this unit of analysis cannot, and should not, be anything less than the world-system considered in its totality—that is to say, in its vastest geographical dimension, which has been, during the last five centuries, either semiglobal or, in later years, strictly global.[9] This means that according to world-systems analysis, it is an important methodological error to consider the nation-state as our analytical frame or as our global unit of analysis—that is, to confine our analysis to the national space within which the problem we are studying has unfolded, a national space that, under the names of "society," the "social formation" in consideration, or "the social structure," always limits our epistemological horizons for the explanation of those specifically national coordinates and processes, be they of Mexico, Argentina, France, Guatemala, Russia, or the United States, among others.

Such an error—to cite only a few possible examples—would consist of attempting to explain the Mexican independence movement solely through those processes specific and particular to Nueva España, or examining and explaining the French events of May 1968 without departing from the consideration of purely French causes and factors, or seeking the purely English elements that unleashed the Industrial Revolution of the late eighteenth century. In a similar vein, it would be erroneous to analyze the fall of the Berlin Wall through purely German explanatory vectors or to attempt to grasp the backward and limited government of Vicente Fox in Mexico through exclusively Mexican conjunctures and circumstances.

In attempting to do so, one loses sight of the underlying global dynamics of these processes and events, supranational dynamics that derive from the functioning of the global capitalist world-system considered as a whole. For Immanuel Wallerstein, this global world-system is the only truly relevant unit of analysis, and it requires that we situate Mexican independence within the broader movement of the general decolonization of the Americas, a movement also provoked and unleashed by the global dynamics of the reorganization of European and global geopolitics at the end of the eighteenth and beginning of the nineteenth centuries, which combine and become imbricated with protonational and local processes in each of the zones of this vast American continent.

Such global dynamics also reinsert the French May into the global cultural revolution of 1968 and England's Industrial Revolution into the broader constitution of the new global hegemonic cycle characteristic of the long nineteenth century, while reposing the fall of the Berlin Wall within the context of the global collapse of liberal ideology or reframing the shameful and impoverished policies of Vicente Fox within the process of the new social and political polarization generated by that collapse of liberalism and the concomitant worldwide resurgence of the bellicose, cynical, militant, and shameless Right and ultra-Right that we have witnessed in recent years and decades.[16]

Against all these standard explanations from those historians and social scientists who assume—consciously or occasionally unconsciously—these limited national frames as their essential unit of analysis, Wallerstein asserts the existence—always present and always fundamental for a proper scientific explanation—of this global unity that is the capitalist world-system in its totality and, with it, the existence of those supranational global dynamics that have always fundamentally determined and influenced all the events, phenomena, and social processes that have come to pass in whatever part of the world during the past five hundred years.

Moreover, and as a second powerful thesis of this historical-critical axis, Wallerstein has defended the idea that throughout its historical life, capitalism has always operated by way of a profoundly unequal and asymmetrical hierarchical structure. This structure takes the form of a tripartite division of the planet into a small nucleus of very wealthy countries or areas that constitute the *core* of the system, a similarly small intermediate zone made up of countries and areas that enjoy a moderate degree of wealth and are deemed the *semiperiphery*, and finally a vast poor and exploited *periphery*. This periphery represents the immense majority of the world's area and nations, and as the broad foundation of the system as a whole, it supports both the semiperiphery and the core of the capitalist system.

This thesis about the tripartite division of the capitalist world already represents a first criterion for distinguishing what is possible and impossible for any given country or nation on this capitalist planet. Hence, the zones at the core will almost always be the generators of new groundbreaking technologies and the center of the great transnational monopolies; they develop the highest levels of income, consumption, and lifestyle and pay the highest salaries in relative terms. Together these indicators are little more than the various expressions and consequences of the greater wealth that these areas hold as a result of their exploitation, through various methods, of the semiperiphery and, above all, the immense periphery that surrounds them.

On the other hand, these multiple peripheries—exploited through various methods, from the age-old forms of unequal exchange and explicit blocking of development of entire branches of production to the most recent form of imposing onerous and unjust external indebtedness on the least developed countries—will always be the poorest areas and countries, with little to no technological development, small and limited industries and businesses with only a local scope, and low income and consumption levels, low standards of living, and the lowest salaries.[11]

The acute economic differences that exist between core and periphery—only slightly attenuated in semiperipheral zones—are also reflected on the social, political, and even cultural levels, placing powerful imperialist states at the core, medium states in the semiperiphery, and weak, colonial, dependent, or subordinate states in the periphery. But these core areas also develop those models of cultural and social behavior that are then imposed as dominant on the planetary scale. So, for example, we now see English phrases like "the American way of life" used as supposed signs of "progress" and, in turn, presenting as backward or underdeveloped all other languages or the cultural habits of all regions of the periphery and semiperiphery.[12]

This is an unequal and hierarchical structure containing three geographical zones of the capitalist world-system. Moreover, during the five centuries of the historical life of capitalism, this structure has proceeded to widen and deepen, rather than to close, the gap and thereby erase the differences between these zones. If the small nucleus at the core of the system is every day more scandalously rich, luxurious, wasteful, and offensively ostentatious, this is only thanks to the fact that the immense periphery becomes every day poorer, more ascetic, more restricted, and more modest in its consumption and its use of the scarce resources not expropriated by the core. The wealth of this core—today as five hundred years ago—is the direct fruit of exploitation, pillage, theft, expropriation, and the systematic impoverishment of this immense peripheral area.

This means—and not only on the theoretical level—that all supposed theories of development, modernization, or progress, or models for the possibility of escaping backwardness or underdevelopment, are totally ineffective and absurd as explanatory theories or proposals for the evolution of the poor and peripheral countries under capitalism. But also, on a more practical and profound level, this means that the countries of the periphery do not have any promising future within the current framework of this capitalist world-system.[13]

A third central thesis of the historical-critical axis refers to the distinct dynamics that, within equally diverse historical times, progressively adapt and set the rhythm of the evolution of historical capitalist becoming. These differential dynamics—while also profoundly intertwined—comprise, on the plane of historical conjuncture or Braudelian medium time, the well-known Kondratieff cycles, as well as the broadest range of long duration. They are, first, the dynamic of the important changes that impose distinct and super-imposed "long centuries" on capitalist history; second, the successive move-ments of expansion and consolidation of the world-system itself; and third, and perhaps most importantly, the global dynamic of the successive hegemonic cycles of this same general path of capitalist modernity.

As Fernand Braudel has shown convincingly—he is followed on this point closely by Wallerstein—the fabric of history is always woven in multiple simultaneous registers, which in their complex interrelation and interplay define the particular configuration of societies in each moment and singular historical circumstance.[14] Therefore, as important explanatory elements, the world-systems perspective returns to the question of whether, in a determinate moment, we are in an expansive or depressive phase of the Kondratieff cycle, as well as to analyze the integration of that moment also within a singular moment of the then predominant hegemonic cycle.

But we are also in an intermediary period of the "second historical twentieth century" that began in 1968, which allows us to explain our current situation in terms of a transition between two long historical centuries—one that blends the declining elements characteristic of the long twentieth century with those elements of the future long historical twenty-first century already in gestation. This historical twenty-first century will without a doubt be characterized by, among many other things, the multiform growth and expan-sion of multiculturalism in all its variants and expressions. But it will also be a century in which we experience, among various possible processes that we could mention, the protagonic irruption onto the front of the world stage of the entire Latin American semicontinent, alongside, for example, the global recuperation of multiple social, political, cultural, and civilizational spaces by indigenous populations the world over.

Equally, it is difficult to grasp the present global situation without con-sidering that we are crossing into a stage that has only rarely appeared in the historical life of humanity, a historical bifurcation that in this particular case falls within our lifetime (the terminal crisis of the historical capitalist system.[15] This is a situation of genuinely systemic chaos of the sort not seen in the past five hundred years, and it provides the explanatory key to the truly terminal and irreversible collapse experienced by an entire vast totality of structures in our society, such as the modern state, the very activity of politics, the economic logic based on capital accumulation, the present class structure, and modern, enlightened, and rationalist bourgeois culture. This collapse even reaches into structures like the global configuration of populations under the framework of the nation or the very structure of knowledges constituted by modernity five centuries ago.

Finally, in order to understand the present state of the world, it is essential to realize that we now live in a period characterized by the decadence of the global hegemonic cycle of the United States, a phase that began more than thirty years ago. This makes it possible to understand both the U.S. defeat in Vietnam and the survival of an independent, autonomous, and sovereign Cuba, as well as the tragic events of September 11, 2001, and the subsequent desperate, irrational, and unjust U.S. invasion of Iraq, which becomes every day more and more of a failure.[16]

Carefully reconstructing all the multiple and imbricated dynamics of this temporal development of the past half millennium of capitalist history, Wallerstein not only recuperates the principal lessons of the past in order to provide a denser and more accurate diagnosis of our present but also forges certain intellectual tools that—on the basis of this precise and dense portrait of the past and present—allow him to keep his eyes on the possible future scenarios of this very same present with a good deal of certainty. This he does through the careful forward projection of those tendencies operating today, tendencies already clearly identified and grasped through this multiple dissection of these distinct dynamics, which constitute the global itinerary of capitalist modernity.

It is precisely on the basis of these three powerful theses—or the three lines of proposals outlined up to this point—that the historical-critical axis of the world-systems perspective is structured. This historical-critical axis, in turn, has provided the originary matrix for the entire approach, functioning also as the most general horizon framing the other three previously mentioned axes, which we will now approach in greater detail.

THE AXIS OF THE CRITICAL ANALYSIS OF THE HISTORICAL LONG TWENTIETH CENTURY

"The 20th century will be remembered for three things: the hegemony of the United States, the political resurgence of the non-Western world, and the revolution of 1968."
        Immanuel Wallerstein, "Last Century, Last Millennium," 2000

The second organizing axis of world-systems perspective is the *critical analysis of the long historical twentieth century,* an axis that, by projecting the lessons of the historical-critical axis onto our own historical century, allows Immanuel Wallerstein to diagnose and analyze in an equally novel manner several of the principal processes and events taking place during the past 140 years. Openly countering those authors who defend and postulate the existence of a "short twentieth century"—running from World War I and the 1917 Russian Revolution to the fall of the Berlin Wall and the reconversion of the Soviet Union into an openly capitalistic Russia—Wallerstein defends the thesis of the existence of a long twentieth century. This long century, having already begun around 1870, would unfold up through the present day and even beyond, concluding at a still indeterminate date but possibly extending beyond 2050.[17]

This important opposition between the thesis of a short and long twentieth century is not reducible to a simple dispute about the number of years in the century; rather, it refers to the essential problem of determining, in each of these positions, the fundamental and determinant processes of the entire chronological twentieth century. Such processes, from their own particular temporality, would then fix the very chronological limits of that possible historical twentieth century, thereby determining whether we are speaking of a short or a long century.

Thus, against the idea of considering the processes of so-called actually existing socialism, which developed during the twentieth century as the central and defining processes of our recent past—this being the basis for the thesis of the short twentieth century—Immanuel Wallerstein instead defends the idea that this long twentieth century has been defined by the long curve representing the construction, definition, affirmation, and then decadence of U.S. hegemony, a century that therefore begins around 1870 and is now living out its final and conclusive stage. It is around 1870—after the end of the American Civil War and at the same moment as the French defeat in the Franco-Prussian War—that we see clearly taking shape the dispute that will later reach truly global proportions, that between the United States and Germany. This Germano-American dispute—over the next seventy years and, above all, during the modern "thirty years war" stretching from 1914 to 1945—would decide the new global hegemonic power that would replace England in the role of the core of the entire capitalist world-system, favoring in the end the United States after Germany's debacle. This would be a process of the slow edification, then the affirmation and decadence, of that same U.S. planetary hegemony, a process that—for the world-systems approach—would define the general meaning and historical significance of this long historical twentieth century.

Therefore, following this logic, the U.S. victory of 1945 would be followed by a period of the powerful exercise of hegemony on the part of the victorious power, a hegemony that would install—between 1945 and 1968/1972–1973—that *Pax Americana* we know as the Cold War. In this way, the global geopolitical pattern would be defined unilaterally and with few significant obstacles by the United States of America. But with the global cultural revolution of 1968 and the global economic crisis of 1972–1973, this powerful American hegemony came to a close, and so began the slow but unstoppable process of the total decadence of U.S. hegemony. This decadence clearly continues into our own times, most dramatically during the two recent administrations of George W. Bush.

In this way, and by reexplaining the entire twentieth century from the perspective of this U.S. hegemony, Wallerstein profoundly relativizes the role of actually existing socialism to the point of arguing that none of the so-called socialist societies were truly socialist, that none could be since all of them were part of the world-system as a whole, and that since it was impossible for them to escape the essential logic of that system, all were doomed to return to an open embrace of capitalism sooner or later and in one way or another. Moreover, Wallerstein even characterizes World Wars I and II as one long, modern "thirty years war," structured around the rivalry between Germany and the United States, whose principal result was precisely the uncontested U.S. domination that existed during the 1940s through the 1960s.

In the same direction, Wallerstein proposes as one of the principal axes for grasping all events and phenomena of the years since 1970 the background provided by the process of the progressive and irreversible collapse of the hegemonic power of the United States. This collapse has created a vacuum in the hegemonic position of leadership within the capitalist world-system, pushing to the front of the world stage the rivalry between, on the one hand, a Northeast Asia enormously developed in capitalist terms and, on the other, a reunified Western Europe under the aegis of German power. This is because, repeating a cyclical model that we have lived on two previous historical occasions, the decadence of the hegemonic power—in this case the United States—on the world scale is again accompanied by the emergence of a new dispute between two possible contenders that hope to occupy the place of the waning power. Apart from this, Wallerstein shows us clearly the explicit organic connection between the first historical-critical axis and this second axis of the analysis of the long twentieth century. Having studied the previous hegemonic cycles of capitalist history—the Dutch cycle of the seventeenth century and the English cycle of the nineteenth century—Immanuel Wallerstein is able to analyze with all certainty the current phase of U.S. decadence; he can even forecast from the present that the winner of this dispute will almost certainly be Northeast Asia, if capitalism itself is not already in terminal and definitive crisis.[18] Thus, in reexplaining the long twentieth century from this dense view—one achieved by studying the entire history of capitalism—Immanuel Wallerstein is able to propose original and novel interpretations of the distinct phenomena, events, and processes that humanity has lived through during the past 140 years.

Alongside this central line of the twentieth century represented by the contours of U.S. hegemony, a second fundamental curve also unfolds: that of the total decolonization of the planet and the progressive achievement of political independence by the many colonial countries that survived into the twentieth century. This process entailed the disintegration of all colonial empires, including the English, the French, and several others, in successive waves throughout the entire "first twentieth century" (running from approximately 1870 to around 1968). This would achieve formal and political independence for practically all nations on earth, thereby erasing from the world map that old and durable colonial relation.

It is crucial to emphasize that this formal and official dissolution of the colonial bond and the concomitant winning of political independence did not in any way dissolve the existing relations of dependency and economic exploitation; nor did it totally eliminate the various existing forms of social and cultural dependence. Still, we must also recognize that, in spite of everything and as a subterranean process that fed into national liberation or independence movements, there developed a vast and powerful process of political consciousness raising and generalized democratization of public life for popular masses all over the world. This is because once the populations of all the colonial countries began to question this relation of dependence with regard to their respective metropoles and mobilized themselves politically to struggle for independence and national sovereignty, those antisystemic national liberation movements that proliferated during the long twentieth century throughout every corner of the planet began to generate and promote, in a profound manner, a clear process of forcing countries at the core and semi-periphery of the capitalist world-system to recognize and come to terms with the fact that all peoples on earth—and, with them, all nations on earth—are active and fundamental protagonists of the universal history of the present. As a result, these actors must be taken into account at the time of deciding the general destiny of our planet.

If it remains clear that these national liberation struggles were partially successful in their general objectives but at the same time incapable of eliminating economic, social, and cultural dependence, it is also clear that in more profound terms they developed, on a local level, crucial processes of democratization of the public life of many peripheral countries. Moreover, this simultaneously created a reservoir of experience and consciousness that continues to manifest today in various ongoing struggles, and these will continue to manifest in various forms of social combat in the immediate future.

Just as the curve of U.S. hegemony suffered a fundamental collapse in 1968/1972–1973—passing from authoritative hegemony to hegemonic decline—so, too, does the curve of total global decolonization culminate around these same years, giving way thereafter, during the past forty-five years, to the systematic and repeated global critique of Eurocentrism in all its forms.[19]

Despite its limitations, this critique—which has occasionally reached absurd extremes and at other times represented a legitimate challenge to the negative consequences of European domination of the globe between the sixteenth and nineteenth centuries—expresses in a general way the profound changes brought about by this process of the complete dissolution of colonial relations on the global level. It is no accident that alongside the real disintegration of these colonial ties, this critique of European domination and its negative consequences unfolded and was largely legitimated. This critique underlies the rejection of the Eurocentrism projected through visions of universal history, models of cultural valorization, methods for distinguishing "progress" from "backwardness," and so forth, as well as the ever more generalized calls for the recognition of multiculturalism in its different variants.

It is further interesting to observe that, from the perspective of this global and long-duration optic through which Wallerstein attempts to examine and diagnose this long historical twentieth century, this same century appears to be divided by a fundamental event-rupture: the global cultural revolution of 1968. We could almost say that this long twentieth century is divided—as was the case with the long sixteenth century—into two twentieth centuries: a "first twentieth century," stretching from approximately 1870 to 1968, and a "second twentieth century," more or less beginning in 1970 and continuing today.

This is because—in opposition to many other analysts who minimize or even ignore the fundamental symbolic importance of 1968 and the student and student-popular movements linked to it—Immanuel Wallerstein underlines the profound global impact of the 1968 revolution. This revolution, unfolding as a radical upheaval throughout the dominant geocultural system, was expressed not only in the collapse of the Old Left movements and the birth of multiple New Lefts but also in the beginning of the definitive collapse of liberal ideology and in the definitive interrogation of the then dominant structures of knowledge, alongside the crisis and transformation of many of the previously dominant models, codes, and principal mechanisms of cultural structures.[20] Following Braudel on this point, Wallerstein characterizes the 1968 revolution—that is, the vast totality of movements between 1966 and 1969 that shook practically every country on earth—as a profound cultural revolution of planetary dimensions—one that also has real civilizational implications, whose effects continue to be felt today in the broadest spheres of contemporary culture, society, everyday life, and politics.

The central characterization of the revolution of 1968 that emerges from the perspective of world-systems analysis is the idea that it was a truly long-duration revolution in the structures of contemporary society. That is, it was a modification of certain structures—in this case cultural ones—that had unfolded and predominated during several centuries and sometimes even millennia, structures that, having persisted tenaciously over long periods, began to come radically and definitively unhinged precisely from the starting point of this global cultural revolution symbolized by the emblematic year 1968. Given that we are speaking of a truly cataclysmic, long-duration mutation of cultural structures—age-old, millenarian structures—it follows that the profound meaning of these 1968 revolutions can only be grasped according to the very same long-term parameters.

The extraordinarily profound implications of the movements of 1968 become clear when we realize that it was thanks to these movements that, for example, the masculinist and patriarchal structure of the then predominant monogamous family was called into question, thereby releasing the process of women's liberation and the different elements of the feminist movement of the present. Hence, by calling into question this masculinism and patriarchy—which had been in force for at least the previous two millennia—the cultural revolution of 1968 began a slow but unstoppable process of revolution in the family cell, a revolution that would logically still require several decades to affirm and develop all of its multiple and complex implications and potentialities.

And something similar has occurred with contemporary educational institutions, which have also been challenged and shaken to their very deepest foundations. The interrogation of the traditional hierarchical relationship between teacher and pupil, as well as other aspects, mechanisms, modes, and relations involved in the processes of generating, transmitting, and appropriating the distinctive knowledges of the collective students, also unleashed a total revolution in the educational apparatus, which today, at every level—from kindergarten to postgraduate education—has entered into a profound global crisis and embarked on the total restructuring of all its elements and fundamental operations. This is a crisis in an educational system that is every day less and less capable of motivating the interest of students and increasingly teaches abstract and useless knowledge, with no connection to real life and in which the intellectual and even personal authority of the professor is increasingly emptied of grounded and real content. This crisis will need to persist for several decades more and will certainly only culminate when an entire revolution and renovation of this same educational structure has been carried out.

The same upheaval occurs in the modern communication media, whose disproportionate influence—positive and negative—dates precisely from this global cultural revolution at the end of the 1960s. Today, the communication media can now decisively influence national and global public opinion, determining, for example, the election or defeat of a president or absurdly justifying an irrational and arrogant invasion by the greatest military force on earth, that of the United States, against a defenseless Middle Eastern nation like Iraq. In this way, emphasizing the profound relevance of 1968, Immanuel Wallerstein rounds out his exceptional explanation of the long historical twentieth century and, with it, the second principal axis of the world-systems perspective.

This second axis divides the long twentieth century into a first twentieth century, which comes to a close around the fundamental period of 1968–1973, and a second twentieth century consisting of the period since then. Moreover, this crucial date also provides us with the connection that links this second axis with the third axis of world-systems analysis, that corresponding to the study of immediate history that has been experienced and occasionally even participated in by Immanuel Wallerstein. He has examined and critically assessed this immediate history as it has happened, while exercising a critical vigilance toward possible prospective scenarios of the immediate and distant future of the evolution of this same capitalist world-system. We must now turn our attention to this third axis.

THE DOUBLE AXIS OF THE ANALYSIS OF IMMEDIATE HISTORY AND THE PROSPECTIVE SCENARIOS OF PRESENT-DAY CAPITALISM

> *"We are now living in an important historical moment: it is the moment of the era of transition of the present world-system toward another, new historical system. In a period like this, we all have the obligation to help clarify which are the possible and desireable alternatives."*
>
> Immanuel Wallerstein, message sent for the inauguration
> of the Immanuel Wallerstein Center in San Cristóbal
> de las Casas, Chiapas, Mexico, September 2004

The third organizing axis of the world-systems perspective is the *examination of the immediate history and future prospective scenarios* of the capitalist world-system. In other words, this axis breaks down into two lines of investigation that are intimately connected but nevertheless differentiated. Along the first line, that referring to the critical diagnosis of the history of the present—that is, the history of the past three or four decades—Immanuel Wallerstein once again distances himself radically from the most popular and widespread explanations available today for the characterization of contemporary capitalism: from the empty and mediatic pseudotheory of globalization and its identical twin, equally superficial and lacking in solid theoretical foundations, the theory of mundialization.

Not only does this radical critique of theories of globalization and mundialization underline the fact that none of the processes supposedly characteristic of this mundialization-globalization are new at all—their existence almost always dates back centuries—but Wallerstein also emphasizes the openly obscurantist function of such theories. This function emerges from uncritical insistence on the "progress," "advancement," "achievements," and enormous and marvelous "accomplishments" brought about by this globalization-mundialization, the result of which is the concealment and even elimination of the vast totality of expressions of the systemic civilizational crisis that we have been suffering and enduring across the entire planet.[21]

This is because it is easy to demonstrate that all of the events and processes that claim to "support" and "underpin" the weak justification for this theory of globalization and mundialization are already very old processes that have, in various forms but with a fundamentally identical essence, accompanied the entire history of capitalism. This applies equally to the disproportionate role of transnational organizations, the planetary diffusion of certain cultural models, the global movement of commodities, and the almost instantaneous flow of news and information. We have been familiar with all these processes for centuries: consider, for example, the dominant role of the Dutch East India Company, or the imposition of cultures and languages by the Spanish and Portuguese in the Americas or by the English in India, or the fact that the network of the global market dates back centuries already and that the invention of the telegraph or the telephone was even more revolutionary and fundamental than, for example, the recent invention of the Internet.

Beyond demystifying those supposedly characteristic features of this globalization, Wallerstein's central critique is directed against these theories' presupposition that we have entered a new stage of the capitalist life cycle. This alleged new stage is one full of technological innovation and social change, which will only fully develop during the next century or more, thereby prolonging by a century or more the historical life of the capitalist world-system. Against this, and in diametrical opposition to such theories, the world-systems perspective affirms that—departing precisely from the double rupture represented by the cultural revolution and global economic crisis of 1968–1973—the capitalist world-system has entered into the final stage of its historical life cycle. That is, this is a historical bifurcation that combines both the terminal crisis of capitalism and all of its constitutive structures with the urgent task of beginning to build—immediately and from this present moment—possible alternatives for the definition of a new historical system that exists now in embryonic form.

Thus, in distancing itself from these theories of globalization-mundialization, which totally omit or refer only marginally to these multiple crises in absolutely every one of the present structures of capitalism, the world-systems perspective also stands against the equally erroneous and superficial theses regarding an allegedly new stage of "empire." Such claims exaggerate, for example, the role of transnational structures at the very same moment when, for example, the United Nations is totally deligitimized and has perished as a historical global structure before our very eyes, an event that already represents clear refutation of these same theses on "empire." Such an approach eventually leads to totally questionable political conclusions and evaluations, like that of undervaluing or even ignoring the specifically national level of struggles of the oppressed the world over. While this level should not be the only one considered, and perhaps not even the fundamental one, it must nevertheless be considered in a central way within the diverse necessary levels of class struggle and the everyday struggle of subaltern classes toward their own liberation.

In stark contrast to these theories of empire and globalization, Wallerstein puts the accent instead on characterizing the present situation of capitalism as one of terminal crisis, a multifaceted and profound crisis of civilizational import that extends from the ecological level and the current logic governing the relation between humans and nature, to the cultural level and dominant structures of knowledge, and even to the technological, economic, social, and political planes more generally.[22] This is because, against the grain of all of these dominant discourses on globalization and mundialization, which emphasize allegedly immense virtues, world-systems analysis will draw attention to the increasingly alarming ecological crisis of the present. This crisis can be seen in the massive air pollution around large cities, in the diminishing atmospheric ozone layer, in the growing filthiness of the planet's rivers, in global climactic changes, in the ever-larger cemeteries for atomic waste, in the desertification of vast areas of the earth, and in the irreversible destruction of jungles, forests, and entire species, all of which is driving us directly toward an ecological catastrophe of planetary dimensions.

This is not the case because the technological means for reversing and resolving these problems do not exist; rather, it is because these technologies are not profitable within the limited logic of capitalist accumulation. And it is equally because these already-existing technological solutions collide directly with this perverse capitalist logic dictating the relation between humans and nature—one that pillages, destroys, and assaults nature as though it were an inexhaustible and passive reservoir of resources—a logic that has now reached its ultimate limits, which are expressed in the present situation. And still this predatory capitalist logic is maintained, as we are confronted with an ecological "boomerang" that now submits the bill for the five centuries of destruction and indiscriminate plunder brought by capitalism to this same world and the natural environment of the globe.[23]

Equally, the focus of world-systems analysis insists on the distinct manifestations of an increasingly acute global economic crisis, which becomes evident as much in the explosive growth of the external debt of the majority of peripheral nations—a mechanism by which the core exploits this periphery—as in the spectacular growth in all countries of the so-called informal, underground, or parallel economy. This crisis is further evident in the galloping loss of real purchasing power of working-class salaries everywhere, as well as in the growing unemployment that is increasingly the norm in all economies on earth. This unemployment—among many other factors—explains the growing and unstoppable migration of workers from the periphery to the core, as well as from the rural areas of particular nations toward their large cities.[24]

This global economic crisis's difficulties are manifold and various. The crisis itself is manifested in the increasingly scandalous and ignominious economic, thus social, inequality that is rapidly swelling the ranks of entire sectors living in poverty and extreme poverty, while the fortunes of a tiny group of magnates grow limitlessly. This group enriches itself swiftly at the expense of the vast majority, which grows more impoverished. This growing social polarization, quite logically, is manifested in a significant growth in crime and other forms of social violence, at the same time as the deterioration of the standards of living of the immense majority of the population, creating a breeding ground for destruction and decline in all areas of the social fabric. This extends from the most elemental of family units to the whole landscape of urban and rural culture and spreads through all types of institutions, including schools, factories, prisons, businesses, government offices, and even the sites of simple social interaction and recreation.

Alongside all this, there also appears an equally total and structural crisis on all levels of politics; this extends to the state level, as states are increasingly incapable of fulfilling their basic functions of providing a minimum level of acceptable services, security, public health, and education for their populations. They are also less and less capable of achieving or maintaining a minimal legitimacy and credibility among these same populations. Such crises also extend to parties, organizations, political actors, and even different political events. Increasingly, the majority of people identify politics as a merry-go-round turning on its own axis, one that in reality does not represent any specific force or social movement, let alone the vast, crucial sectors of the citizenry in general.

This is a total crisis of the political world and of politics in general, which is today emptied of all connection with the social, ethical, or cultural realms. In the near future, in an already approaching noncapitalist society, this will be expressed as the total death of politics—that is, as the complete disappearance of this human activity, born in ancient Greece, which is today moving through the phase of its radical, terminal agony.[25] This will manifest as a sharper, and increasingly difficult, total disillusionment with this politics on the part of the inhabitants of the world as a whole, alongside the proliferation and multiplication of those obvious processes of its emptying and degeneration discussed above. Finally, this terminal and structural crisis of capitalism will also manifest in the cultural sphere, extending from the modification of the most basic structures that produce and reproduce that culture—the family, school, and now the media—to even the totality of all presently dominant structures of knowledge.

In line with this broad global characterization of present-day capitalism—which emphasizes the multifaceted civilizational crisis we have lived over the past three decades and rejects the superficial ideologies of "empire" and "globalization-mundialization"—Immanuel Wallerstein characterizes many of the events, situations, and processes we have experienced recently in a totally original and novel way, again in opposition to the common points repeated by political analysts and social scientists. For example, he insists that the fall of the Berlin Wall, far from representing the death of Marxism or of the socialist project of social transformation, symbolized instead the final and definitive collapse of liberal ideology.

This seems all the more clear now than it did at the time, when Wallerstein first argued as much.[26] This is because it is evident today that the terminal crisis of capitalism has generated an extreme ideological polarization—an expression of, among other things, the equally economic, social, and political polarization engendered by this very same situation of crisis—a polarization that simultaneously invalidates and delegitimizes the liberal and centrist interpretations that prevailed and were dominant in the geoculture of the past two hundred years, from the French Revolution to the fall of the Berlin Wall. This polarization clearly relaunches the two most extreme and radical positions: a now cynical Right, shameless and increasingly aggressive, as well as an interesting range of New Lefts, more creative, tolerant, plural, and effective than the previously dominant Old Lefts characteristic of the period prior to 1968.

These New Lefts, by linking themselves with equally new social movements and the new protagonists of social protest and struggle more generally—from indigenous people and women, to ecologists and students, to new urban groups, pacifists, homosexuals, the retired, the unemployed, farmers, and so forth—have not only recuperated and re-created Marxism but also developed an increasingly rich and interconnected project of truly radical global social transformation.

According to this same logic, we can also mention the heterodox explanation that Wallerstein has offered for the principal consequences and aftermath of the tragedy of September 11, 2001. He posits that these events demonstrate not the immense power, force, and vigor of the United States but rather the contrary, the previously mentioned irreversible hegemonic decadence that this nation has been living since the 1970s. Thus, in his view, the United States did not invade Afghanistan and Iraq because it is powerful, but rather for the opposite reason—because it is growing weaker and weaker by the day, in technological, productive, financial, commercial, economic, political, and geopolitical terms.

It is this accelerating and unstoppable economic, political, and geopolitical decline of the United States that the neoconservative camp, headed by George W. Bush, vainly attempted to reverse, with its arrogant and ostentatious use of the still powerful U.S. military. This has no doubt achieved the toppling of the Taliban and Saddam Hussein governments, but only at the price of breeding resistance and popular hatred among Afghanis and Iraqis, which might very well end up completely undermining the possible intended effects and consequences of these invasions in the immediate or long term. This overthrowing of governments, besides further isolating the United States from the rest of the world, has accelerated rather than slowed the global hegemonic decline of the decadent U.S. power.[27]

In this way, and on the first line of this third analytic axis, Wallerstein then interprets the immediate history that he himself has experienced in terms of this terminal and structural crisis of capitalism as a specific historical system. But equally, and from this same global horizon, he also develops distinct prospective exercises—that is, the second line of this third axis—the goal of which is to teach us about the most feasible futures that we can expect with the immediate and long-term evolution of the capitalist world-system. These prospective exercises, as already indicated, have been largely accurate, owing to the fact that they are supported doubly—by the future projection of the lessons learned from the five previous centuries of capitalist history and by this critical gaze, always distrustful of common explanations and instead attentive to the deep structures and realities of the history of the present.

This double intellectual scaffolding allows Wallerstein to predict, for example, that beyond the illusions propagated by the thesis of an emerging and powerful Pacific Rim becoming a formidable rival to the United States, more likely is the construction of a strategic alliance between Northeast Asia and the United States, but under the leadership of the former rather than the latter. This is because, in the current dispute between Western Europe and Northeast Asia, the latter is likely to triumph, as a sea-air power confronting the European land-air power. Since in the last three hegemonic cycles the maritime power has always won out (Holland, England, and the United States) against land powers (Spain, France, and Germany), this model will very likely repeat itself as long as capitalism survives, transferring the new leadership of the world-system progressively to Northeast Asia. And since the winner of each hegemonic struggle always enters into a partnership with the old declining power (England with Holland, the United States with England), it is quite possible that in the next few years we will see an affirmation of this Northeast Asia–U.S. alliance, whose first manifestations are already clearly visible.[28]

Seen through this optic—and despite its progressive monetary, economic, social, and cultural unification—Western Europe will lose this hegemonic struggle, remaining a wealthy semiperiphery of the system and undergoing within the few decades that remain in the life of the capitalist world-system the slow but already old process of its social, cultural, economic, political, and geopolitical eclipse. This will not prevent it from entering into an alliance with Russia, but such an alliance will not allow Western Europe to reverse this clear tendency toward its global decline.[29]

Such prospects for the evolution of the capitalist world-system will continue to unfold and be confirmed during the coming years and decades, although probably no later than 2050. As Immanuel Wallerstein has clearly demonstrated, all these prospective tendencies for the reorganization of the world briefly described above will develop in combination and coexistence with the equally continuous unfolding of the characteristics and manifestations of the terminal crisis of capitalism, shaping as a whole the systemic chaos or historical bifurcation that always accompanies the conclusive stage or the end of the life curve of any specific historical system.

THE EPISTEMOLOGICAL-CRITICAL AXIS AND THE SOCIAL SCIENCES

"The appearance of independent research institutions in Africa and Latin America, however limited the number at the present, has created an alternative path for embarking upon research."
Immanuel Wallerstein, *Open the Social Sciences*, 1996

The fourth fundamental axis of the architecture of the world-systems perspective is the *epistemological-critical axis.* In contrast to the three previous axes, this one is not related to the others by the logic of successively approaching the present situation—that is, from the perspective of five centuries of capitalist history (axis 1) to the perspective of the long twentieth century (axis 2), then from this long twentieth century to the specific conjunctures of the second twentieth century, present and future (axis 3). Rather, this fourth axis links with the others transversally and, by cutting equally across all three, interrogates them in three ways: in terms of (1) the genetic process of the structures of knowledge corresponding to capitalist modernity as a whole, (2) the process of the institutionalization of the social sciences that developed during this long and still unfinished twentieth century, and (3) the irreversible crisis of both these current social sciences and the so-called regime of the three cultures, as well as, more generally, the entire structure of knowledges, a crisis unleashed after 1968 and ongoing today.

With this fourth axis, Immanuel Wallerstein invites us to question seriously the nonexplicit premises of the specific configuration put forward today by our global "episteme" of cognitive expropriation of the world—that is, our present system of scientific knowledges, with its specific division between natural, or exact, hard sciences, social sciences, and the humanities, but also and afterward, with its organization under the scheme of the distinct disciplines of history, economics, political science, anthropology, geography, psychology, or sociology, to name a few. This multifaceted interrogation of the entire foundation of this organization of scientific knowledge—which could even extend into the interrogation of the division between "scientific" and "popular" knowledges, that is, to the division between hegemonically established cultures and popular and subaltern ones[30]—naturally leads Wallerstein to a radical critique of, and total distancing from, those popular and pervasive perspectives that defend and promote "interdisciplinarity," "multidisciplinarity," "pluridisciplinarity," or "transdisciplinarity."

This is because, far from validating or supporting all these false alternatives to the current crisis of the social sciences, the world-systems perspective instead demonstrates the profoundly limited and superficial character of these ostensible alternatives, which, since they do not attack the true root of the crisis, can only partially repair some of its most immediate and evidently catastrophic consequences. From Wallerstein's perspective, the true root of the present crisis of the social sciences can be found in the very fact of having fragmented and parceled out the study of the social-human into distinct disciplines—supposedly autonomous and independent—each with its own object of analysis, its own theories and concepts, its own particular and exclusive methods and research techniques, with their own characteristic models of interpretation, description, and reconstruction.

Hence, following Fernand Braudel—who would make radical and sharp jokes against all these limited proposals of "inter-," "multi-," "pluri-," or "trans-" disciplinarity—Wallerstein also questions this inquiry into the social, fragmented and autonomized into distinct fields and disciplines, proposing in its place the reconstruction of a new and more complex *unidisciplinarity* and, therefore, the construction of new unitary "historical social sciences."[31] New historical social sciences, constructed on the basis of this unidisciplinary focus, would naturally surpass and transcend the specific criteria through which the different disciplines that currently study the various aspects and terrains of the social were constructed. These criteria today find themselves absolutely questioned and delegitimized, in terms of both the rigid and abstract division between the past and the present and the artificial and equally mechanical separation between the economic, the social, and the political, as well as in terms of the nineteenth-century distinction between civilized peoples and barbarous, savage, or uncivilized ones.

The essential differences between the disciplinary fields and the disciplines themselves were constituted precisely on the basis of these criteria, deriving from them their supposed divergences with respect to objects, theories, concepts, methods, and specific techniques. The autonomy and specificity of the historical discipline were erected based precisely upon the difference between the alleged past and the so-called present, with that nebulous and undefined "past" as the discipline's object. The present, on the other hand, should be studied and diagnosed by the remaining disciplines or social sciences.

In reality, as all genuinely critical social scientists and historians of the past 150 years—from Marx to Wallerstein himself—have demonstrated, it is impossible to separate the past sharply from the present since the latter is, as Fernand Braudel argues, merely the "sum of many distinct pasts," some of which date back only hours or days, others having already persisted for years, decades, centuries, or even millennia. And if it is therefore impossible to say where the past "ends" and the present "begins," as Marc Bloch explains, then this definition of history as "that science which studies the facts of the past" has no meaning at all, just as the division between history and the rest of the social sciences lacks any kind of epistemological meaning.[32] Therefore, all social sciences must be profoundly historical by virtue of the fact that no relevant social fact can be understood and interpreted without a consideration of its own history, just as it is possible and even necessary to continuously historicize present facts, introducing a dense historical view into even the most immediate realities, even those still in development.

If this division between past and present—and with it the division between history and the other social sciences—is completely artificial and questionable, so is the supposed autonomy and clear distinction between the worlds of the economy, society, and politics upon which the distinction between economics, sociology, and political sciences is founded and justified. From the very work of Marx, we understand that politics is not, and never could be, an autonomous and self-sufficient reality since power cannot exist on the basis of power itself. Politics always has been and remains the management of this power toward objectives, interests, forces, and realities that are always extrapolitical or not political at all, be they economic, social, or of the broadest sort.[33]

But if politics is completely saturated by the social and the economic, the economic also broadly exceeds its own sphere of action, providing the essential foundation of social classes themselves and equally impacting some of the most fundamental realities on the political, social, cultural, family, and civilizational planes. This is not a vulgar economic reductionism; nor is it the case that the economic represents the hidden essence of the social. Rather, it is the recognition—as indicated also by Jean-Paul Sartre—of all the complex implications of the structural condition of scarcity that all human societies have suffered, from the moment the monkey evolved into man up to the present.

Since social power underlies political power and economic relations are the root and foundation of social classes and the central conflict between them, it becomes totally artificial and illegitimate to separate economic facts and phenomena from social ones or the latter, in turn, from political dimensions and realities. Therefore, the distinctions between economics, sociology, and political science are equally artificial and illegitimate. All this again delegitimizes and disarticulates the validity and justification of this division of the study of the social—corresponding to its "present" realities—into the economic, sociological, and political fields of analysis.[34]

Moreover, and following this same logic, if the present development of our scientific knowledge renders unsustainable that division between past and present, and with it the rigid separation between economics, sociology, and political science, then the division between "civilized" and "uncivilized" societies also becomes equally questionable and illegitimate. That same division lent support 130 years ago to the foundation of the science of anthropology and all its subbranches, like archaeology and ethnology, among others. If this profoundly racist and Eurocentric criterion could be accepted during the last third of the chronological nineteenth century, the entire chronological twentieth century has developed in opposition to this postulate, relativizing the implicit equation between European civilization and "civilization" per se and demonstrating how human history and historical social development have unfolded precisely as a complex civilizational "tree" with multiple branches, giving rise to as many civilizational paths as there have existed important human groups throughout time.[35] In this way, by conceiving of history as a complex dialectic among multiple civilizations, representing distinct combinations of technological, cultural, ritual, linguistic, scientific, family, and anthropological development, twentieth-century anthropology itself has ended up invalidating the central assumption that gave rise to it as a discipline, allowing us now to have a more universal and cosmopolitan perspective on general human evolution itself.

So when Claude Lévi-Strauss recovers so-called savage thought, showing us the different rationality through which such thought operates, or when he proposes to us that we consider modern bourgeois reason as a simple modern variant of older structures of the myth, he is fundamentally relativizing and dissolving that absurd and unsustainable difference between supposedly civilized and uncivilized societies. This becomes evident at the very moment when contemporary anthropologists begin to study European societies themselves, using the same tools forged to study and examine non-European societies, and even when they at first deem these exercises to be anthropologies of "complex societies." But when this division between the "civilized" and the "savage" or "barbaric" collapses, so does the difference between anthropology and the other social sciences, giving rise to the proliferation of the various current subbranches of anthropology, such as the anthropology of music, clothing, women, and social networks, as well as medical anthropology or historical, political, economic, or symbolic variants, among many others.

We now also see a proliferation of new and previously unknown fields of knowledge that no longer follow criteria defined by the current disciplines or social sciences—consider women's studies, cultural studies, folklore and popular culture studies, modern political ecological studies, or institutions dedicated to studying war and peace, or documentation centers for new anti-systemic social movements—Immanuel Wallerstein insists on the urgent task that we need to assume, as social scientists, in this immense project of the total restructuration of our knowledge of the social, which is today in complete crisis and in the process of total redefinition.

This project, moreover, is inscribed within a broader horizon, one defined by the fact that since the 1970s, various theories, developing from very different intellectual locations, have begun to question the traditional division of these modern forms of human knowledge under the rule of the so-called two or three cultures—that is, into natural sciences, social sciences, and humanities.[37] This multifaceted questioning stretches from the so-called complexity science, as for example proposed and defended by Nobel Prize winner Ilya Prigogine to modern cultural studies that now demand the profound relativization and historicization of the "canons" in which are rooted the classifications and analyses of the various areas of what we know as the "humanities."

In this way—and questioning equally the Galilean and Copernican visions of the so-called exact sciences, as well as those atemporal and abstract criteria that define the system of human arts—the new defenders of complexity sciences and cultural studies even question whether this division of our knowledges according to the criterion of the three cultures is legitimate or productive at present. This has led Wallerstein to study the history of this very separation of human knowledges into three cultures and therefore also to examine the specific criteria of justification that have founded these ruptures of science from philosophy and of philosophy from theorization about the arts, along with the subsequent fragmentation of philosophy into all the present social sciences, as discussed above.[38] This then brings us to a situation in which the dominant element is the end of the epistemological certainty around which we construct all present knowledges—that is to say, our knowledges and structures of comprehension and intellectual appropriation of the complex natural world, of the entire range that surrounds the world of the social, and of the complicated synthesis of realities and dimensions that comprise all of the human arts, or more briefly, the entire rationality through which we learn about the world and the universe, about our all-encompassing and global Weltanschauung.

This end of epistemological certainties—beyond being the most general horizon of this entire fourth axis of the world-systems approach—is also the framework within which this very perspective was born and developed, one that, not coincidentally, we refer to as *unthinking* the current social sciences. But this also means unthinking our understanding of the entire history of capitalism, of the history of the still unfinished long twentieth century, and of the immediate history of the terminal and definitive crisis of the capitalist world-system. This complex process of unthinking many of our most deeply rooted understandings of the problems that, as social scientists, we tackle on a daily basis finds one of its crucial points of support in the perspective of world-systems analysis and also in the intellectual work of Immanuel Wallerstein.

NOTES

1. The Immanuel Wallerstein Center for Research, Information, and Documentation was inaugurated in September 2004 as part of the University of La Tierra, Chiapas branch, and of CIDECI–Las Casas in San Cristóbal de las Casas, Chiapas. It is there that a permanent seminar has also been established with the goal of discussing and analyzing events and situations in Chiapas, in Mexico, in Latin America, and in the world, from multiple critical perspectives, among which the perspective of "world-systems analysis" developed by Wallerstein stands out particularly. The fortnightly commentaries mentioned earlier—in which Immanuel Wallerstein has been analyzing and diagnosing important global events during the past six and a half years, always from a critical and long-duration perspective—can be seen at the Fernand Braudel Center website (http://fbc.binghamton.edu), in the "Commentaries" section.

2. On Wallerstein's biography and intellectual journey, it is worth mentioning his own texts on the subject, for example, the introduction to *The Essential Wallerstein* (New York: The New Press, 2000), as well as "The Itinerary of World-Systems Analysis, or How to Resist Becoming a Theory," in *The Uncertainties of Knowledge* (Philadelphia: Temple University Press, 2004). For a descriptive rather than analytic synthesis of this intellectual biography, see Orlando Lentini, *La scienza sociale storica di Immanuel Wallerstein* (Milan: FrancoAngeli, 1998). For a more analytic and interpretive view of this intellectual journey, see our long introduction to Carlos Antonio Aguirre Rojas, *Immanuel Wallerstein: Crítica del sistema-mundo capitalista,* 2nd ed. (Mexico City: Era Editions, 2004).

3. It is worth insisting that Immanuel Wallerstein's work and the world-systems perspective are not identical, since his work includes, for example, his first books on Africa, at which point this perspective was still in gestation. Besides all of Wallerstein's work after 1973—since in 1974 he published volume 1 of *The Modern World-System,* in which this perspective would come together and be specified for the first time—world-systems analysis would also encompass the contributions of some of his close colleagues such as Giovanni Arrighi, André Gunder Frank, and Christopher Chase-Dunn, as well as the work of some of his disciples, like William G. Martín, Walter L. Goldfrank, and Richard Lee. But what interests us here is to recover the horizon of this perspective as contained in Wallerstein's work, which besides, and in our opinion, constitutes not only its fundamental structure but also its most finished form. On these other versions of the world-systems perspective—which are not necessarily in agreement with and are even occasionally antagonistic to that developed by Immanuel Wallerstein—see Giovanni Arrighi, *The Long Twentieth Century: Money, Power, and the Origins of Our Times* (London: Verso, 1994); Giovanni Arrighi and Beverly J. Silver, *Chaos and Governance in the Modern World System* (Minneapolis: University of Minnesota Press, 1999); André Gunder Frank and Barry K. Gills, *The World-System: 500 Years or 5000?* (London: Routledge, 1993); André Gunder Frank, *ReOrient: Global Economy in the Asian Age* (Berkeley: University of California Press, 1998); and the critiques of this last book by Giovanni Arrighi, Samir Amin, and Immanuel Wallerstein, included in *Review* 22, no. 3 (1999), and Christopher Chase-Dunn and Thomas D. Holl, *Core/Periphery Relations in the Precapitalist World* (San Francisco and Oxford: Westview Press, 1991).

4. The three books are *The Modern World-System,* Vol. 1 (San Diego: Academic Press, 1974), Vol. 2 (San Diego: Academic Press, 1980), and Vol. 3 (San Diego: Academic Press, 1988). On the idea of "long centuries"—which to all be *long* are necessarily superimposed on one another—see the interview with Immanuel Wallerstein, in Rojas, *Immanuel Wallerstein,* 198–99, 228–30, and 265–68, in which Wallerstein explains also how it is that he modified the initial periodization of the book proposed in the introduction to *The Modern World-System,* Vol. 1 (pp. 10–11) and how this change was the result of the process of writing the book itself.

5. If only to realize the accuracy of these prospective exercises, it is worth reviewing some of them, noting their original publication date and comparing them to later events that have occurred and which they sought to anticipate. See, for example, Immanuel Wallerstein, "Europa después del 92," in the political supplement to the newspaper *El Nacional* (November 2, 1989, but bearing in mind that the text was originally written and published in 1988), "La imagen global y las posibilidades alternativas de la evolución del sistema-mundo capitalista," in the *Revista Mexicana de Sociología* 60, no. 2 (1999, originally written and published in 1996), and also the essay "Peace, Stability, and Legitimacy: 1990–2025/2050," included in Immanuel Wallerstein, *After Liberalism* (New York: The New Press, 1995).

6. It is with this that Wallerstein distances himself completely from those projects—so fashionable today—of defending and promoting "interdisciplinarity," "pluridisciplinarity," "multidisciplinarity," and even "transdisciplinarity." Wallerstein's approach shows how all of these represent only very limited viewpoints and only seek to "repair" the present situation without attacking it at the roots: the very division of the study of the social into different, separate, autonomous, and even allegedly self-sufficient disciplines. Instead, Wallerstein defends the much more radical project of a new "unidisciplinarity" and, in

so doing, follows in the footsteps of Fernand Braudel. On Braudel's position, see Carlos Antonio Aguirre Rojas, *Fernand Braudel et les sciences humaines* (Paris: L'Harmattan, 2004), ch. 4 and appendix 2. In general, one could also consult our essay "Rethinking Current Social Sciences: The Case of Historical Discourses in the History of Modernity," *Journal of World-Systems Research* 6, no. 3 (fall–winter 2000), available at http://jwsr.ucr.edu/archive/vol6/number3/pdf/jwsr-v6n3-aguirrerojas.pdf, as well as *Antimanual del mal historiador*, 7th Latin American ed. (Mexico City: Contrahistorias, 2004).

7. On the Annales School, see Carlos Antonio Aguirre Rojas, *La Escuela de los Annales* (Barcelona: Montesinos, 1999), now available in German translation with an updated bibliography, *Die Schule der Annales* (Leipzig: Leipziger, Universitaetsverlagm 2004); Rojas, *Los Annales y la historiografía francesa* (Mexico City: Quinto Sol, 1996); and Rojas, *La historiografía del siglo XX* (Barcelona: Montesinos, 2004).

8. On this broad "genealogical tree," see also, besides the autobiographical texts by Wallerstein mentioned previously, chapter 1, "Historical Origins of World-Systems Analysis: From Social Disciplines to Historical Social Sciences," in *World-Systems Analysis: An Introduction* (Durham, NC: Duke University Press, 2004), 1–22. With respect to the fundamental role of the Marxist and Braudelian matrices, it's no coincidence that Wallerstein dedicated an entire section to Marx and another to Braudel in his book *Unthinking Social Science: The Limits of Nineteenth-Century Paradigms* (Cambridge: Polity Press, 1991).

9. On the importance of this thesis with respect to the relevant unit of analysis, see, for example, the following by Immanuel Wallerstein: "Hold the Tiller Firm: On Method and the Unit of Analysis," *Comparative Civilizations Review*, no. 30 (spring 1994); the article "World-System," in *Dictionary of Marxist Thought* (Oxford: Blackwell, 1991); "World-System Analysis," in *Encyclopedia of Political Economy* (London: Routledge, 1999); and the essay "Societal Development or Development of the World-System?" in *Unthinking Social Science*, 64–79.

10. For the examples referred to here, and in the same order that they are mentioned in our argument, see Wallerstein, *The Modern World-System*; Immanuel Wallerstein, "1968, Revolución en el sistema-mundo: Tesis e interrogantes," *Estudios sociológicos*, no. 20 (Mexico City) (1989); Giovanni Arrighi, Terence K. Hopkins, and Immanuel Wallerstein, "1989, the Continuation of 1968," in *Review* 15, no. 2 (spring 1992): 221–242; Wallerstein, *The Modern World-System*, Vol. 3; "The Collapse of Liberalism," in Wallerstein, *After Liberalism*, 232–251; and Carlos Antonio Aguirre Rojas, "Tres comentarios de Immanuel Wallerstein sobre la historia reciente de México," appendix 1 in Rojas, *Immanuel Wallerstein*.

11. For a broader explanation of these differences, see, for example, Immanuel Wallerstein's *The Capitalist World-Economy* (Cambridge: Cambridge University Press and Maison des Sciences de l'Homme, 1979), *Historical Capitalism and Antisystemic Movements*, and *World-Systems Analysis: An Introduction* (Durham, NC: Duke University Press, 2004).

12. On this social, political, and cultural projection of economic inequality between the core, semiperiphery, and periphery, see Immanuel Wallerstein, *The Politics of the World-Economy* (Cambridge: Cambridge University Press and Maison des Sciences de l'Homme, 1984).

13. On this present situation and the possible future destiny of Latin America, the reader can consult Carlos Antonio Aguirre Rojas, *América Latina: Historia y presente* (Morelia: Jitanjáfora, 2000), and also several of the essays included in the book *Para comprender el mundo actual: Una gramática de larga duración* (Havana: Centro Juan Marinello, 2003).

14. On this point, see Fernand Braudel, "History and Social Sciences: The Long Duration," in *Writings on History*. Also, Carlos Antonio Aguirre Rojas, *Fernand Braudel y las ciencias humanas* (Barcelona: Montesinos, 1996), whose French edition, which includes various appendices and an updated bibliography, we have cited above, and also *Ensayos braudelianos* (Rosario: Prohistoria, 2000).

15. On this situation of historical bifurcation, on which Immanuel Wallerstein has been insisting for a long time now, see the book coordinated by him and Terence K. Hopkins, *The Age of Transition: Trajectory of the World-System, 1945–2025* (New York: Zed Books, 1996); Wallerstein, *After Liberalism*; and "The World We Are Entering, 2000–2050 (32 Propositions)," in *The World We Are Entering, 2000–2050,* ed. I. Wallerstein and A. Clesse (Amsterdam: Dutch University Press, 2002), 9–22.

16. On the tragedy of September 11, 2001, various other contemporary events, and the irrational U.S. response to this new situation that we have been living in since then, see Immanuel Wallerstein, *The Decline of American Power* (New York: The New Press, 1993), and also *Alternatives: The United States Confronts the World* (Boulder and London: Paradigm Publishers, 2004). See also our various essays included in Rojas, *Para comprender el mundo actual.*

17. On this important polemic on a "short" versus a "long" twentieth century, it is worth reviewing the distinct positions developed by the different authors in question. For example, the stance of defending a short twentieth century can be seen in Eric Hobsbawm, *The Age of Extremes: The Short Twentieth Century, 1914–1991* (London: Michael Joseph, 1994), or in Jürgen Habermas, "Our Short Century," *Nexos* (August 1998), and in the collected volume *Le court vingtième siècle, 1914–1991* (La Tour d'Aigües: Ed. de l'Aube, 1991). On the other hand, the thesis of a long twentieth century can be seen developed in Arrighi, *The Long Twentieth Century;* Immanuel Wallerstein, "Last Century, Last Millennium," *La Jornada,* March 10, 2000; and Immanuel Wallerstein, "The 20th Century: Darkness at Noon?," *Eseconomía,* no. 2 (2003). For other interpretations of the twentieth century, it is also worth looking at the texts of Bolívar Echeverría, "El sentido del siglo XX," *Prohistoria,* no. 8 (Rosario) (2004); Edward Said's critique of Hobsbawm's book, "Historical Experience," *Viento del Sur,* no. 8 (1996); the interesting essay by Fernand Braudel, "La faillite de la paix, 1918–1939," in *Les écrits de Fernand Braudel: L'histoire au quotidien* (Paris: De Fallois, 2001); and Carlos Antonio Aguirre Rojas, "Balance crítico del siglo XX histórico: ¿Breve, largo o muy largo siglo XX?," in Rojas, *Para comprender el mundo actual.* Finally, and for the specifically Mexican case, see Bolívar Echeverría's interview with Carlos Monsiváis, "El breve siglo XX mexicano," *Contrahistorias,* no. 4 (2005), and also the introduction to Rojas, *Antimanual del mal historiador.*

18. On this point, see Immanuel Wallerstein, "The Three Successive Hegemonies in the History of the Capitalist World-Economy," in *Historical Capitalism and Antisystemic Movements.* See also Carlos Antonio Aguirre Rojas, introduction to Rojas, *Immanuel Wallerstein,* 51–54.

19. On this critique of Eurocentrism, see Immanuel Wallerstein, "Eurocentrism and Its Avatars," in *The End of the World as We Know It.*

20. For the approach that minimizes the meaning of the global revolution of 1968, see Hobsbawm, *History of the 20th Century,* 322–45. In contrast, for the position that values this revolution more highly in terms of its fundamental effects and historical-universal significance, see Fernand Braudel, "Rebirth, Reform, 1968: Cultural Revolutions . . . ,"

La Jornada Semanal, no. 226 (October 10, 1993); Immanuel Wallerstein, "1968: Revolution in the World-System: Arguments and Questions," cited above as "1968, Revolución en el sistema-mundo: Tesis e interrogantes"; and Carlos Antonio Aguirre Rojas, "1968: La gran ruptura," and "Repensando los movimientos del 1968," in Rojas, *Para comprender el mundo actual.*

21. On this critique of the concepts of globalization and mundialization, see Immanuel Wallerstein, "Globalization or Era of Transition? A Long Duration Perspective on the Trajectory of the World-System," *Eseconomía* 1 (Mexico City) (2002), and Carlos Antonio Aguirre Rojas, "A modo de introducción: Una perspectiva histórico-crítica de la 'globalización' y la 'mundialización,'" in Rojas, *Para comprender el mundo actual.*

22. Immanuel Wallerstein has characterized the various expressions of this multifaceted crisis in several of his essays and books. In this respect and only by way of example, see Wallerstein's *After Liberalism; The End of the World as We Know It; The Essential Wallerstein;* and *Utopistics: Or Historical Choices of the Twenty-First Century* (New York: The New Press, 1998). For a broad synthesis of all Wallerstein's discussions on this subject, see Rojas, *Immanuel Wallerstein,* 72–111.

23. On this point, see Immanuel Wallerstein, "Ecology and Capitalist Costs of Production: No Exit," in *Ecology and the World-System,* ed. W. Goldfrank et al. (Westport, CT: Greenwood Press, 1999), 3–11, and also the essay "Ecology and the Economy: What Is Rational?," *Review* 27, no. 4 (2004): 274–283.

24. On all of these symptoms of this terminal economic crisis of capitalism, see Immanuel Wallerstein, "The Modern World-System in Crisis: Bifurcation, Chaos, and Choices," chapter 5 in *World-Systems Analysis,* 76–90.

25. This, precisely, was Marx's idea: that the end of capitalism is also the complete death of the human activity of politics. This is what is expressed transparently when he affirms, for example, the following: "Only in an order of things in which classes and class antagonism no longer exist will *social evolutions* cease to be *political revolutions*" (*The Poverty of Philosophy,* ch. 2, pt. 5).

26. On this point, see Immanuel Wallerstein, "The Collapse of Liberalism," in *After Liberalism.*

27. On this point, see Wallerstein, *Alternatives.* See also Carlos Antonio Aguirre Rojas, "El 11 de septiembre de 2001: Una puesta en perspectiva histórica" and "Las lecciones de la invasión a Irak," in Rojas, *Para comprender el mundo actual.*

28. On the role of Japan within the present world-system, see his essay "Japan and the Future Trajectory of the World-System: Lessons from History?" in Immanuel Wallerstein, *Geopolitics and Geoculture: Essays on the Changing World-System* (Cambridge: Cambridge University Press and Maison de Sciences de l'Homme, 1991).

29. On this European role, see "European Unity and Its Implications for the Interstate System," in Wallerstein, *Geopolitics and Geoculture.* A more recent version of the same point can be seen in his short essay "Bush's Geopolitical Legacy," Fernand Braudel Center, http://www2.binghamton.edu/fbc/archive/158en.htm.

30. In this last sense, especially relevant is the work of Carlo Ginzburg, who has concentrated his attention precisely on the study and deciphering of the codes and structures of this popular knowledge and its relation to hegemonic culture. On this subject, see Carlo Ginzburg, *The Cheese and the Worms: The Cosmos of a Sixteenth-Century Miller* (Baltimore: Johns Hopkins University Press, 1980), *Tentativas* (Rosario: Prohistoria, 2004), and

Wooden Eyes: Nine Reflections on Distance (New York: Columbia University Press, 2001). See also Carlos Antonio Aguirre Rojas, *Contribución a la historia de la microhistoria italiana* (Rosario: Prohistoria, 2003), and "El queso y los gusanos: Un modelo de historia crítica para el análisis de las culturas subalternas," in Ginzburg, *Tentativas.*

31. For Fernand Braudel's critique of this inter/multi/pluri/transdisciplinarity, see, for example, the interview "Une vie pour l'histoire," *Le Magazine Littéraire,* no. 212 (November 1984), in which Braudel says, "Interdisciplinarity is like a legal marriage between two neighboring sciences. On the other hand, I am more in favor of a sort of generalized promiscuity. Thus, the lovers who believe in making an interscience, marrying one science to another is too cautious. What should prevail here is bad behavior: we should mix all of the sciences, even the most traditional like philosophy, philology, etc." (22). More generally, see also chapter 4 of Rojas, *Fernand Braudel y las ciencias humanas,* 91–108. For Wallerstein's position on this new "unidisciplinarity" and new "social-historical sciences" and their implications, see also Rojas, *Immanuel Wallerstein,* 335–47.

32. On this point, see several of the essays in the book by Fernand Braudel, *On History* (Chicago: University of Chicago Press, 1982), and also Marc Bloch, *The Historian's Craft* (Manchester, UK: Manchester University Press, 1992), and Rojas, *Antimanual del mal historiador.* See also Immanuel Wallerstein et al., *Open the Social Sciences: Report of the Gulbenkian Commission on the Restructuring of the Social Sciences* (Stanford, CA: Stanford University Press, 1996), and Wallerstein's essay "Writing History," in *The Uncertainties of Knowledge* (Philadelphia: Temple University Press, 2004), 126–141.

33. On this problem, it is always useful to reread Marx, for example, *The Poverty of Philosophy, The German Ideology,* or also various brilliant fragments in the *Grundrisse.*

34. This naturally does not prevent us from recuperating the central thinkers of all these disciplinary fields or parceled-out social sciences, and even using the tools they provide to move toward this new unidisciplinary vision of the social, as Wallerstein himself has explained for the particular case of sociology in his essay "The Heritage of Sociology, the Promise of Social Science," *Current Sociology* 47, no. 1 (1999): 1–37.

35. On this critique of the concept of civilization, which is used first in the singular before turning to the plural, it is worth looking over the book *Civilisation: Le mot et l'idée* (Paris: La Renaissance du Livre, 1930), especially the essays by Marcel Mauss and Lucien Febvre; also see the article by Fernand Braudel, "The History of Civilizations: The Past Explains the Present," in Braudel, *On History,* and chapter 5 in Rojas, *Fernand Braudel y las ciencias humanas.*

36. On this rule of the so-called three cultures, see Wolf Lepenies, *Die drei Kulturen: Soziologie zwischen Literatur und Wissenschaft* (Frankfurt: Fischerverlage, 2002).

37. On this point, which is still an open line within the present research of Immanuel Wallerstein and within world-systems analysis, see the following by Wallerstein: *The Uncertainties of Knowledge;* and "The Challenge of Maturity: Whither Social Science?," *Review* 14, no. 1 (winter 1992): 1–7.

CHAPTER ONE

The World-Systems Analysis Perspective

An Interview with Immanuel Wallerstein

Carlos Antonio Aguirre Rojas

BIOGRAPHICAL-INTELLECTUAL SKETCH

CARLOS ANTONIO AGUIRRE ROJAS: Your adolescence and early years were spent in the United States under McCarthyism, which you studied for your master's thesis. How did this McCarthyist atmosphere influence your intellectual development and your studies? What were your arguments and conclusions in your master's thesis? Do you still maintain them today?

IMMANUEL WALLERSTEIN: During that period the atmosphere of McCarthyism was very difficult, but this did not influence my political opinions. My reaction to McCarthyism, which developed when I was quite young, owes more to the fact that I was already on the left. So I was against McCarthy. At that time, everyone was. For example, within the environment of the university, the great majority of people were in opposition to McCarthy, against him. So when I wrote this thesis on McCarthyism,[1] it was very well received. And it was well received because I attempted to discover the political foundations of McCarthyism, in a different way than it had been explained up to that point.

Originally published in Immanuel Wallerstein, *La crisis estructural del capitalismo* (Mexico City: Contrahistorias, 2005), 5–56.

Several professors even found the thesis interesting and cited it. Because what I say there, in essence using the theory of C. Wright Mills—who said that there were two types of right in the United States and the world: in the first place, an intelligent, agile, internationalist right, and on the other hand a narrow-minded right, much slower and more conservative—what I argue there is that McCarthy represented this second right, much more narrow-minded and radical in its conservatism, and as a result the principal enemy of the right that McCarthy represented was *not* the left but rather precisely this intelligent right, which was at the same time internationalist and high up in the social hierarchy. Because McCarthy also expressed a certain ethnicism, since he represented all those people who had suffered a degree of domination by WASPs,[2] and who constituted a dominant sector within the traditional right in the United States.

That was the principal thesis. For me it was a subject that was obviously worth studying at the time. Although the thesis was presented in 1954, and we should not forget that in that year we were already in the post-McCarthy era. At that time, McCarthy had already been removed, which had occurred in 1953. I got the idea of developing this subject when I read Wright Mills, thinking that he provided a way to explain what McCarthy had represented. I carried out a very detailed empirical analysis, and at the same time an analysis of his speeches, of the themes that he had repeated or put at the center of his concerns, working in the realm of what was then called "content analysis."

CAAR: Were you politically committed at that time?

IW: In 1954–1955 I was not a member of any organization, because at that time we were passing through a period of what we could call a certain drowsiness of the American left. I had been politically engaged earlier, in 1951. Then I entered the army to do military service during the two years up to 1953, and when I returned there was very little activity.

CAAR: Your first article, which dates from 1951, is it related to this political engagement that you mention?

IW: The first article that I wrote, entitled "Revolution and Order,"[3] was indeed written in 1951. At that time, I was participating very actively in a student movement that supported the creation of a global federal government. The article was written for the journal of the movement, and what I wanted to say at that time about the problem was that federalism supported another International, but that this new International could not be created without taking into account the existence of a revolutionary movement in the Third

World. Because the federalist movement was at that moment completely blind to the participation or the role of the Third World. For them, the problem was reducible to the United States and the Soviet Union, and the question was one of how to achieve peace between the two, that is, a vision that only considered East-West relations. So at that time what I attempted to do in that article was to introduce into the debate the question of the role of the South in all of this. This was something that also constituted a political commitment: to put the question of attention to the problem of the South, of the Third World, at the center, raising consciousness about its essential role.

CAAR: Let's return to your master's thesis. Do you think that the arguments that you made in that work were correct? Would you support them now?

IW: Yes. Considered grosso modo, I believe that those theses are correct, the idea that McCarthy represented a movement whose principal roots were outside of and beyond the American Northeast, outside and even against the American elite. Obviously, McCarthy was against the communists, but in reality he mixed them both together, always insisting that the people he mentioned were very suspect people. He referred to people, for example, like Alger Hiss, who was one of the most important cases of that period, and who also came from the social group representing the internationalist and enlightened right. That is, McCarthy had simultaneously an *antiestablishment* and an anticommunist position, and what he did was to blend both positions into a single one.

CAAR: What was the influence of having studied at Columbia University, a place that at one point attracted some of the most important émigré intellectuals of the Second World War, people like the members of the Frankfurt School, or like Claude Lévi-Strauss or Roman Jakobson, people who also worked at one point at the New School for Social Research? Did you read these authors in your youth?

IW: This question touches on a potentially confusing point, because on the one hand there is Columbia University, and on the other the New School for Social Research, but these are two different things. There was no relationship between the two except that both are located in the same city, New York. For example, Claude Lévi-Strauss or Roman Jakobson had absolutely nothing to do with Columbia University, and moreover they were there during the war at a time when I was in high school. On the other hand, the Frankfurt School was different, because various members taught at Columbia—for example, Max Horkheimer, as well as Franz Neumann and Herbert Marcuse.

CAAR: And Theodor Adorno?

IW: No. Adorno was in the United States but not teaching, if I recall correctly. He was dedicating himself more to research. Nevertheless, everyone was reading, for example, *The Authoritarian Personality*,[4] a text that was fashionable at the time, at least in Columbia's Sociology Department. I read it around that time. Returning to your question, I will tell you that I had very little contact with Horkheimer. On the other hand, I attended the courses of Neumann, and I was going to take his doctoral seminar when he died in an accident.

On the other hand, Marcuse only visited for two years. He was a magnificent professor, and I attended those courses for the entire two years. The Frankfurt School, in this way, had an important resonance for me. I knew that the school existed, and I had read many of the works of Marcuse and also of Franz Neumann. I read Claude Lévi-Strauss while I was studying for my doctorate, but I wouldn't say that he had much influence on my thought. And I could add that I have never felt attracted to Lévi-Strauss's thought. And I simply had no relation with Roman Jakobson.

CAAR: What other intellectual experiences do you think were important during your studies at Columbia?

IW: On this point, I would refer you to the introduction to the book *The Essential Wallerstein*.[5] These influences were of a broad order, and there was an entire group of professors that were very influential. For example, there was Mark van Doren, a great man of letters, member of a very famous family in the United States. Van Doren had a very original, very global view of things, a bit out of the norm and that influenced me. I also followed the courses of Paul Tillich, who was a great theologian. Because near Columbia there was the Union Theological Seminary, an institution in which Tillich gave courses, which I attended, on the subject of Protestants and Protestantism. Paul Tillich had a very original understanding of the religious message: it was almost secular. And in whatever way, it was Tillich who introduced me to the idea or concept of *kairos* that I would use later. Raymond Bulman published an article in *Review* in which he attempts to demonstrate the influence of Paul Tillich on my own thought.[6]

C. Wright Mills was also very important, first as my professor and later as a colleague. There was also Robert Lynd, famous for two things: in the first place for having written a book called *Middletown*,[7] which was an ethnographic study of a small American city, a study that explained the reality of power and the relations of power in this small city. Later, and in the second place, he wrote a book entitled *Knowledge for What?*,[8] which was a call for committed knowledge, that knowledge must serve to transform the world.

I also have a very important intellectual debt to Karl Marx, Sigmund Freud, Joseph Schumpeter, and Karl Polanyi (whom I knew). And I should add that the three people who have had the greatest impact in my thought—since I knew them personally and directly, and they managed to modify the manner in which I perceived the world—were Frantz Fanon, Fernand Braudel, and Ilya Prigogine. Fanon was the first of the three that I knew personally. He died in 1961, but I saw him on two occasions: the first in 1960, when I was with him for a week in Accra, Ghana, and then the next year, in 1961, when he was dying in a hospital in the United States where I went to see him. I read his work from the beginning, since he began to publish, and I tried personally to make sure that his works were translated in the United States. After that, I came to know Braudel—in the 1970s, perhaps in 1972—and finally Ilya Prigogine, whom I met for the first time in 1980.

CAAR: How much did it influence your work to have been born in New York, a cosmopolitan and "capital" city within the world-economy?

IW: Ah! The role of New York. It's absolutely essential for me. I was born in New York, I'm a complete New Yorker, in terms of my tastes and temperament, and with a great degree of fidelity. And I'm a New Yorker by upbringing, without a doubt. And yes, New York is a very cosmopolitan city and has been, as you say, the capital of the world-economy. But it has also been—and this is something crucial—the seat of the United Nations. This is very important for me: I spent a lot of time at the UN between 1958 and 1963. But in any case, it's true that New York was something special: everyone visited the city. In my intellectual biography it plays a central role, greatly influencing how I saw the world. It was from this city that I was able to perceive the confluence of many different tendencies, many distinct geographies, beyond its location at the very heart of power. The fact of having been born in New York, of having grown up there and lived my first years as a writer and professor in that city, has been absolutely fundamental for me.

Regarding the United Nations, it's important to remember that from 1958 onward I was an Africanist. I was already a professor by then, and 1957 marked the entry of Ghana into the UN. After that, 1958 saw the admission of Guinea, which was very important, and 1960 was the Year of Africa. That year, a significant number—sixteen African countries—became members of the UN. And moreover, there were delegations from the various national liberation movements of still-colonized countries. And they all came to New York every fall to participate in the UN General Assembly. So important African leaders came to New York every September, October, or November for at least a few weeks. And as was the practice, each of the delegations held regular receptions, and since I was on the guest list, I would attend these receptions at the UN after six in the evening, at which there would be about two hundred people. With some small changes, these were generally the same two hundred people every time.

In this way, I got to know those people very well, those leaders who would later be my contacts when I went on to work in different locations in Africa. You could almost say that for a certain period, New York was like the center of Africa. Clearly, a bit later it would become a much less important place for Africa, but during those years—let's say from 1957 or 1958 to 1965—New York was the point at which the greater part of African leaders met, and also the place where many of them made contacts with the rest of the world. So for an Africa scholar, this experience of being in New York was something exceptional.

CAAR: And perhaps also from the informational point of view. I think it would have been very difficult to construct as broad a comparative and global perspective without the support of all the information that is concentrated in New York . . .

IW: Yes, without a doubt. The quantity of information was truly incredible. So, at that time I realized that, in order to find out about the present, it's necessary in any conversation to know ahead of time 80 percent of what is occurring. With that 80 percent of information, it's possible to pose an entire series of small questions to some specific people in a relaxed atmosphere, and in this way one can learn much more, and in an immediate way. Because from this information, one knows precisely which question is the right one to pose, thereby immediately also convincing the other person that they are speaking with an intelligent interlocutor who knows the subject they are discussing, and this makes all the difference. It is from this that one arrives at a certain level, and from there precisely one can begin to construct.

If you look at my first two books about Africa—the first, *Africa: The Politics of Independence,* and the second, *Africa: The Politics of Unity*—you will see that I used and exhausted all of this informal information, to put it one way, but also all of this documentational information.[9] Because these people passed me documents that were not secret but which weren't easy to get. And moreover, I spent two months a year in Africa, during the summer, stopping over in fifteen different African countries. In these stops, I met with various people whom I already knew ahead of time, or to whom I had been introduced or referred, and in this way I had even more information. And in this way I was able to construct contemporary history—and even, in a stricter sense, the immediate history—of the African countries that I was studying, which would have been impossible were it not for this network of intimate acquaintances and close people and the studies mentioned.

You're not an Africanist, but if you read *Africa: The Politics of Unity,* you will see that I develop there a very detailed account of all that happened in those comings and goings of those African leaders and their decisions. I kept myself well-informed in that respect, and while I was more or less committed to certain positions, I had good relations with all parties and was able to maintain sufficient distance so that everyone would consider me to be, if not objective, at least willing to give them the benefit of the doubt and to include their different points of view within the argument of my book.

CAAR: I have the impression, which I share with others, that the contribution of thinkers from a Jewish background has been essential to the construction of European and global culture during the past 150 years, from Marx himself to current Italian microhistory, passing through thinkers like Émile Durkheim, Marc Bloch, Ernst Bloch, the whole Frankfurt School, Norbert Elias, Claude Lévi-Strauss, and so forth. The question is then if you consider your Jewish origin to have influenced in some way your intellectual itinerary or work, and if this is the case, how in particular.

IW: To begin, if you ask me, for example, of these thinkers you have mentioned, if for me it was important that they were Jewish, I would say no. At the time that I read Marc Bloch, Lévi-Strauss, Durkheim, or other authors, I did not think that their work was more or less interesting because of the fact that they were Jews. Nor am I certain that this decisively influenced their respective works or thought, and nor did it affect the attitude that I had toward them. Regardless, I have felt identified as a Jew, and this did not bother me at all. For me, this is a very important intellectual tradition, the carrier of an ethic that no doubt influenced me. And it's also certain that I realized completely that an important number of revolutionary thinkers were Jewish, and that the fact of being Jewish, and as a result never being well received or integrated into society, made them to a certain degree a species of "foreigners." I think that Jews are a bit like anthropologists: at the same time that they are found in the condition of the foreigner, they study the subject to the marrow, which gives them a crucial viewpoint. And alongside this, the fact that Jews were persecuted even after the Second World War has given them a position more or less on the left. They were persecuted for being Jews, but also largely for being poor people, and people were as a consequence very active from their own class condition.

This has all changed after the Second World War, because Jews in Western countries have been able to climb the social ladder both as a result of a decline in anti-Semitism—a decline that may not have been real but has indeed existed in practice, deriving from the war and the reaction it provoked against Nazism—and also because they had been admitted to fill an entire variety of professional positions, and they took advantage of that opportunity. Therefore, the class status of the Jewish population in the United States, France, and England, and in all of Europe more generally, has changed completely. They became members of the middle class and even the upper class, and as a result their political positions have also changed. Perhaps not as quickly as their social condition, but it has changed regardless.

So there exists now in the United States an entire group of people who refer to themselves as Republican Jews, something which would have been completely unthinkable in my youth. Perhaps this or that person in particular could be Jewish and Republican at the same time, but the idea that an entire group of Jews could refer to themselves in this way was impossible. At that time, Jews were either Democrats or on the extreme left: there was no other possibility for them in New York. Today, however, Jews on the far left are somewhat less common, and the majority are either Democrats or Republicans, as a result of the change I mentioned.

Now, if you ask me if this Jewish condition has influenced my intellectual itinerary or my work, I would respond that I believe that insofar as I am committed, be it morally or politically, this commitment is part of a Jewish heritage.

CAAR: I would like to recall that, in some of our previous conversations, you also mentioned that this Jewish condition has made you a more sensitive person, for example, when it comes to questions of nationalism and some related issues ...

IW: Yes, you're completely right. In my youth, the question of Jewish nationalism was central. In the discussions of the time, it was part of the debate over whether or not a State of Israel should be created. Obviously, before that state had been created, and if it was created, what attitude was necessary toward it. I knew very well these arguments pro or contra coming from practically all sectors, from all different positions. And when I began to dedicate myself to studying Africa, I immediately realized that in the African debates one finds exactly the same arguments, for and against the subject of nationalism in Africa. Clearly, the geography changed—it was different—but the substance of the arguments was exactly the same, and the only thing that changed then was the nouns.

So I traveled that path regarding the African debate on nationalism, and one of the reasons that I felt a great empathy for the Palestinian cause from the beginning was because I couldn't see any difference between their arguments and those that the Jews had made. They were exactly the same, and the same logic underlay both positions. I was therefore very sensitized to these sorts of discussions, and that was one of the reasons I was able to fully commit myself to the African process, to the struggle by African countries for their independence. And this helped me to understand that African struggle, at the same time that I grasped its own limits, the limits of this nationalism.

But it's necessary to say that not all Jews took a similar path. Perhaps prior to 1948, but not thereafter, because from the emergence of the Arab-Israeli conflict, or the Arab-Jewish conflict, there came into existence an important group of Jews committed to the Israeli cause, who saw Arabs as enemy number one, thus to a position that brought them closer to the West. Because we shouldn't forget that prior to 1948, Zionism was a clearly anti-Western movement, which rejected the West, but after 1948 it became the absolute opposite. There then occurred a clear swing in Zionism and its whole logic after 1948, which constitutes a new reflection of real political evolution, of the real situation, but which from an intellectual point of view seems incomprehensible.

Well, I don't want to construct an entire discourse on Zionism, although it would be very interesting for me to reconstruct the whole intellectual and historical itinerary of Zionism as a movement. But with respect to me, and I am here speaking strictly of personal experience, the fact of having been immersed within an atmosphere in which the question of the legitimacy of Jewish nationalism was discussed ceaselessly, and with regard to the alternative, which was total integration—what was at that time referred to as an assimilation to the Christian world—the fact of having listened to and passed through all of those arguments made me extremely sensitive, even to the point of having a certain degree of sympathy with those same arguments when I have seen them developed in other places. For example, in the case of Algeria. Because what was the Algerian debate if not a debate on whether or not to affirm itself as a part of French civilization and say, I'm not Algerian, I'm really French, and on the other hand those who said, No, no, no, no way, we will never be truly accepted. And when I heard this debate in Algeria, I was immediately reminded of the similar Jewish debate, developed in an almost identical manner except, obviously, for the fact that the one dealt with Algeria and the other with Israel.

CAAR: I also believe that on another occasion you mentioned, from a more specifically personal perspective, about your family network, for example, the fact that you had an uncle who lived in Mexico, another who lived in Paris, and so forth.

IW: Yes, that's true. Like all Jewish families from Central Europe—families that lived global transformations, above all after the First World War, and later with Hitler, but even prior to Hitler—mine also suffered an enormous dispersion of people and family members. Take for example the case of my parents, who were born in two small cities that formed part of the territory of the Austro-Hungarian Empire, and who had then come to emigrate to Berlin, which was their first emigration and where they met. After that, my parents emigrated to New York, and with the rise of Hitler, one of my uncles was forced to move to Paris. Another of my uncles emigrated to Mexico. But this was a completely normal process: at that time it was something very common, in no way an exceptional situation. So this gave me, for example, a sort of family that was dispersed all over the world. And I also have friends who had relatives, for example, in Brazil, or others with family in South Africa. And there were others who spent some of their lives in China, people who in fleeing Germany ended up, for example, in Shanghai, put down roots there, and began to construct their lives in eastern Asia.

So it was not only my immediate family, but also those of many of my close friends, that had developed this feeling of being part of what were, in a certain sense, global families, living in many different countries, and might visit other family members in far-off places. This is something that I believe is no doubt a different experience from that of other types of families that are born in more or less the same space, and in which even the largest family lives and develops generally within that same space. This makes a big difference even from the linguistic point of view, because this was an impetus, for example, to speak various languages at the same time.

CAAR: Yes. I believe you mentioned this at some point, in the sense that this situation perhaps opened broader horizons for you since childhood, in order to develop certain linguistic capacities, to practice in different languages.

IW: Yes, of course. For example, my family, originating from a German-speaking area, obviously spoke German, but when they came to New York they began to speak English. They even spoke English at home, but it's also true that they often had friends visiting, people who had just arrived in the United States and couldn't speak English, or who sometimes didn't want to, and so my parents would speak German with those friends. This was such that, from a very young age, I often heard German spoken in my own house. But I should say that, despite hearing it often, German was a language that I didn't learn very well, perhaps because as a young American I had a certain resistance to German ...

CAAR: But resistance in what sense? To what exactly? What do you mean by that?

IW: It's often been shown that second-generation Americans, those who were children of emigrants who had come to the country, generally rejected the original language of their parents with the goal of integrating better into the new environment of the United States. It's generally only the third generation that begins to relearn the language, to return to a more open attitude with regard to this original language. But in any case, I heard German from a very young age. It's also true that from this very early period, I had the opportunity to study French in school, and I immediately took advantage of this possibility. However, neither my mother nor my father spoke French; nor could they read it. And Spanish came later. My uncle, who as I mentioned lived in Mexico, obviously spoke Spanish, and I remember that my older brother once went to visit him and spent six months in Mexico, thereby learning Spanish as well. Later, I too began to study Spanish.

So, this is all to say that I was educated within an environment in which many languages were spoken and heard, and this was considered to be completely normal. During their childhood, my parents had also spoken various languages; moreover, they were from the Austro-Hungarian Empire, in which different languages were spoken. So for me, learning various languages was something completely normal.

In whatever case, when I finished high school, I could read French fairly well. I still didn't speak it very well, but I had a good foundation for the language. My Spanish too had developed a bit, and so I had some elements to know how to construct statements in that language. I learned Italian later, and after that, in order to learn Portuguese, I read a book that explained how to convert Spanish words into Portuguese, and this worked more or less. Since I like languages quite a lot, I make an effort to continue improving the various languages that I know, starting with English itself: one could say that I have spent my entire life attempting to perfect my English.

CAAR: How do you go about perfecting your own language, English? Do you work through a dictionary?

IW: Well, yes. For example, if I see or hear a word that I don't know, I turn to the dictionary to look it up immediately, but I also do crossword puzzles regularly, and this teaches me new words. I also occasionally read books about how to use English well, to such a degree that I feel that I have truly attempted to improve my English all the time, up to the present.

CAAR: Just one point to close our discussion of languages: I seem to remember you once mentioning that you became a professional actor and were even paid, performing a play in French. Is this true?

IW: Yes, it is, but that was when I was younger, when I was between ten and fifteen, more or less.

CAAR: But why didn't you continue developing as an actor? Why didn't you continue to work along these lines?

IW: Because what I really wanted to do was to quit acting, to get into university and dedicate myself to something else.

CAAR: But was there ever a moment in which you couldn't make up your mind between acting or doing something else?

IW: Well, I have always adored the theater, right up to the present, but I didn't want to be an actor. This was really more of my mother's desire, since she was an artist. She wanted one of her children also to be an artist, like her. In this way, my older brother dedicated his childhood to painting. But in the end, he didn't want to devote himself to painting, so he stopped and became a doctor. Moreover, it must be said that he was never a great painter. Afterward, I wanted to be an actor for a while, but in the end I didn't want to be an actor. I really didn't want to—although we could say that a good professor is really an actor deep down.

CAAR: You've taught practically all your life, right?

IW: Yes. Let's say from 1958 to 1999.

CAAR: And have you taught since then?

IW: I have continued to lecture, when invited.

CAAR: Let's continue to the next question. How did your experience in Africa influence your point of view?

IW: Africa has been absolutely central to my intellectual experience. To start from the beginning, I will tell you that already from high school I had that teacher I mentioned earlier, who had a truly global view of things, something which was in no way common at the time, but was, rather, very exceptional. This teacher organized a course that I took on Asia, in which she explained to us a bit about Japan, China, and India. At that point, India began to fascinate me: I began to read all about it. I read about Gandhi, I read about Nehru, and later I even visited India, in 1954.

But in any case, what is certain is that at that time I had already been active for a good amount of time, due to my participation in the federalist movement mentioned previously—because the organization had joined the Young Adult Council (YAC), in which I also participated actively. Afterward, I participated via YAC in the World Assembly of Youth (WAY), of which I was at one point named vice president. In 1951, the first time that I participated in a meeting of WAY, the meeting was held in the United States. And this meeting had a large number of African participants, above all from francophone Africa. This large presence of francophone members was abnormal, and it resulted from the fact that the French wanted to increase the number of votes that they had in the assembly. I was twenty-one at the time, but these young Africans were occasionally as old as forty, and they were even senators or national assembly members in France or the heads of various political parties in Africa. And this was how I got to know many of those who would later be presidents of many African countries.

The next year, in 1952, the meeting took place in Dakar, and that was how I first came to visit the city, and after the meeting I made a brief tour around several countries in French West Africa. And this is how, bit by bit, I became an Africa scholar. Later, when I began my higher education, my doctoral studies, I decided to write my thesis on Africa. I was awarded a scholarship from the Ford Foundation to carry out my studies, and I went to Oxford to continue my education as an Africanist. Later, I went directly to work in Ghana and the Ivory Coast, in order to do the research for my doctoral thesis. From there, I began to travel all over Africa, for a period of a dozen years, and always in a double role: as an activist and as a researcher. Because at that time the two blended together, and I was doing both at the same time. This was how I began to get to know the different African nationalist movements, which gave me a different view of the world, an understanding of the world that was completely new to me.

For starters, this experience gave me a view of the Third World that was entirely different from the point of view that centered on East-West relations; it was a fundamental experience that opened my eyes to the characteristic problems of the Third World. And I learned how these same problems are central in the present-day world; this was the first point that I wanted to insist on, and the second was that, after I had been an African specialist for a good amount of time, after I had written several books on Africa and given courses as a young professor on subjects related to Africa, there arrived a moment in which I said to myself that I had spent my time running along behind recent events, and that this didn't make much sense—since there was a new coup d'état in some part of Africa each year, and I was spending my time trying to explain them, and so forth. And I reached the conclusion that this was not, shall we say, the best way of working; nor was it the best way of doing things in general.

This was how I began to reflect on the world-system, although it was clear that, at that time, I still did not have this concept in my head. But it was on this path that I began to think about the role of Africa in the world-system. At that time I had a false belief that would later nevertheless prove, while false, to be useful: that African nations were new nations, and so in order to understand their situation, it would be necessary to study other nations—for example, the first new nations. This led me to the belief that it was necessary to study the sixteenth and seventeenth centuries in order to understand England and France in their quality as new nations.

This idea, in reality, is nonsense, but it got me reading about the sixteenth and seventeenth centuries. This is how I began to develop the idea, later concretized in my book *The Modern World-System,* of the modern world-system and, in this same way, the entire series of proposals that would later constitute "world-systems analysis." So Africa had a crucial importance for me in what came afterward. But as one can already see by 1966, in an article published in the journal *Africa Report,*[10] I was attempting to explain what had occurred in Africa between 1961 and 1966 in terms of what was going on in the modern world-system. And this was in 1966, that is, before I wrote *The Modern World-System.* So, to summarize what I have said a bit, I would say that this African experience affected me profoundly.

CAAR: To get into this a bit more deeply, I wanted to emphasize two questions. Firstly, what was the effect for you of comparing American society at that time with African society during the same period? Because I recall that in the preface to *The Modern World-System* I, you argue that at that point you were already preoccupied with the social problem, and also with the question of the role of ideology within a society. Could it be perhaps that you went to Africa in search of a point of comparison, or elements for comparison with respect to this problem? Or was this not a specific concern for you at the point at which you began to work in Africa?

IW: I have always been preoccupied with the problem of social conflict in the United States, as demonstrated by my master's thesis. And at the same time, I had already become sensitive to the themes that would, some years later, be center stage in the Black movement in the United States. I had already read, for example, Frantz Fanon and Amilcar Cabral, long before great American Black leaders had read them. I have here, and can show you—although unfortunately it has begun to fade due to time—a photo that Amilcar Cabral sent me.

CAAR: What year was that?

IW: The date was 1970—it's written right here. Well, in any case, the relationship, the nexus between all of these movements and what was going on then in the United States, seemed very clear to me....

CAAR: A second point regarding these questions: I believe that I read somewhere the idea that the nation, the national framework, the nation-state in Africa during the times we are speaking about was extremely weak. Do you think that this could have influenced your thought?

IW: It could have, but I'm not completely certain. I actually think it was something slightly different. No doubt, the weakness of Third World states was already very clear at that point, but I was instead reacting against the thesis, which was very much in vogue at the time, about modernization. Because this thesis was one that wanted to impose a specific path or forced itinerary that all Third World countries would be forced to travel and, moreover, sought to explain everything that went on inside these states as the effect of processes that were entirely internal to their borders. That idea seemed to me so erroneous, so far from reality, that I then began to attempt to weave or to construct another way of describing what was going on.

Now, when and where exactly did I come to formulate this idea or this concept of the world-system? I'm not 100 percent sure. But if I try to remember, I would tell you that perhaps it has its origin in the genesis of a course that I will now tell you about. The idea that would later be expressed in *The Modern World-System* possibly began with a speech that I gave in Ghana in 1965 and which I would repeat a bit later. I remember very well: it was a speech not about Africa, but about the world, that I first gave in Accra, and then a second time in Ibadan, Nigeria, and lastly as well in Dar es Salaam, Tanzania. This presentation was very well received in all three places, and so I began to say to myself, I'm going to organize a different course. And during three or four years I gave a course on a different subject than I had taught before. I'm not sure if the course was very good, but in it I attempted to tackle, shall we say, much more global themes, which were analyzed from a much more historical perspective. So when I went in 1970 to spend a year in Palo Alto, the project was to write a short book about the modern world, supported by and setting out from the experience of these courses that I had given during the previous years. And this precisely was my "small" book, which later became what is today *The Modern World-System*.

CAAR: What was the intellectual impact of 1968 on your work and your intellectual itinerary? Is it appropriate, in your opinion, to speak of a "Wallerstein before Wallerstein," that is to say, pre-1968 as opposed to post-1968, the latter of whom would write *The Modern World-System* I in 1974? How did the movement of 1968 impact your worldview more generally?

IW: Well, I should say that this idea of "Wallerstein before Wallerstein" doesn't strike me as very correct at all. No doubt there has been an evolution in my thought, which I have been elucidating to you just now, but I don't believe there has been any real rupture. If one wants to identify me with the perspective of world-systems analysis, then there was truly a moment in which this perspective still did not exist. But whatever the case, what I do indeed believe is that 1968 was for me a second moment of great intellectual resonance. First there was Africa, about which we were just speaking, and in the second place there would be precisely 1968. One could even say, to speak more broadly, that there was perhaps a first period of my youth, which would be characterized by the struggle against fascism and later, let's say, my position toward the left of the social-democratic left. These two elements would represent a first period, followed by a second period comprising my experience in Africa, and then would come the experience of 1968.

In that year, I participated very actively in what was perhaps the most important movement in the United States: that of Columbia University. This was moreover the first in the entire country and even developed prior to the French May, since it took place in April of 1968. That month, we already had students occupying five buildings, and the administration was against them. And between the two, the students and the administration, were the mediators, the ad hoc committee formed to deal with the situation. Moreover, I was the only mediator for the part of the building occupied by the Black students. So I was constantly coming and going between these Black students and the administration. But I believe that I explained this entire experience in much greater detail in my oral testimony about the movement of 1968 at Columbia, in which I explained all the details of my participation. There is also another book, written not by me but by others, entitled *Up Against the Ivy Wall*, which explains everything that happened then, in 1968, at Columbia. This is an excellent book written by student journalists at the time, which can be consulted for more details.[11]

Later, in 1969, I published a book on the university crisis called *University in Turmoil*, and I also wrote a good number of articles on the subject at the time.[12] Since then, the movement of 1968 has been a central element within my vision, and I attribute to it a very important place in the history of the evolution of the modern world. Obviously, I didn't have such ideas prior to 1968. It was the very experience of that year that showed me, as the movement of 1968 itself developed, more and more new things every day. Because 1968 generated for me as well many new ideas—above all, for example, the idea that liberalism constituted the dominant geoculture of the modern world up to the present. And moreover, the thesis that 1968 itself had ruptured or broken that domination occurred to me precisely as a result of the events that I lived through during that same year. So I wouldn't say that I had already had these ideas previously: they emerged from the experience of the movement itself. In the same way that I had learned the importance of the Third World through my contact with African militants, so too did I learn from the movement of 1968 the role and limitations of liberalism in the modern world.

CAAR: In your well-known article about 1968,[13] you say that 1968 represented a profound crisis for the Old Left and, at the same time, the moment of birth, or at least the powerful redeployment, of the New Left. My question is then, don't you think that you yourself, your work, and your theoretical perspective are precisely part of these New Lefts produced by 1968?

IW: Well, I would say yes and no. Because at that time what were literally referred to as the New Left was organizations like, for example, Students for a Democratic Society (SDS) and similar organizations. These were student organizations, youth organizations in which I didn't participate at that point. But yes in the sense that I was much more sympathetic toward these organizations than the great majority of people my age. I was, we could say, a sort of fellow traveler of this New Left. Later, things would get a bit different, but it's true that at that point I was saying very similar things about the Old Left that those from the New Left were saying. I had read Frantz Fanon, for example, before American Black militants themselves. And I was attempting around that time to understand what was going on in the Soviet Union or with European social-democratic parties, even before the New Left posed such questions. But it's also true that they influenced me a bit, forcing me to a certain degree to crystallize this whole type of reflections ...

CAAR: Don't you think, for example, that 1968 radicalized your political perspectives, pushing them, shall we say, to the left?

IW: Yes, I believe so; I would say that's true. Because I believe that 1968 provoked, in effect, two very different answers: I believe it generated on the one hand, in a clear majority of people, a reaction in which these people changed their positions and shifted much more toward the right. And on the other hand, there was a small minority who in response to 1968 moved to positions further to the left. And I believe that yes, I was effectively part of that small minority.

CAAR: And do you not then think that the world-systems analysis perspective would be, in a manner of speaking, an intellectual expression of this movement, a post-1968 intellectual expression?

IW: Yes, certainly, without a doubt. I believe that this perspective is an intellectual response, a way of responding to a vacuum created by the crisis or the collapse of the predominant doctrines of the 1950s and 1960s, particularly theories or doctrines of modernization. But more generally, it is also a response to doctrines or theories of progress and all those other elements that were part of the theory of modernization. So I think that I was profoundly influenced by 1968. With respect to this question, there's no doubt.

CAAR: Do you think that we could also characterize world-systems analysis as a type of neo-Marxism?

IW: This question bothers me a bit, because I think that in order to be able to respond, we must first know, with regard to the person who is asking, what they consider Marxism to be, in order, on the basis of that, then to be able to say if I believe this perspective can or cannot be categorized as neo-Marxist. Perhaps you know how I generally respond when people ask me, "Are you a Marxist or not?" I respond that there exist four explanations or theses about me: some people say I am a Marxist and that this is good; there are also the people who say I'm a Marxist and that this is bad; next, there are those who say that I'm not a Marxist and that this is good; and, finally, there are those who say that I'm not a Marxist and that this is bad.

CAAR: Which of the four do you choose?

IW: I would say, rather, that I have been profoundly and enormously influenced by Marx and that I have a great deal of intellectual debt to him, to his thought. I would also say that I consider him to have been the most interesting thinker of the entire nineteenth century, but that he's not the only thinker on earth, that I don't agree with everything that he says, and that for me it's not important to characterize myself as a Marxist or not. I don't try to avoid or distance myself from that label, but nor do I make any special effort to show it off. Certainly, I wouldn't want to enter into a debate about whether or not I'm a true Marxist, and I believe that I have made a good deal of effort to situate my thought in relation to that of Marx. For example, there is my proposal for a rereading of Marx, developed in various articles included in the book *Unthinking Social Science*.[14] Or also, one could see the introduction to my book *Historical Capitalism,* in which I expound upon the manner in which I believe we should situate ourselves with regard to Marx: as a comrade in the struggle who knew as much as he knew.[15]

CAAR: I understand your point of view, but I wanted to insist nevertheless on the fact that you use in your works up to the present such terms as "capitalism," "capital accumulation," "class struggle" …

IW: Yes, it's true that I use many expressions, terms, and concepts that emerge out of the Marxist corpus and that I do so in a deliberate manner. This means, of course, that I accept the utility of those concepts. And to say it with complete clarity, I would say that if I were a person observing my own analysis from the outside, I think I would say that my work is located precisely at the heart of Marxism. But when I say, in one of my essays, that there exist three stages within the history of Marxism and that the present is the moment of a thousand Marxisms, then to say that something is at the heart of Marxism is no doubt to say something important, but not too important. Certainly, there are people who consider themselves to be generally Marxists, and whom I could also consider Marxists, or at least quasi-Marxist, and who nevertheless have certain ideas that I think are not only wrong but even on some occasions truly terrible—and these alongside ideas that are perhaps even brilliant. And on the other hand, I am willing to make use of the ideas of people who are not Marxists and would never consider themselves as such—for example, Fernand Braudel or Ilya Prigogine, neither of whom was a Marxist. Or even people like Frantz Fanon: could we say that Fanon was a Marxist? I'm sure if you had asked Fanon if he was a Marxist or not, it's likely that he would have given an answer similar to mine. I had a friend who said, and I believe he wasn't mistaken on this point, that if someone accused Fanon of being a Marxist, he would respond by saying he was a Freudian. But if someone accused him of being too Freudian, he would respond by saying that he really was a Marxist. Fanon didn't care too much about this question of labels, and I think that he was as much of a Marxist as I am and, at the same time, as little of a Marxist as I am.

But one thing that I'm certain of is that I'm not a post-Marxist. Someone recently told me that I'm a post-Marxist, and my response was the following: I am as post-Marxist as I could be post-Aristotelian. But what does this mean? Because it is said that I am very much influenced by Aristotle, but insofar as I don't accept all of his perspectives, I would have to say that I'm post-Aristotelian. But in my opinion, this doesn't mean anything, and it strikes me as nonsensical—it has no meaning.

Now, we must remember that to accept that one is a Marxist is like assuming a sort of intellectual stamp—and also, in another sense, assuming a sort of political mark or classification. In this last sense, if you ask me, for example, if I believe in socialism, I would say that yes, I believe. But on the other hand, if you ask me if I agree with all of Marx's political ideas, I would say, no, I don't agree with everything—although it's true that I find many of them much more intelligent and sympathetic than I do many of the political ideas of those Marxists coming after Marx himself.

CAAR: So to finish with this point, you wouldn't characterize the world-systems perspective as a Marxist perspective?

IW: I would say that it's a perspective influenced by Marx's thought, but also by other perspectives and other different thinkers. It is a mix of influences, because, for example, the Braudelian element is present within it. Or there's also the core-periphery element, which has been derived from the thought of Raúl Prebisch, who was not a Marxist thinker. And the same can be said of the dependency theorists, although the majority of them considered themselves Marxists. So there's a whole variety of influences incorporated into the world-systems analysis perspective. It must also be said that, even among those who presently utilize or attempt to apply world-systems analysis, there are some who consider themselves Marxists, but there are also others who don't. Personally, I don't ask for a profession of faith from those wanting to work within the perspective of world-systems analysis. To continue then, with respect to this problem, I can tell you that there are analyses from the world-systems perspective that claim to be Marxist, but there are also others who claim to develop this perspective from a non-Marxist point of view. In any case, world-systems analysis refers to a whole set of elements that have been developed in a series of articles already published.[16]

CAAR: But then, can the personal perspective of Immanuel Wallerstein regarding world-systems analysis be characterized as Marxist?

IW: If you or whatever other person call my personal perspective Marxist analysis, then I have no reason to object....

CAAR: And if we label it post-1968 Marxism, would you agree to that as well?

IW: Yes, of course. If you describe me in this way, I would have no problem with such a label or qualifier being attached to my work. It wouldn't bother me at all.

CAAR: Good, on to the next question. How did the year you spent in Paris affect you, especially your direct contact and discussion with Fernand Braudel in 1975–1976? What were the mechanics of the discussion of your book *The Modern World-System* I? Who attended that seminar, and how did such an unusual review process influence your historical vision and the argument of the book? To what degree do you believe that this seminar influenced Braudel, his understanding of capitalism, and his work in progress on capitalism?

IW: Things went more or less like this: I had almost finished writing the book when Braudel read it. At that point, he was very enthusiastic about the work and proposed that we do a seminar together on the basis of my book. So, what did it mean more specifically to organize a seminar based on my book? It meant, for example, that I gave an exposition in the first session of the seminar, and afterward there was a whole series of people who made interventions, or who directed specific debates in which I was present, as was Braudel, on the basis of which more general discussions were arranged. These expositions or interventions referred to subjects that I had dealt with or approached in the book. The experience was excellent, and from that moment Braudel and I began to have much more frequent contact. Then Braudel arranged to have the book published in French.

CAAR: Who was in this seminar? For example, which economic historians participated?

IW: There was, first of all, a group of faithful followers of Braudel's seminars, who had attended for many years and who continued to attend all of his seminars. They weren't very well-known people. Then there was a group of various scholars who taught at the École des Hautes Études des Sciences Sociales or who were involved in various research centers at the Maison des Sciences de l'Homme; they only participated occasionally, sometimes in one or two, sometimes in many seminars. The only person who attended in an absolutely regular manner, without missing a single session, because Braudel himself had personally invited him, was the historian Krzysztof Pomian....

CAAR: So the general framework of what you discussed was the problematics characteristic of the "long sixteenth century"?

IW: Yes, that's true. That was sort of the general subject of the seminar's discussions. Now, on the question of how much the seminar influenced Braudel, that's really a difficult question for me to answer, because I wouldn't be able to say to what point the experience of this seminar could have influenced Braudel. Perhaps I had a certain impact in the sense that, as Braudel himself has said, while he and another group of people had thought a whole series of things for a long time, none of them had up to that point connected all of these ideas or elements in the specific manner that I had. So perhaps this connection was useful at that moment.

On the other hand, Braudel discusses the arguments of my book directly in the third volume of his book on capitalism. We need to recall that during those very years, he was probably in the process of writing that very book. Or perhaps he even wrote it after the seminar, because the book was published only in 1979. Now that I think about it, we could presume that Braudel had not yet written volume 3 prior to the seminar. Regardless, what needs to be said is that it was above all I who benefited from this contact with Fernand Braudel. If, beyond that, he benefited a bit, then all the better.

In any case, what should be said is that on the basis of this shared seminar, we began to weave a friendly relationship. A bit later, Braudel introduced me to the Settimana di Studi that took place annually in Prato. As its director, he invited me to participate and suggested that the following year the Settimana di Prato, which was being organized at the time, have as its central subject the core-periphery relations in Europe and also a bit outside of Europe. Putting these core-periphery relations at the center of the debate was a way of introducing my ideas and arguments into the discussions of all of the historians and participants of the Prato discussions.

CAAR: Looked at more generally, then, what was the nature of this important relationship of academic interchange with Fernand Braudel, and what did it contribute to your intellectual trajectory? What was the general impact of this ten years of dialogue with him, between 1975 and 1985?

IW: This interchange was continuous from 1975 onward and was very frequent, since in those years after 1975, I came regularly, every year, to Paris. So I was able to see him and to chat and discuss with him.

Now if we speak of the general balance sheet of this ten-year relationship, what I could say would perhaps have to do with what lessons I personally learned from Braudel. Although this isn't necessarily reducible to those ten years but is rather more general, what was relevant for me, what is important within my thought that I believe I obtained from Braudel. So the two most important things would be, in the first place, the idea of multiple social temporalities and, in the second place, the scheme for explaining capitalism in terms of three levels—that is, the material level, the level of the market economy, and finally the level of capitalism—and in particular the idea of this capitalism as an anti-market.

He was also reticent, however, and even, I think, opposed to the idea of a fundamental rupture emerging in the sixteenth century regarding the origins of capitalism, since he thought instead that this rupture should be pushed back to the thirteenth century. Moreover, I believe that he also disagreed with the idea that capitalism was a phenomenon that had only existed in the modern world. But I believe that, more generally, Braudel posed these disagreements with my points of view very clearly in that first chapter of the third volume of his book mentioned above.

CAAR: Turning to another question, I wanted to ask how important the founding of the Fernand Braudel Center and the journal *Review* has been for the development of the perspective of world-systems analysis?

IW: I believe that the foundation of the Fernand Braudel Center and the journal *Review* has been fundamental for us. Because it has been on the basis of these nuclei that the group in Binghamton had been able to enrich our analyses, to deepen them empirically, and then had allowed us to create and produce a whole series of works that filled new spaces, with studies that, even if they haven't always had an evidential nature, thus nevertheless allowed us to launch a debate regarding each of these new themes, which have been tackled in a successive manner. The list of all of these subjects and the results of the investigations can be found in synthetic form in the *Intellectual Report* that I wrote after fifteen years of life of the Fernand Braudel Center (FBC).[17] This report, which you know well, is an essay in which I attempted to summarize in a very concentrated manner the role played by the Fernand Braudel Center.

I also believe that the FBC has become well-known all over the world. I think that for many it is like a symbol of something important, something that is simultaneously very open but that nevertheless has a very definite point of view about things. And I think that our journal has also come to be very much respected in the world and considered a publication of high academic quality. Because I think that for the people who read it, it is also useful in terms of establishing and maintaining contact with us.

With respect to myself, it was primarily with the FBC that I carried out all of my activities and work regarding world-systems analysis. And while there exist other people in different places who are more or less close to this type of analysis, I nevertheless think it's the case that if the FBC didn't exist, it would have been very difficult for us to have done the work we have done during all these years. On the other hand, the FBC has also been, in my opinion, an excellent educational space for many people; a great number of people have passed through it. And I'm not only speaking of students, although no doubt they are important, and there have been a good number educated here, who have worked among us and spent a good deal of time there. But alongside them, there are also people who come to the FBC for one, three, six months a year, just to listen, to read, to work, and to edit articles. And I believe that there are various cases in which it's clear that their stay had an important impact on their form of thinking, their way of analyzing things and seeing problems in general.

It's clear that many came because they already had a clear idea of what it was we did and were interested in our perspective. Moreover, I should mention that we did not pay them to come and work at the FBC: they always came with their own resources. In this way, we have always had four, five, or six people at the FBC each year since its foundation.

CAAR: Here's something interesting: while it's clear that you openly combat the "disciplinary" division of the social sciences and its fragmentation of the study of the social, it seems to me that outside the Fernand Braudel Center and outside of Binghamton, most people identify the journal *Review* as above all a journal of economic history. And if one looks at the list of authors who have written in its pages during its existence, it's clear that a large number of the most important economic historians of the last three decades have collaborated, with a text, essay, or article for *Review*.

IW: What you mention is curious. Because I can tell you that there was someone in the past, a person who claimed to be a Marxist and self-identified as such, but who was very negative toward world-systems analysis and claimed exactly that—that this whole approach was little more than a pretext invented by sociologists so that they could dedicate themselves to economic history. There's no doubt that economic history has played an important role within the journal, but it's equally necessary to point out that we try to develop economic history in a manner that is a bit different from the traditional or previous approaches. Yet, it's also certain that of the entire totality of social scientific disciplines that exist presently in the modern world, many practitioners of economic history have tended to find our work and our approach useful.

However, if we analyze more closely all of the articles published in *Review*, you will find within its pages a whole series of texts that would never in your life have been published in a classical journal of economic history. This is a first point. We could add also the fact that, if you look at the editorial committee of the journal, not one member was originally educated as an economic historian. So, if there are people who think that we are running a journal of economic history, it's fine for them to think that—and, in any case, I suppose that would be a compliment for us. But I believe deep down, personally, that in reality it's a journal that can't be labeled, that would be difficult to pin down.

So, for example, and to refer to an anecdote, I will mention to you that recently, when the National Library of France was created, the holdings were increased, and a section was formed for new journals, and they also decided to include our *Review.* When the library opened to the public, I went and discovered that they had placed *Review* in the sociology section. So I spoke with the director of that section and told her that, in my opinion, *Review* should instead be in the section devoted to general social sciences. She answered that yes, she agreed; she thought there must have been some error and said they would correct it. Later, I discovered the reason for this original classification: it turns out that the person responsible for classifying journals, especially the sociology list, was a woman who had studied sociology. When she was organizing the classification, she asked directly that *Review* be included in the list of sociology journals. In the end, despite this little story, *Review* was transferred to the general social science section, and in fact this is how I understand our journal, as a general social science journal.

CAAR: I have another question, derived from reading an article that you published in the first issue of *Review* in 1998, in which you define what you consider to be the future tasks of world-systems analysis. How do you see the future of this perspective during the next twenty-five or fifty years? Also, does this analytical perspective already have other serious establishments outside of the group at the Fernand Braudel Center, perhaps at the University of California or among the people who regularly participate in the Political Economy of the World-System (PEWS) conferences,[18] or in other parts of the world, and in the latter case, where and how? What role should the Fernand Braudel Center and *Review* play in the future for the maintenance and dissemination of this perspective?

IW: I would tell you that I hope *not* to be still talking about world-systems analysis in twenty-five years. Because I trust that by then world-systems analysis will already be a constitutive and incorporated part of the historical social sciences. I am confident that world-systems analysis will no longer be seen as a separate thing, like something different from these same historical social sciences....

CAAR: Do you mean to say that you are in favor of the dissolution of the world-systems perspective?

IW: No, it's something much more pretentious than that. I hope that this perspective will end up conquering the intellectual world. And this is why I have always said that world-systems analysis is not a theory, not a paradigm, but is better considered as an intellectual protest against the dominant mode of analysis in the social sciences during the past 150 years. We have wanted precisely to attempt to *unthink* all this, all these dominant forms, and on the basis of this to derive new ways of thinking new historical social sciences. If we finally triumph in this objective, people will begin to develop the historical social sciences in a new, different way, and at this point the existence of a perspective known as world-systems analysis won't make any sense, because we will then have new historical social sciences.

So, I consider this perspective as more of an intellectual movement, and I use the term deliberately because I think it's a movement that propels a transformation of the mode of doing things that has prevailed up to the present. And if it triumphs, then it will cease to exist from that moment. Because the world-systems perspective is not a subsection of the social sciences; nor is it a variety among others of these social sciences. It's better considered as a proposal for another way of developing and constructing the entire totality of the historical social sciences.

CAAR: Since you insist on this definition, I wanted nevertheless to remind you that in your prologue to *The Modern World-System* II, you argue that the history you are dealing with is part of a theory of capitalist development, which will in turn be part of a theory of social change . . .

IW: Okay, but in this case we are speaking of the book *The Modern World-System,* not the world-systems analysis perspective . . .

CAAR: But, they aren't the same thing?

IW: No, of course not. For example, world-systems analysis can also be applied to develop an analysis of ancient history. I don't do this personally, but it's theoretically possible. In empirical terms, I only work on the modern world. Therefore, the history of the modern world-system is an attempt to elaborate an analysis of capitalist development . . .

CAAR: But you clearly say that it's a theory, and if it's simultaneously a theory and an application of the world-systems perspective, in the sense that you just finished defining it, then there would seem to be a contradiction here. . . .

IW: Very good, you might be right. Perhaps I wasn't always sufficiently careful in choosing the words or the terms that I used during the 1970s. Later, I became much more prudent in the use of these terms. What I am saying now is that world-systems analysis is not a theory of world-systems, but this doesn't prevent us from having a theory of capitalist development, and the book *The Modern World-System* is a proposal for the latter.

CAAR: A theory?

IW: No, not a theory. It's better considered a path toward theorization, developed on the basis of a historical analysis of how things occurred. Because in order to carry out a complete theorization—and this is part of my epistemological perspective—I believe it's necessary to begin *not* from making the a priori distinction between concrete historical analysis and abstract theory. It's necessary to develop both elements at the same time. Hence, for example, I have other books besides *The Modern World-System,* like a small book titled *Historical Capitalism,* which is much more abstract and has practically no empirical references. It is a way of dealing with a whole series of elements, expressed abstractly, and in this sense I don't think I've managed yet to elaborate a definitive theory on this problem, a theory of capitalist development that is completely satisfactory. I think that we are on the way to elaborating such a theory, that we are in the very process of constructing such a theory.

CAAR: To keep insisting on this point, you claim that the world-systems perspective is above all a protest against the way of doing things characteristic of the nineteenth century, which perhaps would imply that you put the emphasis on the negative character and not the positive character of this proposal.

IW: Not necessarily. I emphasize the negative character only in the sense of the need to make an effort to clear the playing field, to then be able to carry out one's work ...

CAAR: Okay, but once one has swept the field clean, it becomes necessary to construct.

IW: Yes, without a doubt. And in this sense *The Modern World-System* is a contribution to this process of constructing something new, as is the entire totality of other things we have written and, moreover, all that we have organized, set into motion, and completed. Hence, I believe that practically all of the books produced in the Fernand Braudel Center could be considered as different efforts on this path of attempting to construct something new. But lastly, one constructs by simultaneously critiquing. So when we say that theory is simultaneously critical, we would have to remember that in reality, in a certain sense, all theorizing is necessarily critical.

With respect to this question, you can see my article "Hold the Tiller Firm,"[19] which is a critique of the positions of my friends, since what I say there is that, at the very heart of those who work in the world-systems perspective, there are those who fish here and there for *other* elements. Of course, I don't think the point is to exclude them, because when we speak of the perspective of world-systems analysis, we are not speaking of an orthodoxy, and this is why I critique them directly. And it is clear that they too, for their part, sometimes think that I am myself or all of us are mixing up the perspective, incorporating into it other elements that we have found outside it.

Moreover, inside this very same world-systems analysis group, there are people who think that we should be much more nomothetic, that we should work much more on quantitative factors, and there are also those of the opinion that we should focus on developing the comparison between different world-systems, as is the case with Christopher Chase-Dunn, and who think that in the long run this would be much more fruitful than, for example, what we are doing presently. And it's worth recalling that Christopher Chase-Dunn, in contrast to us, does speak directly of a theory of world-systems in an explicit manner. Moreover, there exist other people, like André Gunder Frank, who have returned to the idiographic perspective of arguing that there has never existed more than a single world-system in history and that this comprises all of human history. And clearly, all of these authors whom I mention consider themselves to be working within the lines or perspectives of world-systems analysis. And logically, we are in constant discussion.

CAAR: Don't you think that this perspective runs the risk, one that is common to all perspectives, of having been born and developed in determinate circumstances but beginning, after a certain point, to be vulgarized or simplified?

IW: No doubt this is a real risk. Personally, in this respect I have tried to follow a prudent strategy; I don't think it's necessary to be so strict, because that might provoke people to reject us and withdraw quickly from participating in the different things we are doing, and we would thereby run the risk of becoming a small sect. But on the other hand, I don't think it's necessary to be so exaggeratedly open that one ends up in the end without any clear and well-defined point of view. I believe it's necessary to try to move forward a bit between these two extremes, and this is precisely what I have tried to do, both in Binghamton and inside the group that participates in PEWS, and even all over the world, with colleagues who, more or less closely, are considered to work within this same world-systems perspective. And I'm very clear that I don't want in any way to be converted into a sort of pope or pontiff of this approach.

CAAR: I understand what you're saying. So you believe that, considered generally, the PEWS program can be considered to be within the world-systems perspective?

IW: Well, in theory this perspective was the very reason for which the PEWS section or program was created. The group was created in 1977, with the idea of following or carrying on the perspective of world-systems analysis. But it's true that there was a moment in the history of the program when a group of people came up with the idea of changing the official name of the subsection, to rename it something like the development program—I'm not sure this was the exact name that was proposed. Then there was a reaction from another group, which said, No, we don't agree, and if the group is renamed, then we're going to abandon it and create a new and different group, since if we rename the group, it loses all meaning.

But regardless, the PEWS Section of the American Sociological Association is in reality quite broad—I am a part of it, as is Christopher Chase-Dunn and as was André Gunder Frank—and I think that the PEWS conferences reflect this variety, this diversity. I should confess that sometimes I'm not too enthusiastic about some of the contributions, but I think they are useful, because in general, they maintain a certain degree of camaraderie and also represent a permanent intellectual discussion, which is pretty healthy. I believe that the same has happened on the international level, since while a formal structure doesn't exist yet, we have nevertheless managed to hold thirteen International Colloquia on the World-Economy between 1978 and 1995, which has been very useful.

CAAR: Where have these colloquia taken place?

IW: In different places all over the world. These colloquia were cosponsored by our Fernand Braudel Center, the Maison des Sciences de l'Homme in Paris, and the Max Planck Institute in Starnberg. We have met every year and a half, and through these meetings we have traveled almost the entire world. We first met in Europe, then in some parts of Africa, and later also in some Asian locations, in Latin America, and so forth. And we have always met with the clear objective of stimulating and maintaining an international debate. For me, this activity is extremely enriching. It's even to the point that I have become a sort of defender of these types of events, even if they aren't arranged very regularly or very strictly focused.

CAAR: I also wanted to ask how it was that you came to the thesis that characterizes the situation after 1972–1973 as one of "historical bifurcation."

I think, for example, that if we compare your vision of things, first in your contribution to the book *Dynamics of Global Crisis*[20] in 1982, then in "The Lessons of the 1980s," which opens *Geopolitics and Geoculture,* we can see an important shift with regard to the final objective, the "socialist" objective. Does Immanuel Wallerstein still think that the final objective is communism or socialism? How did this shift change your vision prior to 1989, and what are its principal stages and inflection points?

IW: So you see a difference between my points of view expressed in *Dynamics* on the one hand and *Geopolitics and Geoculture* on the other. Yes, I think you're right, and I even think that I can date this shift more precisely, because the concept of the "situation of historical bifurcation" derives from the terms used by Ilya Prigogine, and I heard his name and first got into contact with him in 1980. I recall that in that year I was with a group of people to whom I was going to give a presentation, and Ilya Prigogine was also there to give them another. So I decided to listen to it, and upon hearing it, I found it truly brilliant. And so I said to myself, I've had ideas very similar to those posed by Prigogine for many years, but I had never had the terms to express them until that moment, so now I had the language that allowed the expression of these ideas deep inside me, a language that moreover had been developed by a man whose origin was in the so-called hard sciences.

From that moment onward, I began to read Prigogine's work, began to have more frequent exchanges with him and to use his language. I can even remember the precise moment in which I used Prigogine's language for the first time: it was, I believe, in one of the meetings of the PEWS annual conference, probably the sixth, and I think I remember that it took place exactly in Arizona, in Tucson. I think it was at that conference that I began to speak of the situation of bifurcation.

CAAR: In what year?

IW: I believe it was 1982. And from that point I began to develop the group of ideas that I maintain to today. So it's really a development of my own ideas, an evolution in my thought.

CAAR: What then of the change with respect to what would be the final, socialist objective?

IW: On this point, I can tell you that for me, the final objective hasn't changed. But yes, there has been a certain conversion within my understanding in the sense that during a period I was still very full of Enlightenment ideas, and

I believe that, bit by bit, I have shed some of these. You can see how this conversion emerges, for example, in my book *Historical Capitalism*, which contains a series of talks that I gave in Hawaii, I believe, in 1982. The first three parts of the book are transcripts of these talks, while the fourth part is a text I added a bit later. I remember in a given moment during the talks that I said I wanted to pose a series of important questions about the concept of progress, and I explicitly added that this would provoke a powerful reaction in the auditorium. It's clear that ten or fifteen years after that, a critique of the idea of progress would hardly bother anyone, but in 1982 the idea of opposing the idea of progress was not a particularly widespread point of view.

But if one ceases to believe in the idea of progress as something inevitable and begins to think in terms of bifurcations and unpredictable consequences, then we can no longer continue to affirm that within fifty or one hundred years we will be in socialism. Socialism can be maintained as an objective to accomplish, but without being affirmed as a certainty. So I now reject those points of view that argue that socialism is something absolutely certain that will arrive in the future, and in this sense there was a clear shift, but it didn't occur in 1990; instead, it was developing little by little from 1982 onward.

In this way, you will see that in some of my earlier texts I still use a language in which I say that modern society proceeds toward socialism, while later, and above all now, I say instead that we are headed for a fundamental transformation, one that can end up in a better situation, but which can also end up in a worse situation, and whichever of the two alternatives comes to pass depends precisely on the struggles that we will develop. So there certainly is a change in language.

CAAR: So, how did the fall of the Berlin Wall and, more generally, all of the changes begun in 1989 influence your theoretical and political perspectives in general? How did these processes and events impact world-systems analysis?

IW: It needs to be said that the fall of the Berlin Wall has not had the slightest impact on my point of view. In fact, I was expecting something of the sort— obviously not in terms of the details or concrete elements but, yes, with regard to the general contours of the process. This can be seen easily by looking back at several of my articles that even date as far back as the early 1980s. Already in those years, from the early 1980s if not earlier, I was expecting a phenomenon more or less like that represented by Mikhail Gorbachev, although it's true that I expected a phenomenon in which Gorbachev would have been more successful, managing to stay in power in order to continue developing a sort of smooth or gradual change in the direction of the social-democratization of the regime, converting it progressively into a social democracy in accordance with its general reintegration. It's true that things didn't turn out exactly in this way, but nor were they totally different.

I even predicted the reunification of the two Germanys at least two year prior to the fall of the Berlin Wall. I demonstrated at that point that such a unification was inevitable, although I thought that this would emerge out of a negotiation between the two regimes, instead of how it finally happened. So the fall of the Berlin Wall changed absolutely nothing for me—if anything, the opposite was the case. This is why I have always maintained the thesis that this process of the Berlin Wall's falling was a fact that we had foreseen some time before, because for many years we had always insisted on one idea—and this was our argument that provoked the most reaction from the global left—which we had since the 1970s when we argued that the Soviet Union had been part of the capitalist world-economy in an integral and absolute manner throughout its entire existence.

We said that the Soviet Union had never, in any moment, left the capitalist world-economy, and as a result it never represented a different social system. And we added that it represented instead a country that had developed a clearly mercantilist policy, but one that was always internal to the capitalist world-economy. Practically the entire world declared their opposition to this position. But in the end, after 1989, many people began to say that perhaps we were right, perhaps it was true that the Soviet Union had never left the space of the capitalist world-economy. Now there is even an entire series of written testimonies that have cited me, or other authors within the world-systems perspective, to say that we were right even though they had not believed us earlier. I think, for example, that perhaps Frederic Jameson has made some statements to this effect.

So the impact of the Berlin Wall on my own understanding is absolutely zero; there has been no impact. Other processes that we have already mentioned, like the experience of 1968, clearly changed my point of view, but 1989 and the fall of the wall didn't at all. This is precisely what I was trying to say in a way in my preface to the book *Geopolitics and Geoculture*.

CAAR: When you say that you have always insisted that the Soviet Union formed an integral, constitutive part of the capitalist world-economy, I want to ask the following: under what condition was this the case? Under the status of a semiperipheral country?

IW: Yes, as a semiperiphery.

CAAR: But you didn't say that then.

IW: Of course I said it. If you look at one of my articles in the book *The Capitalist World-Economy,* where I make a long list of the countries currently in the semiperiphery, you will see that it includes the Soviet Union.[21]

CAAR: Insisting a bit on the influence of Ilya Prigogine on your perspective, I would ask, what would you reject or salvage in more detail from his hypotheses and proposals? What are the implications, in your opinion, of this transferring of a theory born within the field of physics to the so-called social sciences?

IW: I have already said that his influence on my thought is really quite important. Now, what do I reject of these proposals. It's clear that I don't feel competent enough to indicate the limitations or insufficiencies of his proposals with respect to the field of physics, chemistry, and the like. What I try to do instead is a sort of application of his ideas within the field of the social sciences, something that I have already done for the most part. I believe that at a speech I gave in Mexico in 1998,[22] I attempted a sort of synthesis of the ideas that I recover from Prigogine, explaining moreover how I understood this question of applying his ideas to the social sciences. So you could consult this text for a more detailed response to the question.

I think that I proceed with Prigogine more or less in the same way that I do with Braudel. We can say that I take some ideas from him, which for me constitute 80 percent of an argument, and then I add a series of elements and obtain a whole group of derivations, which provide the other 20 percent of the argument. However, I'm not sure, and often even seriously doubt, that Braudel or Prigogine would have agreed with this 20 percent that I add.

CAAR: This process is very interesting, so I would be interested to know, incidentally, what Ilya Prigogine himself says about these derivations and applications that you make of his work in the social sciences.

IW: I think that for the most part he doesn't say much about it, because in general he discusses it less than Braudel did. But Ilya Prigogine was very friendly toward me. I can say that when I was at his university—he worked at the Université Libre de Bruxelles—they decided to spend a few days celebrating the Day of the United States, inviting someone from Belgium and someone from the United States. The Belgian was Prigogine himself, and he suggested that I be invited as representative of the United States. So I attended and gave a speech, and moreover on the same occasion I received an honorary doctorate from the university. The speech I gave that day is a text that you know, in which I compare the points of view of Fernand Braudel with those of Prigogine.[23]

Ilya Prigogine's reaction to the talk seemed to be that he found the comparison interesting and entertaining. I think he had more or less the same attitude about me as Braudel—that is, he understood me as someone younger than him, but as someone whom he accepted within his general approach. Apart from that, it should be said that Prigogine was someone who was very open to the idea that people who aren't chemists or physicists could also work around him or even alongside him. This is why, for example, he also invited philosophers, historians, and so forth, to the colloquia that he organized or in which he participated. Because I believe that he thought his ideas could be applied beyond the sphere of physics or chemistry, and this is how I was included in the group of people who surrounded him.

CAAR: With regard to a possible periodization of your entire intellectual itinerary: when one considers it as a whole, it could seem that you cross through four stages, which in turn would represent the distinct areas or thematic axes within which you have worked. So, in a schematic manner, prior to 1968 the accent seems to be on questions related to Africa. Then, during the 1970s and 1980s, your attention is focused on the book *The Modern World-System* and work in the area of economic history and the history of capitalism more generally. In a third moment, during the second half of the 1980s and the first half of the 1990s, the center of gravity seems to move to studies of twentieth-century history, what could be deemed the "contemporary axis" and the analysis of more recent phenomena. Finally, the fourth stage would be the decade of the 1990s, in which your work seems to shift again, this time toward the theme of the restructuring of contemporary social sciences.

IW: If we look at things a bit schematically, then I don't think you would be mistaken with this periodization. But if we look at the whole of my work, it might be possible to add a fifth period, one developed approximately between 1968 and 1970 or 1971 and in which I wrote a great deal around the subject of the university.

CAAR: So you think there would be a fifth period, which in those years would represent a stage of its own.

IW: Insofar as that was the only period in which I wrote a significant amount on that subject.

CAAR: And which is an important time for such questions.

IW: In reality, we are speaking of the immediate effects of the experience of 1968 and of a period after which I began to work on the project of *The Modern World-System*. But regardless, I want to emphasize that I don't think of the move from the period of Africa to that of *The Modern World-System* as a change. For me it's better understood as a process of evolution, because it was the logic of what I was studying and researching in Africa that brought me toward the problematic of the modern world-system. So, if you want to sketch a bit my intellectual itinerary or evolution, perhaps you might also need to add, prior to my work on Africa, the period consisting of my work on McCarthyism.

On the other hand, I think it's important to emphasize that during the entire time, three considerations have been present in simultaneous form: in the first place, the question of the political present considered in the broadest of terms, that is to say, comprising themes like McCarthyism, or what was going on in the Soviet Union, or the problems of current geopolitics, and so forth. There was also, in the second place, a sense of the need to reconstruct the history of the modern world, and if you look at my articles and books on Africa, you can already see present this second concern. And there has been, already from that period, the problem of considering epistemological questions. So, in my point of view, I have been working on three levels, or "axes," the entire time.

CAAR: I agree, but with different emphases.

IW: Let's look at this point in more detail. I wrote the book *The Modern World-System* in 1970 and 1971, during my stay in Palo Alto, and I really got excited about that work. I got so involved in that effort that when I finished writing the first volume, I wanted to continue immediately by writing the second. Moreover, this personal enthusiasm has been well rewarded since I think that people appreciated this effort of mine. So I think this is what explains the focus on the question of history during the 1970s. But it's also the case that when I would give speeches in different parts of the world, to attempt to explain and defend the ideas that I had developed regarding the history of the world-system, there would always be people who asked me about the political implications of my arguments. This then led me to begin to work on and discuss the present, the element that you identify as more characteristic of the 1980s. But it's worth remembering that while I worked on this field of contemporary questions, I was also working toward preparing and writing *The Modern World-System* III.

Regarding the question of epistemology, the process is very simple. As I presented and defended my own explanations, there began to emerge two nuclei, or principal centers, of resistance to these interpretations. In the first place, there was the nucleus of the establishment, which said that my arguments were fine but that, in reality, I had not proven those arguments, adding that I didn't practice the social sciences as they should be practiced; that is to say, they would pose a series of objections that were, above all, of the epistemological order. A second nucleus consisted of those critiques from the Marxist left, voicing objections that I had violated certain laws of analysis—for example, that I wasn't insistent enough that the proletariat consisted of people who were wageworkers.

In attempting to respond to these two types of objections, I discovered that what was behind their critiques was an erroneous understanding of both reality and epistemology. I realized that in order to be able to respond to all these people, it was necessary to enter more deeply into epistemological problems. It was upon immersing myself in all this that I began to speak of the need to restructure the contemporary social sciences. That is, my heading in that intellectual direction was above all a reaction against a series of critics, one that allowed us to continue advancing intellectually in our research, while simultaneously making it possible to explain what was going on in the world of the present.

A crisis in the world-system, in the capitalist world-economy, leads inevitably to a crisis in the structures of knowledge. And if you look back at an article I wrote in 1982, entitled "Crisis: The World-Economy, the Movements, and the Ideologies,"[24] you will see that I was attempting there to say that if there was a general crisis within the world-economy, this would provoke, at the same time, a crisis within antisystemic movements and also a crisis at the heart of ideologies in the broadest sense. And the epistemological question was already present there, because I remember well that this was the first work that I wrote in which I cite Ilya Prigogine. You can check and see that this text ends precisely with a quote by Prigogine. Whatever the case, this was the first time that I attempted to connect, to blend, these three elements of my analysis. That is, I attempted to connect what was occurring at that time in the capitalist world-economy, as a structure both economic and geopolitical, with what was going on with antisystemic movements and, finally, with what was occurring in the world of knowledges and ideologies. My point was to argue that, if it was true that each of these levels had its own internal crisis, or one that corresponded to its own level, it was also the case that, at the same time, they were all part of the same broader global crisis. I believe that this was the first time that I argued this, and since that moment I have tried to work on this basis, this general framework.

CAAR: I think one important point is the fact that the different and successive contexts in which you have lived, at both the national and global levels, have also influenced the definition of these different emphases and the diverse themes that you have discussed.

IW: Yes, without a doubt. So, for example, since the first year that we arrived at Binghamton, in 1977, we would request financial support from the National Science Foundation, and we really worked hard to prepare the applications, which were finally rejected. When we asked what criticisms were made of our applications, the reasons for which they had been rejected, we saw that there was, on the one hand, a group of very enthusiastic people who supported the project and, on the other, a group of people who had a much more negative view of our proposal. These two groups were divided approximately fifty-fifty. And if one looks closely at the critiques of those with a negative view of our project, one realizes that they emphasized epistemological questions, that their critiques were above all of this order. And it was then that we realized that we could not in any way disregard this aspect of our work.

In summary, I believe we are speaking of levels and questions that are absolutely intertwined. I believe one cannot do one thing without doing the other at the same time; it's not possible to work on one level without simultaneously working on the others. But it's true that I didn't fully see this interconnection of levels in a very clear way until 1975. This interrelation of all the elements came to be sketched in my mind only insofar as my own work advanced and I received certain critiques of that work.

CAAR: So, this more recent emphasis on epistemological themes, was it not perhaps linked to certain questions of a more theoretical kind, or perhaps to the work at the heart of the Gulbenkian Commission?

IW: It was more of the opposite. The research and the final report of the Gulbenkian Commission were among the results of this emphasis on epistemological themes. In fact, I wanted to do something regarding these themes from an organizational point of view, and I was trying to look for a much broader base of support for the diffusion of this group of ideas, as well as a framework to deepen their discussion and elaboration. In this way I tried to push the project, following these proposals to combine different people, choose members, and put together a series of discussions that were really very interesting and stimulating; and then also to edit from among these a final report, which we hoped, and which I still hope, will have an important intellectual and practical impact.

DISCUSSING THE HISTORY OF THE CAPITALIST WORLD-SYSTEM

CAAR: In this second part of the interview, I hoped to transition to a discussion of your interpretation regarding the history of the capitalist world-system.

I think that *The Modern World-System* seems to be your best-known work. Do you believe that your most essential contributions to contemporary social thought are included within this book? Could you go a bit more deeply into how the developments within this book connect to your more epistemological developments about the restructuring of the contemporary social sciences?

IW: If you are asking if *The Modern World-System* is my most important work, I would say that undoubtedly it is. The journal of the American Sociological Association, *Contemporary Sociology,* made a list of the ten books that have had the greatest impact on the field of sociology in the last quarter century, and among the ten books they selected, they included mine, *The Modern World-System* I, more than twenty years after its first publication.

CAAR: To enter into the argument of the book, one thing that leaps out at the reader is that the periodization announced in the introduction to volume 1 changes once we reach volume 2. I wanted to ask, why this change in the essential dates of the periodization?

IW: Perhaps it was a slight error to have announced this periodization ahead of time. I would add that today I completely renounce it. In fact, it was when I began work on volume 2 that I realized that I *couldn't* begin my research from 1640, and so I pushed the beginning of the study back to 1600. Moreover, from that point I could see that it was useful to structure the whole project through a certain overlapping between periods. And on the other hand, I should point out that volume 3 was not meant to be up to 1848 but rather up until the 1840s.

CAAR: So, volume 4 won't include the period up to the present?

IW: Definitely not. In fact, this fourth volume will essentially focus on problems of the nineteenth century, and it's very likely that later on, after finishing it, there will eventually be a volume 5, and even perhaps, although it's impossible to know at this point, even a volume 6. The only thing that I know for certain is that I now reject having attempted to establish a periodization prior to having written the corresponding volume. Because I believe it is only when I am fully submerged in the work and the research that it is possible for me to establish, on the basis of this same work, the logic of the processes that I am examining, and it is this very logic that also tells us which are the adequate criteria for establishing its own periodization.

Moreover, I will say that this periodization is not connected to the study of economic cycles and long waves. Rather, it has to do, as I have already mentioned, with the fact of having submerged myself in the analysis of empirical processes, in concrete historical analysis. It is from there that I began to discover the proper logic that imposed the cuts of the periodization on me.

CAAR: I believe that your argument regarding capitalism, characterizing it not as a stage of progress but instead as a true historical step backwards, is very powerful, as you explain it in, for example, your book *Historical Capitalism* or in your article "The West, Capitalism, and the Modern World-System." But what happens to Marx's thesis of capitalism as a "historical-progressive" stage of the evolution of humanity? What is your position on Marx's argument? Do you believe that it's invalid or that it hasn't been correctly interpreted? Or is even Marx a victim of this notion of progress, a notion that must be overcome?

IW: The question of progress represents my greatest disagreement with Marx. Marx is a thinker still very much within the framework of the Enlightenment. For him, history is inevitable progress, and hence, in his understanding, capitalism represents an evolution with respect to feudalism, and the socialism to come will in turn be an evolution with respect to capitalism. I don't accept the idea that capitalism represents a step forward. Instead, it has been a fundamental shift that has transformed the entire world, but it is far from progress, which isn't in any way to idealize or romanticize the Middle Ages or those societies existing prior to capitalism. We can agree that there has been, without a doubt, technological progress—this is clear—but in terms of human progress, I don't believe this was the case in any way.

CAAR: But, for example, don't you think that the development of the individual was a very important advance?

IW: I'm not certain that progress necessarily consists of this. If what you want to say is that the role of the individual in our society, in capitalist society, is much more important than it had been in any of the precapitalist worlds, then I agree completely. But there is a big difference between this and arguing that this constitutes progress; they are not the same thing.

CAAR: But you don't think that, without the development of the individual and individualism, democracy and freedom are perhaps much more difficult to construct?

IW: It is possible that in a future society, just as we would hope, the affirmation of all the possibilities of the totality of people will be something fundamental. I am in no way certain that in order to arrive at that point, it's necessary to cross through the sort of egoistic individualism that we live with in present society. I think that to be able to understand the question of whether capitalism represents progress, it's necessary to take stock of the system as a whole. And from this global perspective, I don't conceive of the modern world as progress.

CAAR: And, for example, in the sense of having been able to conquer what Jean-Paul Sartre called scarcity, scarcity in material life, and crises of an older type: don't you think that this all represents a fundamental progress toward being capable of constructing a new society?

IW: No, not at all. Because I don't accept the idea that man should dominate nature: this language is totally characteristic of the Enlightenment, the Century of Light, and it is also part of that Marxist language that has accepted this message of the Enlightenment. But this is, deep down, the language of capitalism itself, the vision of capitalist society, and it is on this very point that Ilya Prigogine has introduced a different element. Because this idea or conception of man's domination of nature is really the result of the dualism of René Descartes, who argues that on the one hand man is active, intelligent, and a spiritual being, while on the other hand nature is dead, inert, and above all a threat, and as a result we need to dominate it.

But in the two hundred years after Descartes, a great number of people have said that this dualism is not accurate, because human beings are also elements who function in mechanical terms, like atoms, and as a result it's necessary to study both in the same manner, to analyze them in a similar way. Many have rejected this view, saying that it is terrible, and so forth. So the way to try to counterbalance this understanding of the two cultures as separate, to counterweight a bit this emphasis on the difference between people or human beings on the one hand and nature on the other, has therefore advanced not only by the approximation of human beings to nature but also through the inverse—drawing nature closer to certain traits of humans. The latter is precisely what Prigogine argues, the thesis that nature in itself is also creative—the idea that nature makes choices and that, as a result, it possesses a series of characteristics that we traditionally attribute only and exclusively to people.

So it's fundamentally the same argument, but now it's about arguing not so much that people are also mechanisms but rather that nature is itself something alive. Marx was trapped within a classical understanding characteristic of the nineteenth century. As a result, I don't see this as constituting progress, and moreover, I believe that this idea represents our central obstacle today.

You also asked if Marx was a victim of this notion of progress that we must overcome, and I would definitely respond yes. And to return to one of your earlier questions, I would add that this is perhaps one of the reasons why it is difficult for me to respond to the question of whether I am a Marxist or not, or about whether the world-systems perspective is a Marxist perspective or not. Because in my point of view, this perspective is in certain ways clearly Marxist, but on the other hand, in some things, such as on this last point, it isn't. And I think there's one dimension in which I have effectively attempted to break with a Marx who was still a prisoner of the Enlightenment. If you look back at the rereading of Marx that I propose in my book *Unthinking Social Science,* you will see that there, at a given moment, I argue not merely that everyone has their own Marx but rather that, in fact, everyone has their own *two* Marxes, and I attempt to show that there was, on the one hand, a first Marx, who was still a classical economist, a man within the legacy of the Enlightenment, and on the other hand, a second Marx, who had a much broader perspective, one very different from the first Marx.[25]

CAAR: You explain the relationship between the concepts of the world-system and the world-economy in chapter 7 of *The Modern World-System* I. My question is, how do you understand in more detail this relationship between capitalism and the world-economy, between the world-economy and modernity, and finally also between the world-system and capitalist civilization?

IW: For me, prior to the sixteenth century there had been many world-economies in the history of humanity. I don't know how many there have been because I haven't counted, but the problem was that these world-economies were fundamentally unstable after a short period. Either they would disintegrate or they would be devoured by and absorbed into a world-empire. Then, for a whole set of reasons that need to be analyzed, and which I tried to analyze in one of my articles originally published in *Review,*[26] it occurred that, for the first time, a world-economy managed to survive and was then even able to deepen its development, eventually becoming capable of conquering the entire world. I would also say that for capitalism to be able to exist, it needed to take the form of a world-economy. That is to say that there was a correlation between the two faces of the same coin. As a result, I wouldn't say that I establish any distinction between the capitalist world-economy and the concept of modernity.

CAAR: So you think that the concept of modernity is equivalent to that of the capitalist world-economy?

IW: To be more precise, I would say that deep down I don't really like the term "modernity" because I think that to use it implies accepting that there exists a difference between the capitalist world-economy and modernity. But for me, this difference simply does not exist. What is generally called modernity is nothing but the modern world-system, which is the same as the capitalist world-economy.

CAAR: So, for you all four terms are practically equivalent?

IW: I believe that they are different ways of designating the same thing.

CAAR: But, for example, Marx does make a distinction between, on the one hand, the capitalist mode of production and, on the other hand, modern bourgeois society.

IW: Yes, but this is something else that I don't accept from Marx—because I believe that here we are dealing with a typically liberal understanding, that is to say, the idea that the modern world is for the first time a clearly differentiated world, which clearly distinguishes between an economic segment, a political one, and a sociocultural one, which is the base of the structure of the social sciences in the modern world. My intention is exactly to surpass these distinctions.

CAAR: To finish this point, why is it that you don't often use concepts such as modernity and civilization?

IW: I believe that in reality I have indeed used the term "civilization" several times. For example, I used the phrase "capitalist civilization" in the title of some lectures that I gave in Hong Kong. So I think that I do use the term "civilization" with some frequency, and in fact it is incorporated into the name of the Fernand Braudel Center. On the other hand, I have used the term "modernity" much more rarely, and this is because I don't think that it adds anything new. Regardless, there is, for example, an essay that I wrote some years back, which was published in the collection of articles entitled *After Liberalism,*[27] in which I try to speak a bit about the two faces of modernity: modernity understood on the one hand as technological transformation and on the other hand as liberation. But for me, what is important is the fact that we are presently living within a capitalist world. So I am completely willing to speak in terms of capitalist civilization, or capitalist society, or the capitalist world-system, or the capitalist world-economy. These all seem to me to be very similar, and yes all of this is modernity....

CAAR: When I insisted on discussing the use of this term "modernity," I was also thinking a bit about the discussion surrounding postmodernity.

IW: But then it is necessary to point out that, in any case, this so-called post-modernity is not postmodern but rather an integral part of modernity, and this is moreover a whole other discussion. On this point, I would direct you to the beautiful book by Bruno Latour called *We Have Never Been Modern*,[28] which puts both the theory of modernity as well as the theory of postmodernity, and even that of premodernity, all into the same bag, attempting to show how they all utilize the same premises.

Therefore, this question of postmodernity is another problem. I should say that I find it interesting as a cultural movement aimed against certain theses, but only in this very delimited sense. That is, I find it interesting to speak of postmodernity only against the equally limited concept of modernity and, moreover, only in the sphere of the humanities, within literature and the arts. Besides, we shouldn't forget that in its origin, the term "postmodernity" proceeds from architecture. In this sense, perhaps we can accept the term, but on the other hand, postmodernity considered as sociological analysis has absolutely no value.

CAAR: If I understand you well, you oppose postmodern positions within history, sociology, and so forth.

IW: No. It's not so much that I am against such positions but rather that I oppose those who think that we have entered a postmodern era. In my opinion, we are instead within full modernity; postmoderns are totally modern, not postmodern. Apart from that, I share some of their critiques, but the idea that we have arrived at a new or different epoch seems to me to be absolutely false.

CAAR: What do you think of the idea that we have arrived at an era of the end of the great metanarratives and the grand theoretical constructs?

IW: This all seems to me to be complete nonsense, because even this posture regarding the end of grand narratives is itself a grand narrative. Furthermore, I believe that the only really interesting narratives are the grand narratives.

CAAR: Also, when you spoke of the concept of civilization, I thought a bit about the book by Samuel Huntington and the debate provoked by its publication.

IW: I don't accept the positions offered by Huntington either. I think that in reality, he reifies civilizations, and this implies ignoring everything that has happened historically since the fifteenth and sixteenth centuries. I believe that we live in a world in which there exists only one civilization, capitalist civilization. No doubt there exist certain different cultural heritages in China, India, Western Europe, and so forth.

Moreover, I get the impression that deep down we are really dealing with a geopolitical thesis. Because what Huntington means is instead that White men, those of European origin, need to form an alliance with peoples of the Far East in order to maintain domination over the Third World. I really have little patience for Huntington's arguments.

CAAR: But then on this point you would distance yourself also from Fernand Braudel. Because I am of the impression that he maintains the idea that there exist, even up to the present, multiple civilizations on the planet, as proposed, for example, in his book *Grammaire des civilisations*.[29]

IW: The book *Grammaire des civilisations* was written for students in high school, and its principal objective was to open their eyes to the other worlds that had existed historically. So I wouldn't say that it makes a powerful or very well-developed argument. I believe that Braudel occasionally departed from what he himself deemed *histoire pensée,* reflective history. But in any case, that's my personal opinion.

CAAR: I think that the division of the world-system into core, semiperiphery, and periphery is a thesis that everyone identifies with the work of Immanuel Wallerstein. There are even those who argue that Fernand Braudel learned this division from Wallerstein. But in a heavily circulated interview from 1982, in the journal *L'Histoire,* Braudel claims to have invented the idea. Where did Immanuel Wallerstein derive this division between core, semiperiphery, and periphery? What relation exists between this thesis and the position of André Gunder Frank on the core-periphery relation? And between this thesis and the Latin American dependency theory of the 1960s? And finally, how does it relate to Braudel's ideas regarding the world-economy?

IW: The terms "center" and "periphery," in the sense in which they are used today, are really derived from Raúl Prebisch. It is perhaps the case that Prebisch himself derived these from some German authors who had written during the 1920s and whose works had also been forgotten, but in any case these two terms had a father, and this father was Raúl Prebisch. On the other hand, and with regard to the term "semiperiphery," I think it was I who invented it. And I did so above all because I found it difficult to explain things without reference to this intermediate level, without using this new term "semiperiphery."

Gunder Frank himself took the terms "core" and "periphery" from Prebisch, and moreover, it's clear that Gunder Frank was not the only one to do so. In those years, a great number of people spoke in these terms; this was part of the common and current phraseology.

On the other hand, I took from Fernand Braudel, above all, the concept of the world-economy. I think this was the principal element that I took from Braudel in those years, and afterward, a bit as a counterpart to that term, I invented "world-empire." But the concept of the world-economy was derived directly from the works of Braudel—there's no doubt about that.

CAAR: I now recall an article I read recently, written by a geographer, who attempted to draw the spaces corresponding to the core, the semiperiphery, and the periphery in the world map. And then the author said something that I believe has been repeated many times by many other authors, which is the idea that the most difficult space to define, with respect to its limits, is the semiperiphery.

IW: Yes, I think this is true. But I should also say that it's an exercise that I have decided to stop doing. Because when, for example, the point was to make a list of countries or zones in the periphery, semiperiphery, or core, there were always some other people who would come and try to propose a different list to me. In reality, the difference depends on the exact criteria used for the classification. The division is better understood as a heuristic.

CAAR: That is, what you consider important is the qualitative distinction between the three levels and not so much the specific decision as to whether this or that country, in this or that moment, is part of each level or not.

IW: Exactly, that's right.

CAAR: Another difference between yourself and Braudel might perhaps be your notion of system as a strong concept or, perhaps, the incorporation of your notion of the external arena and its function.

IW: Yes, I believe this is partly true. I think the origin of our differences might be in my education as a sociologist and his as a historian. It is true that he had a certain resistance to the concept of a system and, more generally, to strictly defined concepts, which he saw as overly closed. Because he liked to work on the basis of slightly more open concepts. So whereas I used the term "system," Braudel on the other hand never used it, and in the same way I had some resistance to using the concept of society, for which I proposed substituting the term "historical system." So yes, I believe there is a difference between Braudel and myself.

But this is not a profound difference but rather more of a cultural difference. And the same can be said of the idea of an external arena; since Braudel resisted the term "system," he also resisted the idea of speaking about the borders of systems. But for me, on the other hand, to speak of an external arena and to mark the distinction between the periphery and an external arena seemed very important.

CAAR: And you derived the idea of a system from the work of Ludwig von Bertallanfy?

IW: No, not especially. I attempted to define the system as a real entity, with a certain content and in which all parts are interdependent, and if some were separated or cut out, this would change the whole entity, the whole system entirely. It's true that it is a bit difficult to define and establish what a system is in practical terms, but at least on the level of theory, it's pretty clear to me what a system is.

CAAR: I wanted to move to another question that alludes to a big debate and that I think is very important. This is the question of why European civilization, rather than China, Africa, Islam, or America, moved toward capitalism. You take up this question in the first chapter of *The Modern World-System* I in order to respond through a combined explanation that is long-term and conjunctural at the same time. But then you return to the same question in a different manner in the book *Historical Capitalism* and, above all, in the essay "The West, Capitalism, and the Modern World-System." What explains this change of position toward a more negative view of said passage in the 1980s and 1990s? Moreover, in your article "Historical Systems as Complex Systems"[30] you argue that the problem is not resolved and that your own response seems unsatisfactory to you. What implications does this unresolved hole or open subject have for world-systems analysis?

IW: Rather than a change of position, this was an evolution of my position in this respect. Moreover, I don't think the second position is any more negative than the first but is instead just a much clearer position. When I say in the 1987 article that my own response is not totally satisfactory, I refer, above all, to *The Modern World-System* I. Because in reality, I found my argument a bit weak on this point in volume 1. So when I began to rework the problem later in order to write the article "The West, Capitalism, and the Modern World-System," which I wrote around 1990, my explicit intention was to replace chapter 1 with this new explanation, one that was much better thought-out, much more reflective. So my position at present is the same as the one expressed in that article published in 1992.

CAAR: Something calls my attention when reading this latter article, and it's the fact that you reject Max Weber's explanation and that of others like him, with the argument that they are too general, constructed on the basis of processes that are too long. This rejection is noteworthy because you have always persistently defended general explanations and approaches based on *longue durée* historical perspectives.

IW: That's right, but I believe this is because it is necessary to distinguish between "*longue durée*" and "very *longue durée*," which are not the same thing. On this point I agree with Braudel: I believe that the *longue durée* exists at the heart of a historical system. To speak of *longue durée* means to speak of the structures of that historical system. For me, this is the very duration of the life of a determinate historical system, and therefore, as I often repeat, I believe that within this *longue durée* of a historical system, there is a period of genesis, then the period of the life of the system itself, and finally the period of its terminal crisis.

Therefore, in order to explain, for example, the period of the terminal crisis of a system, it's necessary to appeal to the *longue durée*. But on the other hand, *longue durée* has absolutely nothing to do with explaining the genesis of a historical system, because this genesis is precisely the change, the end of a long-duration structure and its substitution by another. And this is what is meant, in my opinion, by the creation of a new historical system: the rejection of prior long-duration structures, characteristic of the previous system. And while it's true that the new historical system might preserve this or that element of the previous system, there is no doubt that the fundamental, general, organizational premises of the new system have changed profoundly. But then, from that moment onward, it is no longer possible to continue speaking about continuity.

This is what happened at the moment of the birth of capitalism: we completely departed from the previous historical system, because it had collapsed, and therefore a new and different system, the capitalist system, was created, which in its own moment has its own characteristic *longue durée* that corresponds to it. So, when I argue that postmodernity is nothing but a simple element of modernity, I support this through these long-duration structures, structures that the defenders of postmodernism have of course not been able to break.

CAAR: But this doesn't answer the question of why it was Europe that took this step toward capitalism and, moreover, did so in the fifteenth century.

IW: I don't believe that. What I say is that we are talking about a situation in which the old system had collapsed, and at that moment, in an exceptional manner and due to a combination of accidental circumstances, at the same time there was no other group prepared to invade the collapsing system; nor was anyone able to dominate it and attempt to reconstruct a system like the old one—like, for example, what had occurred in China, where a group of the Manchu carried out this reconstitution. And I add that then, at that moment and within that momentary vacuum, the capitalists were able to take control of the situation and construct a situation in their way and to their benefit. But this doesn't have anything to do with European history or with the specific character of European civilization. The question is rather one of a sort of breach, or open space, on the battlefront of the permanent struggle against the capitalists, a struggle that has always existed in all regions and all parts of the world. And within this breach or open space, the "virus" of capitalism quickly entered and ended up taking possession, in a manner of speaking, of the entire body of society.

There was absolutely no necessity of any kind for this to have occurred, but rather just the opposite. It's a question instead of something totally unexpected. There was really no way of anticipating that this was going to happen. For me, this can be seen as an example of what is called by Stephen Gould punctuated equilibrium, or, for example, what Ilya Prigogine calls creativity— that is to say, in certain moments, there are determinate situations in which opportunities are possible. At such moments, sometimes something totally surprising and unexpected occurs. And when this is analyzed a posteriori, when it is seen after everything has happened, then one can say either that it was something inevitable, which I don't generally believe to be true, or that it was something very interesting but not in any way inevitable.

CAAR: This means that, according to you, this "historical causality," to put it that way, could have occurred in any other place.

IW: Yes, I believe that this event, the emergence of capitalism, could have never occurred, or it's also possible for it to have emerged, for example, in China, in the Middle East, or somewhere else. At least theoretically, it could have occurred anywhere. Now, in real terms, the place where it emerged was Europe, and I tried to explain precisely why it occurred exactly in a determinate historical moment and also why this event, this birth of capitalism, came to pass precisely in Europe.

CAAR: That is to say, it could have happened in a still premodern or pre-capitalist system?

IW: Exactly. And it would even have been possible for us to continue living that way forever. Of course, we need to say that once it occurred, everything changed completely. Because in this case we are speaking of an *Aufhebung*, a process of surpassing that implied the creation of a new and different field of possibilities, on the technological level as well as on many others, which brought with it an entire series of changes that created what is the modern world. We are dealing with a transformation that changed many things, but although it provoked enormous changes, it can't necessarily be considered progress. So I think it would be useful to reread my article "The West, Capitalism, and the Modern World-System," because that is my present position on the problem. I remain firm today regarding the arguments and the explanations that I develop in that article.

CAAR: Let's move on to another of your arguments. I think that your critique of Max Weber's celebrated argument, developed in chapter 3 of volume 1, is interesting. Nevertheless, it is a very radical critique, since there you argue that there is no necessary connection between the Protestant ethic and capitalism, and you even say that this connection is only accidental. While I agree with critique of Weber, in the sense that the Protestant spirit did not cause capitalism, we are nevertheless left with doubt regarding whether or not there exists a relationship of greater necessary correspondence between industrial capitalism and Protestantism. And on this point, I wanted to ask, what do you think of Marx's argument that Protestantism represents "the religion most suited" to capitalism, an argument later taken up by Lucien Febvre? And also, what do you think of Fernand Braudel's argument about the two Europes and, therefore, about the two long-duration cultural sensibilities that have manifested in any given moment in the division between Catholic Europe and Protestant Europe?

IW: On this point, I don't think that I'm saying exactly that there exists no connection between Protestant ethics and capitalism. I really say that it would also have been possible to find certain elements within other logics—in other, different religions—that would support the development of capitalism. The link that Max Weber establishes between Protestant ethics and capitalism is at the same time something that awakens our curiosity, something that seems at first glance convincing and even seductive, but that is at the same time too *recherché*. In the place of this, what I say is still much more radical, in my opinion: that is, the idea that if capitalism had emerged within a country or countries within the Greek Orthodox tradition, or Catholicism, or the Muslim tradition, it would have been possible to find in the writings of thinkers from these different traditions arguments to justify the birth and development of capitalism. That is to say, it wasn't Protestantism that created or caused capitalism; rather, capitalism was able to find justifying arguments for itself within the culture in which it originally developed.

We also shouldn't forget that the capitalists who existed, for example, in Italy already by the fourteenth and fifteenth centuries had at the same time a clear and well-developed Catholic consciousness. I am thinking of the cases of Francesco Datini or even Jacques Coeur. So they had been simultaneously good capitalists and good Catholics, not Protestants. And on the other hand, we need to consider present-day Japan, in which there exist right now people who speak of great capitalist development in Japan and who, upon investigation, argue that we can see how in certain Confucian positions there exist a series of elements that permit the development and advancement of capitalism and that these elements explain the powerful capitalist expansion in Japan. But exactly fifty years ago, precisely the opposite was said, and it was argued then that this predominance of Confucianism in Japan was one of the things that had impeded the capitalist development of the country.

In my opinion, such arguments imply a misunderstanding of the true role played by religions. All the great religions on earth—absolutely all, with no exceptions—are partly anticapitalist, since they demand a whole series of conditions that fundamentally go against the central tendencies of capitalism, like the need to share what one has, the need to not be totally subordinated to money, or the need to believe above all in God. But at the same time, they all in some way or another justify the present status quo, the powerful, or things as they are at present.

CAAR: I'm not speaking in the sense of a mechanism that everyone rejects today, including myself, of the mechanical determination of the superstructure by the base. I think this is the thesis of vulgar Marxists, not Marx himself. Rather, I'm referring to the problem, of a more general order, of what relationship exists between the forms of social consciousness and certain economic formations or relations.

IW: When all is said and done, it's necessary to make two distinct elements agree—perhaps not immediately, but yes, at some given moment. So I try to argue that all religions have a certain corpus of writings, an enormous series of works that corresponds to each religion, such that it is always possible to find within this vast work elements that can be used to construct updated versions of these religions. For example, I believe that in the nineteenth century—whether it be in Protestantism or Catholicism or in Hinduism, Judaism, or Islam—in all these cases, at the heart of each of these religions, versions were created that despite their differences and details corresponded more or less to the Enlightenment. We could call this an Enlightenment variant of all of these religions, which were even granted special names, and this is why beginning in the nineteenth century there appeared what was deemed a liberal Protestantism or a Reform Judaism, or in the case of Catholicism, a social Catholicism. This is to say that each had its own different name, but all were part of this totality of versions that are present all over the world without exception.

So in that epoch, in each of these religions, we had theologians who had in some manner revised the old traditions by saying that it was necessary to return to such and such a text and who, on the basis of that rereading, could discover elements that showed that things were really this way, and so forth. And in this way, these theologians all arrived by various paths at liberalism, at liberal understandings or versions of their respective religious traditions. They were able to do so, moreover, with a bit of effort, as it was not very complicated.

I assure you that if, for example, the entire world of the nineteenth century was fascist, perhaps they could find justifying elements for this fascism in all of these religious traditions. So, to return to the original point, I think that Protestantism in that moment looked for the means to put itself in agreement with capitalism, on the basis of the fact that capitalism was developing and strengthening within a Protestant area. In this moment, it became inevitable that Protestantism would adapt to this development and growth of capitalism.

CAAR: Does this mean that you think the new historical system, which will be born as a result of this situation of historical bifurcation within which we are living, will of necessity entail the end of all religion?

IW: I don't believe that it would be the end of all religion, and in fact I rather doubt it. In reality, it's very difficult to foresee now, but I believe that, without a doubt, this is not something necessary or inevitable. But it is also the case that religion could come to have in this future a new and different character, which in reality depends on the historical system created at that point. Because I believe that the current religions have various fundamental problems that still have yet to be resolved. The first is the question of sexuality—because on this point they have positions that were first established nearly five hundred years ago and definitely do not correspond in any way to the situation of the world in which we live. And I think that coming to terms with this question will require a sort of small revolution at the heart of each of these great religions, a small revolution that I believe is beginning to sprout at this very moment.

CAAR: My question is, could you specify for us how it is that you understand the absolutist states of the first sixteenth century, and more generally, would it be correct, according to that understanding, to speak of this first sixteenth century as a stage of historical transition or not?

IW: I think that yes, we could call this period between 1450 and 1550 a century of transition, insofar as in these years the dilemma at play had still not been resolved or decided in a definitive manner. In my opinion, the entire project of Charles V was deep down a failed attempt to create a new world-empire. That is, in those times the alternative was still open; it was still not decided if, as a result of this whole undertaking, we would have a capitalist world-economy or merely another new world-empire.

I believe that Charles V did not succeed in this effort to create a new world-empire, and this partly explains his renunciation of the throne in 1557. And from this moment onward we have the process that I explain in *The Modern World-System* I, which I call the shift in the center of gravity from Seville to Amsterdam. In this shift, we see taking root and growing in strength that nascent structure that we could call properly a capitalist world-economy. With respect to absolutism, I think we are really speaking of a manner of constructing modern states.

CAAR: So it's not a matter of, to put it one way, transitional states?

IW: No, not at all. No, because in reality these all came after 1550. It was after that date that the so-called absolutist states were created, and the same word applies to those states of the second half of the sixteenth century and, above all, the seventeenth century, which means that they are an integral part of the new, modern world-system. My point of view is that absolutist states are fundamentally weak, that they merely try to appear both centralized and strong. In its totality, the absolutist state is a creation of the modern world. We are in no way speaking of a phenomenon of the premodern world and much less of a feudal phenomenon.

CAAR: I wanted to focus on the characterization of the long sixteenth century as a possible century of historical transition. In your first volume, after the failed French and Spanish attempts to create a new world-empire, there follows a stage that prepares the conditions for the subsequent Dutch hegemony within the world-system, which was the first situation of hegemony in the history of the world-system and which followed the long sixteenth century. Would not all of the sixteenth century, then, and not only the first sixteenth century, have been a transitional period? But if so, wouldn't a project of capitalist modernity have been born in the Mediterranean?

IW: Since you are forcing me a bit in that direction, I would say that the period between 1450 and 1550 was a period of transition and that from 1550 onward we are already within the present, modern world-system. When you ask me if there was a project of capitalist modernity at the heart of the Mediterranean world, I would say that without a doubt there was. But it existed because, in reality, there have been various projects to create this capitalist modernity during the past five centuries in very different parts of the world, in the sense that there have always been capitalists, throughout the entirety of human history. Although it is true that they were never able to create a system that would guarantee them, that is, themselves, control over society. So there has been this sort of project in the Mediterranean, as well as in Greece, in China, and India, and also in Africa. This is to say that there have been capitalists everywhere, but they have always been a minority and always in a subordinated and compromised position, and it's even the case that for a long time they were robbed by kings, and so forth.

While this all existed, there had nevertheless never before been a true capitalist system. But since there were individuals who owned businesses and had a capitalist point of view, and so on, then it's easy to say that there has always been capitalism. But I believe that this is an error, because capitalism didn't exist at that time; what did exist, then and always, was capitalists. This is where the fundamental difference lies: in my opinion there was no capitalism prior to the existence of a system that gave priority to the ceaseless accumulation of capital, a system that therefore allows those people carrying out this very accumulation to prevail, that is, the capitalists themselves. So I think that there definitely existed capitalists in the thirteenth, fourteenth, and fifteenth centuries in Italy, for example, but they were incapable of creating a capitalist system. They were able to earn money and all that, but this is not the same as creating capitalism.

CAAR: In this sense you would indeed agree with Fernand Braudel's thesis regarding the existence of two clearly differentiated Europes, one Mediterranean and one Nordic, with very distinct dynamics.

IW: Yes, and I say exactly the same in my *The Modern World-System* I, where I argue that since the late Middle Ages there existed, on the one hand, a Mediterranean world and, on the other hand, another more or less Baltic world, like, for example, the development of the Hansa, and I add that there were certain relations between the two through a sort of European dorsal spine. I also affirm that outside these spaces, there was a less developed world, and that these more developed zones represented separate world-economies themselves, although neither managed to impose itself on the other.

CAAR: So, according to you, what explains the "inferiority," to put it that way, or the incapacity of this Mediterranean Europe to develop capitalism?

IW: I think this results in part from the geographic element. Because at that time, the task that had to be completed was to establish a link between this Baltic space and the whole of the Americas. On the other hand, I think we are also speaking of nations and spaces that were generally quite young. A third element is that we witnessed, already at that time, a certain exhaustion of Venetian power. So I believe it's around these reasons, plus others, that I attempted to construct the argument of my volume 2, of how it was that Holland managed to build, piece by piece, the elements of its domination. And, among others, there is also the question, for example, of the construction of ships that would allow them to carry out these tasks and that derive from their own prior traditions, from the experience they had acquired through their activity of navigating the whole North Sea zone.

CAAR: Let's move on. After the publication of your first volume, the Fernand Braudel Center was founded. There, crucial work was developed regarding the study of cycles, long waves, phases A and B of the economy, and so forth. This would seem to have been a new element, a crucial addition to the transition from volume 1 to volume 2. My question is if you believe that these studies influenced the central argument of volume 2 and the changing of your original periodization, and also if you derive your polemic around the concept of crisis from this.

IW: Definitely. It's worth noting that at the time of writing volume 1, I had not yet integrated this question of Kondratieff cycles and all that concerns this problematic into my framework in any kind of fundamental or prioritized manner. But regardless, I think that this was all nevertheless somehow already implicit in my thought. So I worked on writing volume 1 in 1970–1971, and I came to Binghamton in 1976, and it's clear that between these dates I was moving forward a bit in writing part of the argument of volume 2, at the same time that I began to have some contacts with people in the group at the Starnberg Institute and with Samir Amin and André Gunder Frank, with whom I began to discuss the present.

And it's true that, partly due to this, the question of Kondratieff cycles had become increasingly important and central for me. But I think that, regardless, this was already implicit in the argument in volume 1 and in some later works. Because I had already found references to Kondratieff in the writings of many economic historians whom I had read; perhaps they didn't call them Kondratieff cycles, but they referred to the same processes. And we must remember that this question of phases A and B of the economy, the famous cycles of François Simiand, were in fact present in the thought of the entire Annales School. So, I took, on the one hand, studies on Kondratieff cycles, which had been created above all to explain the nineteenth and twentieth centuries, and on the other hand, studies of phases A and B, which above all corresponded to the periods prior to the nineteenth century, and I united them, arguing that in reality they dealt with the same issue. And it's true that this had a value for me and also for the works generally developed in the Fernand Braudel Center, and so forth. And I believe that these continue, to the present day, to be extremely important for us.

CAAR: Perhaps to conclude our discussion of phases A and B, I would mention that when you speak of these movements in the long term, you qualify them with the term "hegemonic cycles."

IW: I do indeed speak of hegemonic cycles, and I should point out that this idea is not to be found in the proposals of Fernand Braudel. Here, I do believe that my position is a bit different from his and is quite clear. In my opinion, there have only existed to the present three hegemonic situations: that of the United Provinces, that of the United Kingdom, and later that of the United States, to always speak of unity.

And in order to characterize these hegemonies, I have also spoken of a cycle with four phases, the same as with other cycles: a first ascending phase, which is moreover a struggle between two powers, followed afterward by a phase that is generally and almost always a "thirty years' war," in which the confrontation is already direct. Then there is a phase of true hegemony by that power that was victorious in the "thirty years' war" and, finally, a phase of decline. And after this, there is another new phase of initial competition, developed between the two powers fighting for succession of the now-declining hegemonic power.

This is a thesis that I elaborated and sketched in one of the articles included in the book *The Politics of the World-Economy*.[31] There has followed an entire literature devoted to discussing these theses and explanatory proposals of mine, but this has been a different literature, quite apart from what has been written about the world-economy, and it has been produced mostly by people who are located in international studies departments within universities. But whatever the case, this hegemonic cycle is, in my opinion, another great cycle of the capitalist modern world-economy, of the modern world-system.

CAAR: But then, is this hegemonic cycle for you the concrete manifestation of this secular trend, or is it something different and separate?

IW: In reality, to state it clearly, I prefer to speak of a "logistic" of the system. But what's important is that these logistics exist; they are there and represent another reality of the hegemonic cycle. But all systems have cycles, and the very duration of the system already implies the existence of cyclical rhythms and secular trends, but not in the sense that economic historians use the idea but rather as a true tendency that unfolds over the course of centuries.

CAAR: That is, in the Braudelian sense of a secular trend.

IW: Yes, in exactly this sense.

CAAR: But for Braudel, the passage from Amsterdam to London is crucial because he says that with Amsterdam we witnessed the last fundamentally urban domination. Do you agree that this passage from the Dutch hegemonic cycle to the English hegemonic cycle represented a fundamental difference?

IW: I think that this idea that there did exist a major difference between the United Provinces and England originates deep down from a thesis that I explicitly reject, which is the idea that between these two structures of domination there occurred the Industrial Revolution, and as a result, from the nineteenth century onward, everything changed absolutely. This is the idea that at that moment there was a great rupture, and as a result, by speaking of before and after 1800, one is really dealing with two completely different things. Those who argue this even say that everything that occurred prior to 1800 should be included within a determinate period that is distinct from the period following 1800. I think that even Fernand Braudel was a prisoner to this idea, due to his original education, and this is clear from the fact that he concludes his research and his subjects of interest precisely with the French Revolution.

For my part, I should make it clear that I don't find this distinction particularly useful, since in my opinion we need to analyze what occurs in the period between the sixteenth and twentieth centuries. On this point I disagree with Braudel, and not only with him, but even with—

CAAR: Marx?

IW: No, not Marx. In my opinion, this isn't against Marx, but it's against most Marxists and also, more generally, the majority of historians and even social scientists. Because I believe that this thesis that 1800 represents a massive rupture is sustained by 90 percent of the groups I just mentioned. Marx, on the other hand, never said this. I believe that if one rereads Marx carefully, one will see that he says explicitly that the transition to capitalism takes place in the sixteenth century. In my opinion this is very clear. Although we must also accept that he didn't always or on all occasions express this idea that I just mentioned with sufficient clarity or sufficient force. Because also in this sense, perhaps Marx himself remained a prisoner of the world around him, of his atmosphere.

CAAR: I recall another element that Braudel highlights as a decisive difference between the structure of domination of Amsterdam and London: the presence, beginning with the case of London, of the internal market, arguing that prior to the nineteenth century the role of this internal market hadn't been as relevant, whereas it begins to be a fundamental element from the nineteenth century onward. Would you also disagree with this idea?

IW: Yes, I disagree. I think the internal market centered on Amsterdam was already quite considerable, and I think this was one of the reasons that they used the canal structure, precisely with relation to this internal market. On the other hand, I believe that the significance of the internal market, in terms of the percentage it represented in the English case, has always been exaggerated with regard to its importance and quantitative magnitude. Apart from that, I believe that this distinction between internal and external markets was very rarely made by capitalists themselves: for them, the market was simply the zone or the space that they were able to conquer.

On this point, it's important to indicate that the concept of an internal market is typical of the nineteenth century, and this is more or less Karl Bücher's argument, which is moreover shared by a majority of people. That is to say, there first existed a series of small local markets, later national markets were constituted, and finally—for example, today with globalization—a large international market ends up being constructed, which comes to crown this process in a way. I should tell you that this way of seeing things is absolutely in no way how I see the problem. In my opinion, the process began instead with the construction of an international market, and later came the process of constructing national states at the heart of this international market. And even, it was later possible to "close" these states, but only in an ephemeral way, because in reality the market had always been, from the beginning, the market of the entire world-economy as a whole. This has been the case for any capitalists who wanted to make a profit, throughout this whole period, from the sixteenth century to the present.

So in my opinion, the movement proceeds instead from the exterior to the interior and not vice versa. In no way does it move from the interior to the exterior, in terms of markets. It is not the case, for example, that one first conquers France or the French market, and later the market of the whole world-economy. It's always the opposite: one first gains domination over the world-economy, and only then and on the basis of this domination can one eventually conquer France and the French market.

CAAR: Does this mean, for example, that the Soviet Union or, to take another case, communist China under Mao Zedong, never left this space of the world market?

IW: Yes, I think you're right. In my opinion, both China and the Soviet Union attempted to construct a traditional mercantilist market, to gain strength at the heart of this world-economy. And I have been making this argument since the 1970s. Therefore, once they had strengthened themselves, they began to leave their borders. In doing so, they repeated a pattern that was fundamentally the most traditional way in the world of doing things with respect to those markets.

CAAR: Do you think that this same framework applies to the case of Latin America during the period of the Second World War and the process of "industrialization" that began during those years in Latin American nations?

IW: Yes, I believe this is precisely the same pattern. This is even the old idea of infant industries, of industry in its initial period as posed already by Friedrich List. From my point of view, the perfect example of List's argument is exactly the case of the Soviet Union.

CAAR: Let's move on to another question. I don't believe that your attempt, in volume 2, to delimit the concept of crisis and understand it only as systemic crisis has been successful. But you insist on the importance of differentiating between crisis and contraction or slow growth.

IW: On this point, I would say, to begin, that the nucleus of my idea is that there exists a whole literature that uses the concept of crisis to characterize the seventeenth century, and I am directly opposed to such a characterization. For me, and against this literature, there is no crisis in the seventeenth century. To schematize a bit, we can see that this literature says that there was a great forward push by the European economy during the sixteenth century, which is followed by the great failure of the seventeenth century and therefore the crisis of this century with all its effects, and later in the eighteenth century this will finally lead to the French Revolution, the Industrial Revolution, and all of these processes.

For me, on the other hand, what we see in the seventeenth century is quite simply a phase B of the structure of this world-system, that is, a logistical phase B. And although there is a clear stagnation of the world-economy, there isn't, in my opinion, a crisis of the world-system or the world-economy as a whole but rather an absolutely normal manifestation of the general mode in which the capitalist system functions. Because this system only works through cyclical rhythms, so that this period is nothing more than one of the normal moments of the cycle, which corresponds to the phase B of the general cycle of the system.

This is the idea that I attempted to demonstrate in *The Modern World-System* II, that is, to insist that in the seventeenth century we hadn't departed from the logic of the capitalist system; rather, to the contrary, we were within the full functioning of that system. And so, all of the phenomena that are described as characteristics of the seventeenth century—for example, the case of Latin American haciendas or the reinforcement of serfdom in Poland—these constituted in absolutely no way processes of de-capitalization, flight, or departure from this capitalist logic, but rather, to the contrary, these were ways of surviving under the conditions created by a period or phase B of the functioning of the system.

This is to say that the haciendas were in reality a mechanism of producing for regional markets and concentrating on these, instead of continuing to function for transatlantic markets, which was a process that resulted from determinate reasons that I have attempted to indicate in more detail in my book. So volume 2 attempts to refute that entire literature that tries to characterize these processes as "the crisis of the seventeenth century."

CAAR: But then this attempt of yours to eliminate this notion of the concept of crisis, and to speak in its place of slow growth or contraction, seems in the end not to have been very successful. Because I have the impression that everyone continues to speak in terms of a "crisis of the seventeenth century."

IW: This is true, and it's a problem. I think the best way to grasp my point of view of the problems implied by this concept, and even of the term "crisis" itself, is to consult the article included in my book *Dynamics of Global Crisis*.[32] There I attempt to explain how, in reality, everyone uses the term "crisis" to refer to very different types of things or processes. That is, every time that, for whatever reason, things don't function too well, people immediately say there is a crisis. Personally, I propose trying to limit its use only to systemic crises, and I add that crises understood in this way only occur once every five hundred years, approximately.

So when cycles enter into their phase B, this is not a crisis but rather a stagnation, a decline, or whatever else, but not a crisis. Because from my perspective, a true crisis is something that is impossible to resolve within the system.

CAAR: Just to make your point of view absolutely clear, would you therefore consider your concept of systemic crisis as equivalent to what you now call a situation of historical bifurcation?

IW: Yes, these would be for me two ways of designating the same thing.

CAAR: Marx explained the industrial cycle, which in his time lasted approximately ten years, as the time of the rotation or wearing out of fixed capital. As for yourself, you have explained the cyclical dynamic of the evolution of the world-system, with its phases of expansion and then slow growth. My question is, why are the durations of the expansive and slow-growth phases unequal, with the first lasting approximately 150 to 200 years and the latter approximately 100 to 150? What explains this duration or the determinate magnitude of said phases? What is their material foundation, considering moreover that these phases would seem to become shorter as we approach the present?

IW: On this, I would like to say that Marx's idea of the ten-year cycle of the wearing down of capital might perhaps have been true of the moment in which he was writing, but I doubt very much that this cycle still continues to be ten years. For example, I interpret Kondratieff cycles instead, and I think that their dynamic and their duration are very closely linked to an element of monopoly. I say that for there to be a new A-phase of the Kondratieff cycle, it's necessary to have various leading products, and what really constitutes a new leading product is in part its monopolized or relatively monopolized character. That is to say, for example, I begin to produce product x, for which I have or almost have a global monopoly, with which I can earn an extraordinary amount of money over a few years. Now, if I begin to produce this product, and from this I earn enormous quantities of money, it's logical that many people the world over will try to imitate me and enter this market: this is very clear, since we are within a capitalist system. Because if I see that other people are producing such and such a product and making huge profits, I will obviously also try to produce the same. And it's obvious that this other producer is going to attempt to stop me from producing the same item, through the law, through force, or through all sorts of mechanisms. And it's also likely that I will find, toward this end, the support of some state or a possible variation. And perhaps, finally, I will manage to enter the market, and after me will enter a third, and then a fourth, a fifth, and so forth.

I argue that this type of process takes approximately twenty-five years. That is, after this period, the imitation and entry into the market will have multiplied such that the production of this product is no longer a quasi-monopoly, and then this product will cease to be as profitable as it had been at the beginning. This opens, in my opinion, a new period of twenty-five years, because producers will require approximately this amount of time to discover and innovate new products, to create corresponding markets, and to find consumers for these markets, and so on, and therefore to create the basis for new quasi-monopolies.

In general, I believe that I am much less focused on questions of technology than were the majority of nineteenth-century thinkers. Rather, I focus much more, for example, on questions of monopoly, such that with respect to this point, I am here much more Braudelian than properly Marxian.

CAAR: Would the same be the case for hegemonic cycles?

IW: No. This is a process that is at its base similar to that of Kondratieff. That is, in my opinion, underlying this hegemonic cycle is another type of quasi-monopoly. Because when we speak of hegemonic power, we should ask ourselves how this is constituted, and I believe that there are two elements: the first is purely economic, because I believe that one arrives at a situation in which the production within a hegemonic country reaches such a level of efficiency that it can profit not only in peripheral markets but also in other powerful countries in that sphere of the market. So for example, in the 1950s the United States was capable of selling the cars it manufactured much more cheaply in England, Germany, and France than those sold by even local producers in those countries. This is the foundation of everything, although it dissipates over time.

The second element lies in the fact that if a power has managed to become so powerful on the economic level, it is also because it has been able to not spend too much on military expenses. For example, up to 1939 the United States had spent relatively little on military affairs, and as a result, it had been capable of investing in many other things. Of course, once this power had become the hegemonic one, then it began to increase military expenditures, but not right from the beginning. I believe that between 1945 and 1955, the United States was still spending relatively little in military terms. Even after the Second World War, we had a president like Eisenhower, who allowed for an important reduction in military spending and did so for fundamentally economic reasons. Of course, later the United States began to involve itself in wars, and then came the Vietnam War; then, in order to maintain U.S. hegemony, it was necessary for Americans to begin to spend more money on the military, and they began to spend more lives on this as well.

In reality, maintaining hegemony costs, and these costs erode the basis of that hegemonic power, and so in the period since the late 1960s, the United States has progressively lost its productive monopoly. Because, on the one hand,

Western Europe and, on the other, Japan have begun to compete with the United States economically, at the same time that the latter has found it necessary to spend an extraordinary amount on the military, which has not been too fruitful in economic terms. And this has begun increasingly to undermine the basis of its hegemonic power: that is, the very fact of having managed to triumph is the element that provokes its decline. In this sense, it is a process very similar to that which we have described for the case of Kondratieffs.

CAAR: Your interpretation of the Industrial Revolution is very critical of prior understandings. In volume 3, you say that this revolution did not modify the capital-labor relation; nor did it unleash "accumulative and accelerated growth." But Marx, in *Capital,* argues that the Industrial Revolution produces "the mode of production *technically adequate* for capital." What is your opinion of Marx's argument? Do you think it's erroneous or that it has been badly interpreted? Do you think it's compatible with your general explanation, or does it instead move in a different direction?

IW: Marx says that the Industrial Revolution creates this mode of production that is technically adequate for capital, and with respect to this claim, I agree. But I say that the Industrial Revolution is therefore not that process that occurred in England at the end of the eighteenth century. In my opinion, the so-called Industrial Revolution is instead a continuous process, which began in the sixteenth century and has been unfolding in a permanent manner, and as a result nothing particular or exceptional happened at the end of the eighteenth century in England. Perhaps there was a small increase, but in my opinion and just as Schumpeter has demonstrated, such forward leaps have developed in successive form before and after this leap at the end of the eighteenth century.

I want to insist upon the fact that in every phase of the Kondratieff cycle, immediately before the latter unfolds, there is always a technological leap that makes it possible. So these leaps are constant and correspond to A-phases of the Kondratieff cycle, and they repeat continuously. And I think therefore that there is absolutely nothing special, that there is no exceptional process between these years of approximately 1780 to 1830, but rather that, in any case, this was a moment like the other eight, nine, or ten comparable moments that have occurred in the history of the capitalist system. This is the dynamic of capitalism, and it is fundamentally this that I argue.

CAAR: I wanted to insist on the difference that I believe Marx makes between simple manufacturing in small workshops and the large industry characteristic of the factory. And I think of this not in quantitative but rather in qualitative terms: that is to say that until the eighteenth century, the skill of the worker within the labor process is fundamental, while after the invention of the machine tool and the factory, the worker begins to have a function that is more like the living appendage of said machine.

IW: This process of the development of what we could call veritable factories, of great industries, comes after the death of Marx and is developed above all at the end of the nineteenth century and during the twentieth century. And with respect to this point, I think, for example, of the beautiful article by Raphael Samuel, published in the first issue of *History Workshop Journal,* in which he demonstrates that the establishments that correspond to the meaning traditionally given to the term "factory" come to exist and develop in England only after 1870. So even if there is in this development of the factory a fundamental qualitative change, it doesn't develop in this period that we are discussing, between 1780 and 1830, either.

I believe that these technological leaps are part of a more general process of the concentration of capital and also of production, which is a continuous or permanent process within which there arrived a given moment of assembly-line production; then this phase was surpassed by the use of machines, and later this stage of machine production would be surpassed again by one of computerized production. And these have certainly been important phases, because they have changed certain fundamental aspects of the sociology of labor, thereby also producing changes in the political structure.

But we need to analyze these changes from a more profound perspective, and in this sense I am truly and profoundly Braudelian in my affirmation that many of the changes that we have seen, including some that are very important, are not always necessarily true transformations of *longue durée* structures. So with respect to the process called the Industrial Revolution, I don't believe in any way that this constituted a long-duration change. Instead, I think that it has represented a new phase of expansion of capitalist businesses.

CAAR: But what about Marx's thesis, in which the appearance of the machine is a principal element in this change that we are discussing and whose irruption into the labor process represents, in a potential if not real way, the liberation of the worker and, even beyond, the very dissolution of the need for the laboring activity as such?

IW: Yes. I believe that Marx shared the idea, so characteristic of the nineteenth century, that what was really relevant from even the psychological point of view was the process of simplifying ever more difficult tasks. And this is part of a line of reflection that goes in the direction that, at the point of departure, men worked very hard to be able to feed themselves, while later and with the appearance of different tools, machines, inventions, and so forth, work came to be a bit less arduous. But, for example, in this sense there exist some very interesting texts, written by certain feminists, with respect to the domestic labor of women and the role of machines in this type of work. These feminists have been able to show that, with the advent of the different machines that were incorporated into this sphere of activity, like the washing machine or a whole group of other machines for domestic use, their labor did not decrease but rather, to the contrary, actually increased.

It's clear that we aren't speaking of the same labor—the type of work has changed—but what does happen is this: if before they only washed once day a week, or if, for example, certain things in the house were only washed once or twice a year, now this is done every day or every two days, and moreover new tasks and jobs appear that were not done before but now must be. So the total number of hours that domestic workers now have to dedicate to this type of work is much greater than it was, for example, one hundred years ago.

So I think that this idea that machines are going to liberate us is part of the utopianism typical of the nineteenth century. I don't think this is the case at all: rather, we should say that machines will liberate us from certain tasks, but only to create in their place other types of work. Machines are not, in my opinion, the solution for humans. The true solution lies instead in the capacity to carry out rational decisions about how we want to distribute the time in our lives, in having a totality of political structures that rightly grant us the freedom to carry out and implement these rational decisions about the use of our time, and to do all of this in a social way.

Therefore, the idea that everyone is going to dedicate themselves, for example, to dancing and collecting flowers in the fields, while a bunch of robots perform the various sorts of labor that we do today, seems to me like a totally unrealistic idea that will never be carried out in practice. Moreover, I don't think it's a good idea at all, because if you ask anyone who is already retired if they really enjoy having left work, I believe that the majority will say that they aren't happy—except in those few cases in which the work they carried out was extremely onerous and their leaving it could be perceived as liberation.

There even exist statistics about this that show us that the people who take their retirement too seriously die shortly after retiring, while those who, on the other hand, live many years after retirement are those who continue to work in one way or another. This is the case even when they don't do it to earn money, but just if they perform some activity more or less regularly. Because it is precisely this regular activity that keeps them alive, since total idleness is essentially harmful for the health. So the idea of a society in which everyone is idle all the time is not a real idea, and if it came to be a reality it would be, in my opinion, truly terrible.

CAAR: I understand, but I think that Marx's idea instead goes in the direction of the idea that we need to reduce the time needed for obtaining our material needs so that there exists a lot of free time, which allows us to dedicate ourselves, for example, to scientific activity or also to social interchange between people.

IW: And do you really think that scientific activity isn't also another type of work?

CAAR: No. I think that for Marx scientific activity isn't work.

IW: Well, for me it is work—and, moreover, very hard work. Because it's a work that demands a lot of time, which consumes a great deal of energy and also requires a high degree of concentration.

CAAR: Yes, I agree that it's a very difficult activity.

IW: But then you're using a very limited definition of work, and deep down what you want to say, or what others want to say, is that the work you don't want to keep developing is that of peasants. And in this sense, I think the position is totally correct. I believe that in the future the work carried out by peasants will no longer exist: this will disappear later, and all over the world. Then, there will no doubt exist machines that will be capable of obtaining the things we need to eat or also those things we use to fuel ourselves in other ways. But the nonexistence of this form of labor will bring with it, and in its place, other different types of work.

CAAR: In volume 3, the French Revolution is characterized as an "ideological revolution," which put the ideology of the world-system into harmony with its economic base and its political system. But then, how would you characterize the Reformation and the Renaissance, which many authors, from Friedrich Engels to Lucien Febvre, have described as "bourgeois revolutions"?

IW: Regarding this question, I should tell you that I have no doubt about the great impact that both the Reformation and the Renaissance had within the whole of European life and the history of European thought, which flowed together to open a space for the evolution and development of modern ideas. Nevertheless, we must insist that between the sixteenth and eighteenth centuries, the people, a large sector of the people, continued to use, in a broad and extensive manner, a language that in reality comes from the earlier feudal system. Moreover, and here I should indicate that the question of the legitimation of power interests me very much, I am of the impression that neither the

Reformation nor even less the Renaissance seriously called into question, in a complete and fundamental way, this legitimation of established powers, this right that certain people had to power. And if it is the case that one can take up certain elements of the Reformation in order to renounce the legitimacy of this power (which is not the case at all for Renaissance thought), it's also the case that this reading or special use of the Reformation against established power was only used by very few. Because many people used this same Reformation as a mechanism for the legitimation of power.

On the other hand, with the French Revolution the genie finally escaped from the bottle, a process I have described on many occasions. In the first place, on the basis of this Revolution, the idea of continuous political change is established, not necessarily the reality of this change but at least its normality. In the second place, the idea that sovereignty resides essentially in the people is secured, that it is no longer exclusive to the sovereign. We are speaking here of two ideas that were widely accepted after the French Revolution.

What I am saying is that, at that moment, it became necessary to respond to that new reality in relation to the equally new modes for the legitimation of power. At that moment, ideologies—and I emphasize the fact that I am using the latter term in a very specific way—constituted the response to this legitimacy crisis by offering new forms of legitimation and proposing liberalism, conservatism, and radicalism, each with its respective theses, as the new modes for legitimizing power. In this sense, it was precisely the French Revolution that created this enormous change that developed within the political-cultural plane and that finally ended in the creation of the geoculture of the modern world, a geoculture that justifies our historical system, that has created our current system of ideas and has been the source of our diverse ideologies and our structures of knowledge.

So, for example, what we call the social sciences emerged directly as a result of the French Revolution. They are products of neither the Reformation nor the Renaissance. So without ignoring the importance of the Reformation and the Renaissance, I think that regardless we must recognize the particular impact of the French Revolution.

CAAR: By arguing against other interpretations, you argue quite emphatically that from the sixteenth century onward, everything that exists within this system is capitalist, and you therefore oppose, for example, the thesis that feudalism still existed in Latin America. Or also, when you speak of the realities of the twentieth century, you reject totally the idea that the Soviet Union was no longer capitalist but rather socialist, and so forth. So, in light of these examples, you say that since the establishment of the capitalist system, absolutely everything included in it is capitalist. Following this logic, we could assert that since the Reformation developed within what we could characterize as the period of life of this capitalist system, then the so-called Reformation would necessarily have to be equally a capitalist cultural or religious manifestation.

IW: Yes. In truth, I don't have anything against this claim. Although we should add that from this perspective, I would instead see the Reformation as a sort of revolt from the periphery of the system, developed in the sixteenth century, against the core of the system. Because deep down this movement was organized by the poor populations or sectors of northern Europe, who saw their money flowing toward Rome and also toward the Mediterranean, and who in a given moment said, "Enough! From this moment, we're keeping this money for ourselves."

And it's because of this that, in the case of Martin Luther, the original impulse for the whole movement was precisely the problem of religious indulgences. Because it's obvious that the sale of indulgences represented a permanent flow of money, for example, from Germany to Rome. Here we find the essence of the problem. And then there came the moment when they said no, and from there they invented an entire theological argument, asserting that it's not necessary, nor is it even possible, to purchase one's own blessing with earthly money and that salvation comes only from faith. This is what Luther said, and from that moment indulgences ceased to exist, and with them so too did this flow of money to Rome. And at the same time, this whole process also becomes, afterward, part of the more general process of creating the premises of the modern world, also on the cultural level.

CAAR: What do you think about Marx's argument, as developed in *The German Ideology,* that the French Revolution creates the "bourgeois political state par excellence," the "pure and adequate form of bourgeois democracy"? Would you agree with this argument or not, for what reasons, and with what implications?

IW: I would say that, in general, I don't disagree with Marx's claim, except perhaps for one small difference. You will see this in the analysis that I develop in *The Modern World-System* IV: I call this state that was characteristic of the nineteenth century the liberal state, and I argue that the creation of these liberal states is a process proper to the nineteenth century. Moreover, I add that the cases of England and France are the original and most important examples of this process, alongside perhaps the United States. I also think that this is all, without a doubt, a series of results that derive from the French Revolution and from the geocultural development that accompanied it, and I argue therefore that the creation of these liberal states is a way of rooting and concretizing all of these processes in general. So Marx calls it the "bourgeois political state par excellence," and I call them instead liberal states, but in essence we are dealing in substance with the same thing.

CAAR: So, would you say that the liberal state is the most adequate political form for the capitalist world-system?

IW: Yes, but with the clarification that this is only for states located in the core of the system.

CAAR: Changing level, then, would you say that the problems of the formation and strengthening of liberal states, for example, in the case of Latin America, would be the consequence of their peripheral condition? And to reach the end of my reasoning, I would also ask if, in your opinion, we will never accomplish the formation of a true liberal state?

IW: Well, I wouldn't say never, but yes, effectively up to the present, relatively liberal states have only existed, in strict terms, exclusively among wealthy states.

CAAR: Then, has this also not occurred in semiperipheral zones, in semi-peripheral states?

IW: No, in reality it hasn't occurred there either.

CAAR: At the same time that you characterize the French Revolution as the source of the "geoculture" adequate to the world-system, you also claim that this was the first antisystemic movement in history. Could we say, then, that the first antisystemic thought in history was Marxism? And moreover, what explains this contradiction between the ideological character of the French Revolution and its social nature?

IW: I wouldn't say that it's the first example of antisystemic thought. I would indeed say, on the other hand, that it's perhaps the most important, but not necessarily the first. Because calling it the first would depend a bit on which criteria would indicate that we are in the presence of such a movement. And on the other hand, these movements are not antisystemic forever, and this condition also depends on the conjuncture. Perhaps the antisystemic character of a movement only exists during a conjuncture and can change when the conjuncture changes. So perhaps we need to say that these antisystemic movements have only existed from a certain moment.

And what I say is that this entire enormous group of people who participated in the French Revolution did so as an antisystemic movement. Although there's no doubt at all that they weren't Marxists—nor could they have been in that period. Therefore, on a more general level, I think that Marxism has been an antisystemic form of thinking at a certain historical moment, but it has been neither the first nor the last. Nor has it been the only type of antisystemic thought.

CAAR: Right. But I think that if, for example, we speak of peasant movements in the sixteenth or seventeenth centuries, it seems clear that these movements have not engendered antisystemic thought.

IW: And I would even go further, because as a matter of fact they weren't even movements. I believe that we are speaking instead of structures of a much more spontaneous character.

CAAR: So, perhaps the first organic thought that veritably structured an entire theory and an entire system for explaining the world would be that of Marx.

IW: I'm not very sure of this. Because then, what do you do, for example, with a group like the Blanquists or other similar groups?

CAAR: But in these cases we aren't speaking of a real system of thought, an entire Weltanschauung, or understanding of the world.

IW: Well, I don't in any way want to diminish the importance of Marxism, because it is clearly, simultaneously, an intellectual reality and an organizational structure. But this said, we mustn't forget that, for example, during Marx's own life, Marxism wasn't a more important movement, shall we say, than the Proudhonist movement, which was its contemporary.

I would say that, from my point of view, if we are speaking about Marxist movements, there have been two phases in which these have represented something much more serious. The first phase would be from approximately 1880 to the First World War, in which the role of the German Social Democratic Party was the central element, although it existed alongside other less powerful social-democratic parties, which then began to sprout and develop, and so forth. And a second phase would be that of the Third International, which would last approximately until 1945, until the end of the Second World War. In my opinion, these are the phases in which there have truly been important Marxist movements. Perhaps the second phase has continued, after the end of the Second World War, with the case of the Chinese Communist Party.

CAAR: So, maybe the Marxism of Mao represents a third stage that is also important.

IW: It could have been a third stage, but I think it was really a derivation and a belated prolongation of the second stage, by a party that had freed itself from the control of the Soviet Union, and would be a variation of this second phase. So I would be willing to consider Mao's Marxism as simultaneously a Marxist movement and an antisystemic movement. Obviously this only extends to the late 1970s, because from that point I believe that this movement ceased to be such and was no longer either Marxist or antisystemic.

CAAR: Very good. Let's return then to one of your prior claims. You say that Marxism was without a doubt antisystemic thought, though not the first, nor the last, nor the only form of such thought. But you would accept that it has been the most important form of antisystemic thought up to the present.

IW: Yes, I believe we could say that it has been the most important. Although we would need to mention that there also exists, in a parallel manner, an entire strand of thought whose name could not be associated with a single person, which is national liberation thought and which has been as important as Marxism itself. In this sense, for example, it's very significant that when I visited and gave talks in Cuba,[33] no one, or nearly no one, spoke to me about Marx, or spoke very little; nor did they speak to me much about, for example, Lenin, while on the other hand everyone spoke to me about José Martí. And the Cubans told me that José Martí was the most important thinker of all of Latin America.

Now, I certainly like José Martí, and he is without a doubt an interesting thinker, but we must also recognize that Martí is above all a nationalist thinker, perhaps with a certain dose of socialist elements. Fernández Retamar, who is an important specialist on the work of Martí and also a Marxist, has explained to me at length that Martí assimilated many of these socialist elements during his stay in New York. Fernández Retamar gives credit to the leftist movements in the United States as the great inspiration or great guides of Martí, who in turn, according to Fernández, has been the most important thinker of Latin America. Now, who did he mean when he referred to leftist movements in the United States? He was referring of course to the syndicalists, to the socialists, and even to the American nationalists of that period. Because in truth, we are speaking of a combination of influences.

So in my opinion, during the whole latter part of the nineteenth century, and even more generally between 1848 and approximately 1968, there exist two big nuclei that give rise to the development of antisystemic sentiments and positions, two large spaces of concentration that were, on the one hand, a nucleus we could call Marxist or quasi-Marxist and, on the other hand, a fundamentally nationalist nucleus. And we should add that if these were in the beginning clearly separate and even, during an early period, in competition with one another, in a second moment, in fact, they begin to mix together and become at times a single thing. I believe, for example, that this is the meaning of the 1920 Baku Congress, in which these two elements were fused into one. Then, from the point at which they merged into one, after 1920, it turns out that one could not be a Marxist without being a nationalist at the same time, and vice versa, that one could not defend nationalism without at the same time holding Marxist positions. In my opinion, Mao is a clear example of this blend, as was also the Vietnamese communist movement as well as the movement led by Fidel Castro.

Notice that the most important slogan of the Cuban Communist Party is "Homeland or Death, We Shall Conquer." And I insist that it's necessary to look more closely into this question: the slogan isn't "Proletariat or Death," it's "Homeland or Death." In my opinion, it's necessary to realize what this means and to come to terms with the fact that this is not precisely within the spirit or the line of thinking offered by Marx. Marx was in no way a nationalist.

He was a radical internationalist, a well-defined universalist, and has said very clearly and emphatically that "the proletariat has no homeland." So while Marx was in no way a nationalist, on the other hand, we cannot say the same of the Marxist movements emerging after his death. I even think that there are certain nationalist elements within the German Marxist movement, as in the Marxist movements in the Soviet Union from Lenin's time to the first stage of Stalin, but above all after these periods. To return then to the starting point of your question, I would say that yes, there is no doubt that Marxism has represented one of the most important and essential antisystemic movements, but we would need to add that it has only been so as part of a bipolar whole, as one among two principal nuclei of the antisystemic movements that we have seen.

CAAR: Let's follow this line of reasoning: do you think that in the future there will come to exist new movements that we could really and strictly deem Marxist? And even, do you think that there exist at present movements that we could characterize as Marxist?

IW: I believe that today there exist different movements, some small, some large, that derive an important part of their ideas directly from the work of Marx. Now, are these movements really Marxist or not? I can't say for certain.

Although it's clear that some do indeed explicitly claim to be Marxists, while others don't claim to be such.

CAAR: Perhaps to respond to the question, we could begin by asking ourselves if Marxism as such has a future or not. Personally, I believe that it does.

IW: On this, I also believe that a form of thinking that has had such a decisive impact will always have an important place in the future. In a certain sense, your question is similar to asking if the thought of Aristotle or Plato has a future. And in response, I would say yes, without a doubt. But on the other hand, if we are speaking directly of these new types of antisystemic movements that are going to develop, I believe that we are entering into a transitional situation, and as a result we are going to attempt to construct slightly different movements. I believe therefore that the global left will follow in the future one of the two following alternatives: either to end up dissolving into complete ineffectiveness or to construct a "broad-front" sort of movement. And I think that the latter kind of movement couldn't be linked directly or exclusively to what, in the opinion of some participants, could eventually be seen as a form of thinking that we could say is, up to a certain point, sectarian. As a result, my sense is that within this movement there will coexist both Marxists and non-Marxists, alongside groups, for example, like greens or many other similar kinds of people, with all of these living together inside this broad-front-type movement.

But even, and to attempt to get to the very bottom of my thought, I would add that if we ask ourselves what have been the Marxist movements of the past, and if such a thing has existed, I would respond that, in my opinion, there has not existed up to today a single truly Marxist movement. From my point of view, what has existed after Marx has been, on the one hand, a social-democratic movement and, later and in the second place, a Leninist movement. So therefore, and to reformulate your question, if you posed me the question directly of if, in the future, such "Marxist-social-democratic" movements would emerge again, I would tell you that I don't think so. And equally, if you ask me if we will see a return of "Marxist-Leninist" movements, I would also tell you clearly and emphatically no. But on the other hand, if we ask ourselves again if maybe it would be possible for movements to exist in the future that are directly inspired by Marx's thought, then I would respond perhaps, that it is possible, that it might come to pass.

CAAR: I recall that when you discussed the Latin American movements of the early nineteenth century, you called these "decolonizations" rather than independence movements. Moreover, you show how those that are more radical are marginalized or defeated, whereas those that triumph are the more moderate movements. Could you get a bit deeper into the central implications of this thesis for the history of Latin America during the past two centuries? And given its peripheral situation, what future do you see for it?

IW: On this point, I would like to say a few things. In the first place, and to get to the essential question, I would clarify that I did not intend to characterize only Latin American movements as such, but rather I was attempting to analyze the entirety of the movements emerging during that period on the entire continent, including both North and South America. My intention was to show how, through these movements, there developed a whole series of decolonizations, across the Americas as a whole, and to show the shared or common characteristics present in all of these decolonizations, equally in Latin America as in what was then North America.

So, I found, for example, that the first shared characteristic or trait of all the movements of this approximately fifty-year period is that all of them were carried out by European colonists, and as a result, within these movements, all of the non-European elements were generally marginalized. That is, these groups were pushed to the margins, first Blacks and secondly indigenous people. Although it's obvious that in the case of North America, this problem of Blacks and Indians wasn't even posed, despite the fact that these groups played a certain role, one more important than generally considered. And I believe that it would be worth returning to this point in more detail.

I think then that equally in the case of the revolution in the United States as in those of Latin America, these European or directly European-descended groups that were organized shared certain traits in both cases. For example, in both cases these groups were for independence, but they were also in favor of the creation of a new European-type state, constructed much in this style. This was such that we are dealing with independence movements in the sense of decolonization, but in no way were these movements like what would be called, in the twentieth-century, movements of national liberation. And I believe that this shared character of these two decolonization movements, with the sorts of traits I have just mentioned, influenced in a crucial manner the entire subsequent history of Latin America, even up to the present day.

Of course, this needs to be qualified, depending on the different countries in Latin America or the different cases in America as a whole that I have discussed. In the case of the United States, for example, I believe that the status of African-Americans is the central problem since its very origin as a nation. Because from the very beginning there has existed in the United States a very large Black population, which has always been oppressed, while on the other hand the oppression of the Native Americans has not dominated U.S.

consciousness to the same degree. On the other hand, for example in Mexico or Guatemala, and even for a long list of countries in Latin America, the social and political rights of the indigenous peoples have been, in my opinion, the truly central problem.

CAAR: And you believe that this is the central problem, even up to the present day?

IW: Yes. And moreover, I think that this whole phenomenon in Chiapas is precisely a manifestation of this indigenous demand for equality and self-government. The indigenous peoples feel that up to the present they don't enjoy complete recognition or legitimacy, a true *droit de cité* within their own country. And I also believe that the civil war in Guatemala had to do with something approximately similar, that is to say, a war of the Mayan peoples against the so-called Whites.

CAAR: Do you think that the question is the same in Peru?

IW: In essence, I believe it's the same. Because looking at things more generally, it seems obvious to me that in all those places in which there exists a large non-White population, their very existence and their situation of marginalization constitutes the central problem, which moreover has not been resolved up to the present. Their governments have been seen by a large quantity of the population living within them as racist regimes, as regimes that oppress them.

CAAR: Now this is clear. Let's move on to the next question, still thinking along this line of attempting to "complete," or prolong up to the present, the arguments developed in the first four volumes of your work. You speak of a first expansive wave of the world-system, which would go from approximately 1450 to 1650, followed by a period of stagnation or slow growth, which goes from 1600 to 1750, and then a second expansive wave that runs from 1750 to more or less 1850. My question would be if, after 1850, there is a second stage of stagnation, which perhaps reaches from 1850 to today.

IW: No, I don't believe this is a second period of stagnation. Because we can't forget that the expansive wave that I speak of is considered from a territorial point of view. I argue that from this perspective, there exists still a third wave, also expansive, and which refers to the process of the inclusion of the territories of East Asia. I believe we are dealing here with the final expansive wave, and it includes more or less the process of incorporation of China, Japan, and Korea, which develops from 1850 on.

CAAR: What will be the general implications of, to put it this way, this "geographical" end to the expansion of the world-economy?

IW: Well, I believe that this fact forms part of the beginning of the creation of the situation of bifurcation. I believe that here we are speaking of one of the limits, one of the asymptotes, that constitute the limits of expansion for the system itself—a limit that arrives at some point and thereafter begins to narrow the possibilities of continuing the existence and reproduction of this historical system.

CAAR: Let's move on to the last question in this second part of the interview. I wanted to bring this second part to a close by asking you about the overall meaning of the contribution offered by your book. If we situate *The Modern World-System* at the heart of debates in economic history since the 1960s, what constitutes, in your opinion, your greatest and most original contribution? What can we say are your most fundamental contributions and novelties?

IW: I believe that this originality lies in the selection of the unit of analysis. And I also believe that therein lies the fundamental contribution of what I was arguing then—that is, that it was necessary to analyze and discuss the world-economy as a whole, not individual states, and that it was therefore necessary to include in this discussion things like the analysis of the social sciences themselves, elements of economic history, and many other such things. And I believe that in that era, at that time, people recognized very clearly that this was where the originality of my work lay. Because the readers who, for example, have praised my book have mentioned or cited precisely this element. But exactly the same has occurred with critics, since the criticisms directed at my text also said that this affirmation was not true, that it was impossible to accept this thesis, but they concentrated equally on this element of the unit of analysis that I just mentioned.

CAAR: And do you believe that this is valid not only for the economic level but also for the political and cultural levels?

IW: Yes, of course. And I even think that this is perhaps a second important element of its originality: the fact that I rejected from the outset this idea of seeing the economic and the political as separate fields and of seeing culture as a third field, arguing to the contrary that, in truth, we are dealing instead with realities that are completely intertwined with one another. So I think that we could find in this second idea a second original contribution of my book.

TWENTIETH-CENTURY HISTORY,
IMMEDIATE HISTORY, AND THE FUTURE
OF THE CAPITALIST WORLD-SYSTEM

CAAR: I would like to tackle now, above all, those questions related to the history of the twentieth century, the immediate history of the capitalist world-system, and also the question of the very future of this historical capitalist system. My first question refers to your analysis of Leninism and the historical role of the Russian Revolution, which you only seem to perceive as a radicalized national liberation movement that achieved power. You then trace out the similarities between Lenin and Woodrow Wilson, considering both as "ideologists of the twentieth century." Moreover, you had previously criticized the possibility of "socialism in one country," given the interdependence of nations within the world-system. Regarding all of these premises, I wanted to ask the following: What is the relationship between this destiny of the Russian Revolution, the impossibility of its triumph, and the situation of Russia in that period and the semiperiphery of the system? In the second place, isn't it necessary to make a radical distinction between Leninism and Stalinism, with only the latter representing this defeat and impossibility of socialism and, as a result, simply a movement of national liberation in power?

IW: You make one point that isn't accurate. I don't consider the Russian Revolution to be only a movement of national liberation, and I even think that it wasn't originally a movement of national liberation. It was a movement organized by a Marxist party, understood itself to be the party of the working class, and was, at the same time, an organization that managed to achieve such a large popular response not for being a working-class party, or not in its quality as a party of the proletariat, but rather because it was rightly seen as the party of Russian national liberation.

Therefore, in my opinion, the true basis for the great popular support the party enjoyed was this second characteristic as the party of Russian national liberation. And lastly, I believe that as a result they operated with this great popular support, in the end defending and proclaiming the expansion and consolidation of the new Soviet state. Note that this was the Soviet state, not the Russian state. And all this was happening already in Lenin's time, but above all and much more in the era of Stalin. And I think this is the idea that I highlight, the importance of the industrialization of the Soviet state, or the importance of the state of the Soviet Union as victor in the Second World War, or also that of the construction of a military power, that was invincible on the global level, a power that was again that of the Soviet Union.

In all these proposals and defenses, there existed an extreme degree of national pride. This is also evident in the thesis and the defense of the project of "socialism in one country," a thesis that was truly, deep down, the construction of socialism in that concrete country that was the Soviet Union and which already represented, from the beginning, a betrayal of the central ideas of Marxism and even of Leninism. Although we should also make clear that this betrayal was very clearly imposed on the Soviet leadership by history itself. It was no longer possible to continue waiting for the arrival of the German revolution after 1920, a revolution that in the end never arrived.

CAAR: Does this mean that you think that the revolution cannot be anything but a necessarily global process?

IW: No, not at all. Because I think that when the question is formulated in those terms, one gets the impression that we are going to organize an assault on a global Winter Palace. But it's clear that no such Winter Palace exists for the world as a whole, and besides, I don't think that such an assault will take place. Instead, what exists today is without a doubt a capitalist system on the global scale. Now, we say that this system is going to come to an end some day, one way or another. Therefore, when this end comes, the system will begin to transform, and this transformation could go in the direction of the creation of a relatively democratic and egalitarian society, but it could also give rise to a different historical system that might reproduce all the worst features of our present system, perhaps in a harsher form. But it is indeed clear that there won't be a revolution in the traditional sense, that is, a movement and insurrection carried out by an armed group that is responsible for the transition from capitalism to socialism on the global scale.

To construct socialism only within a single country is impossible. Now, if you ask me, on the other hand, if the Russian Revolution has had an important historical and political impact, I would say yes. And I would say yes because from my perspective it was a great national liberation revolution, which afterward inspired a number of other revolutions, also geared toward national liberation. Whether this is good or bad, that's another question. Also, if you ask me if, from the perspective of the *longue durée,* this was a success or not, I would reply that this remains to be seen.

CAAR: Was Russia, prior to 1917, a semiperipheral country?

IW: Yes, without a doubt. But while it was semiperipheral, it was also the most powerful country within that category, both on the economic and above all on the military levels. Before 1917 Russia was a very important country from a military perspective.

CAAR: So, was this semiperipheral situation in Russia the reason why the revolution had to lead to or turn into a national liberation revolution rather than a socialist one?

IW: It was due to this semiperipheral situation that the revolution took place in Russia, but this is also why it became a national liberation revolution. For Marx, the first socialist revolution had to take place in England. But despite the fact that Marx himself argued this, already by 1890 Marxists had rejected the idea of a revolution in England. Instead, at that time, Marxists were expecting the revolution to occur in Germany. Why Germany? Because at that time the strongest party existed in Germany. But why did the most powerful party exist in Germany? From my perspective the answer lies in the fact that, at that time, Germany was still not part of the core zone of the world-economy but rather found itself in the process of deploying all of its efforts and struggle in order to become part of it.

When the Russian Revolution broke out, the Russian revolutionaries were as surprised as anyone because they had repeatedly told themselves their whole lives that the revolution would start in Germany. And even after the triumph of the Russian Revolution, they spent three whole years awaiting the arrival of that revolution in Germany. Of course after that time, in 1920, people began to say that it didn't look like a revolution was coming in Germany and to ask themselves what they should do and if they should abandon the whole thing. And they replied that they shouldn't abandon it; rather, they needed to change the entire logic of their position. And it was then that they began to speak of "socialism in one country."

I believe that already by 1920, the idea and substance of this term was present in Zinoviev, Lenin, Bukharin, and so forth, and I believe that therein lies the importance of the famous Baku Congress. This congress was originally conceived as a meeting where the various European workers' groups were going to give a whole series of important lessons to the poor peoples of the East whom they had invited to the congress. But precisely the opposite happened: those from the East dominated the congress, and so the Soviet leaders, like all good leaders, ran behind the masses saying, "We are your leaders." But then we can ask ourselves, what did they become leaders of? And the answer is that they became leaders of national liberation movements.

What happened was that, at a given moment, there was a clear collapse of a rotten regime within an enormous semiperipheral country. There, the army collapsed at a given moment and the popular masses began to demand "bread and peace," because all they wanted was bread and peace. Alongside this, there existed a whole series of pretty ephemeral and weak regimes, and so at a given moment, there was a small Communist revolution that ran the risk of losing, that very well could have proven unable to maintain power. Since the other powers and the other groups were in a position of great weakness, this revolution managed to triumph and remain in power. But the problem is that, in order to maintain power, it was forced to compromise all that had sustained it previously.

This revolution ended up compromising all of its positions, and it even came to abandon the idea of a proletarian revolution in Western Europe. It had to accept the interstate system that was operative at the time and to industrialize on the basis of the repression and the sacrifice of the whole rural population, as well as at the expense of maintaining very low living standards for its own working populations. And only at this cost did this revolution manage to stay in power for sixty-odd years—and all this just to lose power again. But this was all done, paradoxically, in order to construct something that was at that time called socialism, although, as a matter of fact, they never constructed it.

CAAR: Do you think therefore that the Soviet Union remained a semiperipheral country during its entire history, including even the Russia of today?

IW: Yes, that's what I think. And I think it's only semiperipheral at best, because Russia now confronts the risk of losing this semiperipheral status and declining even more. I think that this is where its principal problem lies. But we should say that, for now, the Russian nation continues to be semiperipheral, above all because it has maintained its military power. But we should also mention that it has a good amount of collective social power, which could eventually regroup itself and succeed in transforming present-day Russia into an important actor on the world stage, which isn't impossible at all.

CAAR: To try to follow this line of thinking, I wanted to ask what you think of prerevolutionary China. Was it in a peripheral or a semiperipheral situation within the world-system?

IW: I believe that it was undoubtedly peripheral.

CAAR: Do you believe that it remains that way today?

IW: No. One of the effects of the Chinese Revolution has been to change the peripheral situation of the country. I think, for example, that when the

Chinese Revolution managed to recover the unity of the whole country—a national unity, which was at that time, in my opinion, the central problem and which I think remains the central problem today. It has reinforced at the same time its infrastructure, in the first place militarily, but also more recently its economic infrastructure. The Chinese Revolution without a doubt achieved the country's rise on the world scale.

CAAR: You have proposed the argument that socialist ideology, since 1848, has begun to blur and become subsumed within liberalism merely as a radical variant, a sort of "social liberalism." But if this is the case for a large part, or even the majority, of the socialist ideologies of the twentieth century, I would ask, how then would you situate, firstly, the Marxism of Marx, and then the entire lineage of critical Marxism, which represented a rupture from the Second International and, in my opinion, goes from Rosa Luxemburg to Mao Zedong, passing through Lenin, Karl Korsch, the Frankfurt School, and Antonio Gramsci, among others? Wouldn't this lineage of critical Marxism, despite being a minority during the twentieth century, be the true representative of socialist ideology during the past hundred years?

IW: With respect to this question, my point of view is that all of Marx's Marxism, throughout his life, represented a continuous effort to resist this conversion of socialist ideology into a radical variant of social liberalism. We shouldn't forget that one of the most important pieces of the last period of Marx's life was his famous *Critique of the Gotha Program.* Marx notes that this movement, which considers itself socialist and also claims to be a radical movement, and so forth, at the time of formulating a political program, adopts a program so reformist that Marx considers it unacceptable, and he comes to the conclusion that it is necessary to publicly denounce it. However, I believe that this personal denunciation by Marx shows precisely his own political weakness within the heart of this movement.

He was in a position of an intellectual who was fundamentally external to the movement, an intellectual who carried out an analysis of the situation and denounced the limits of this movement because deep down he did not function as its leader.

With respect to the list you mentioned in your question, citing, for example, Rosa Luxemburg, Mao Zedong, Lenin, Karl Korsch, and Gramsci, we shouldn't forget that they all shared a position of rupture with and opposition to the Second International. They wanted to dissociate themselves in some way from the Second International. And this is why they denounced the German Social Democratic Party, and not only the moderate groups but also the left of the party itself, represented by Karl Kautsky. And they denounced them for selling out the revolution and for converting to liberal positions.

This whole group said that they wanted to do something entirely different, so they dedicated themselves to denouncing the irrationality of the First World War, and later they organized the Third International around the twenty-one points. At its base, this was a genuine effort to create a new and truly socialist movement that was really antisystemic. Nevertheless, I think that if they had defended this position at the time of the First World War, by 1920 or 1921, even Lenin himself found it necessary to renounce this spirit, or the original intentions of this project. Because I believe that Lenin realized that neither he nor the whole Soviet party was capable of maintaining, under such difficult conditions, that truly socialist spirit of the movement.

In my opinion, Lenin realized that the price for maintaining this original radical position would be the loss of power by the Bolsheviks. I think he was conscious of this. And he also realized that the price for maintaining said power was the abandonment of this original radicalism, sliding into this same process of "liberalization," or the conversion of the movement, which ended up transforming increasingly into a simple variant of these liberal movements. I have attempted to show in a whole series of essays the way that the Soviet party felt increasingly obligated to give way to liberal arguments on point after point.[34]

CAAR: Hearing you say all this, one would get the impression that there was no other alternative and that we are dealing with the bad luck of a tragic situation, in which the radical individuals and movements were forced, with no other choice, to give ground, to abandon and renounce these radical positions.

IW: I think you're right, and to explain this situation I would refer to the argument put forward by Ilya Prigogine. I say that, in effect, when the system is in conditions of equilibrium—that is to say, when it functions normally—attempts to disrupt it are only able to produce minor deviations in its functioning. It could therefore be the case that people make an enormous effort and only manage to shift the system slightly with respect to these general conditions of equilibrium. On the other hand, when the system begins to come undone and crumble, and when these conditions of equilibrium no longer exist, we enter a situation of bifurcation, and the exact opposite occurs. Within such conditions, a very small accident, fluctuation, or noise can provoke major deviations and can have an enormous impact on the system.

To return to the point we proposed, I would say that during four or five centuries, the totality of revolutionary movements only managed to modify relatively little the general course of the life of the system. But I want to clarify, so there's no confusion, that I'm not arguing that they don't modify the system at all. But they weren't able to have a profound impact on the reproduction, the equilibrium, and the history of the system. As a result, throughout these four or five centuries, thirty, forty, or fifty years after the different revolutions, people began to ask themselves what had really and substantively changed. They felt that after all was said and done, they had essentially returned to the previous situation, and the more things seemed to change, the more they ended up reinforcing and reproducing the old situations.

On the other hand, it's also the case that all systems arrive in a determinate moment at situations of bifurcation, and so, when we are far from equilibrium, the smallest action or gesture, the tiniest transformation, can launch the system as a whole in totally unforeseeable directions. If you look over my texts again, you will see that I never in any way criticize those people or those positions. Never in my life would I use, for example, the term "betrayal" to characterize these people—nothing of the sort—because they didn't have any other alternative, they had no choice, and I believe that they acted—

CAAR:—in the only way they could? How long will this situation of bifurcation last?

IW: Perhaps to 2050, although it's difficult to say exactly. Moreover, from this analysis I simply propose that we attempt to gain more clarity with respect to what is going on now.

CAAR: I want to ask you then if you have a more concrete idea of how to organize a new social movement that is truly antisystemic, according to these new circumstances of bifurcation. It occurs to me that perhaps the neo-Zapatista movement is advancing in a more or less similar vein. I'm not sure what would be your opinion in this respect.

IW: I agree with you completely. I also believe that the case of the neo-Zapatistas could be a good example of this attitude, on the way toward constructing a broad front. Because while it's true that for the moment the base of the neo-Zapatistas is a single movement, they are also putting great efforts into attracting general support, to constructing a much broader basis of support. I'm convinced that we can already find in this attitude and this posture the germ of an absolutely different spirit from that of prior movements. One of the things that most impressed me when I came into direct contact with them was that they are one of those extremely rare, organized movements that assumed and understood the meaning of this lesson. To the contrary, this is not the case with a great number of movements that also claim to be of the left . . .

CAAR: You speak of three phases in the history of Marxism: the chiliastic period of Marx himself, the orthodox period of parties, and the period of a thousand Marxisms. My question is then, where would you situate the lineage of critical Marxism that we mentioned previously, if you indeed accept that it represented an autonomous tendency within these multiple Marxisms?

IW: It depends on whom you are referring to specifically. Because I believe that, for example, Rosa Luxemburg, Mao Zedong, and Lenin can be classified, all of them, as orthodox—each with his or her respective variations and shades—but I believe that they would all fall within the group of representatives of orthodox Marxism.

CAAR: And the Frankfurt School?

IW: We shouldn't forget that the Frankfurt School was above all an intellectual school and not a political movement. Now, in this condition as an intellectual school, they were essentially critics of orthodoxy, in their argument that the intellectual analyses of this orthodoxy and its distinct variants were not correct, allowing them to sense that the political lines of these orthodox parties were not exactly the best. But while it's clear that the members of the Frankfurt School distanced themselves critically from the political line of these orthodox parties, they never indicated which was the political line to follow. I have never read a single text by someone pertaining to the Frankfurt School that could be considered as a sort of political manifesto. Their writings are always of the sociological or philosophical order.

CAAR: What would you say about the case of Gramsci?

IW: We all know that Gramsci was an important thinker of the Italian Communist Party, who grasped the fact that the Italian situation did not correspond to that which had been theorized by the various orthodox positions. In the case of Italy, there existed a semipeasant country that had a fascist dictator. Through this, Gramsci arrived at the conclusion that in Italy one could apply neither the German medicine nor the Soviet remedy—which meant that he was a very intelligent thinker, a thinker who during most of his life had no other occupation than thinking, since he was imprisoned and spent a good part of his life in prison.

I think that Gramsci has written some very intelligent things, which his party has been progressively applying within Italy since the Second World War. But if it has done so, where was it attempting to go? If we look at the results, it was to transform into the great Social Democratic Party of Italy. I would even go further and say that the group Rifondazione Comunista is nothing more than a sort of further left social-democratic party.

CAAR: Let's move to another point. I seem to recall that in your essay on 1968 you characterize this date as a "revolution in the geoculture of the world-system," and from there you explain its planetary nature. Why was this geoculture modified, as you say, in 1968? Is this linked with the process of declining United States hegemony? You have talked of the similarities of 1968 with 1848, which was perhaps the end of English hegemony. Or is it instead connected to the situation of bifurcation after 1972–1973, or both, and in either case with what implications?

IW: I would say that I don't believe that it was the end of U.S. hegemony that provoked the situation in 1968. I would say instead that the second element you mention gave rise to this geocultural rupture. I remind you that on several occasions I have argued that, beyond the diversity of the movements of 1968, beyond their great differences all over the world, two themes repeatedly appeared in these movements and are common to all of them: in the first place, they are against United States hegemony over the planet, and at the same time they are against Soviet complicity or collusion with respect to U.S. hegemony. This is the first repeated theme, while the second element that repeated in all these movements is the critique of the Old Left, from the perspective that these Old Lefts are part of the problem and not part of the solution.

So all those movements were in favor of the creation of a New Left, at the same time that they criticized the Old Lefts prior to 1968. Why this critique of the Old Left? This is something that I have attempted to explain in several of my articles, in which I propose that at the end of the nineteenth century, two types of movements began to take form, and these were national liberation movements and the socialist movements. Both in effect began to formulate and defend the strategy of two stages—a first stage directed toward the taking of power within each state, and a second stage in which, and only after this conquest of state power, the true transformation of the world would follow.

Practically all movements have accepted this two-stage strategy. So if we look at the situation in general terms, it turns out that between approximately 1945 and 1968 and nearly everywhere, both socialist and national liberation movements managed to triumph with regard to what we have deemed the first stage. In this period, a third of the globe was governed by the various communist parties that had taken power, while in the so-called Western world, various social-democratic parties had gained power as well, alternating power to be sure but one in which the conservative parties more or less accepted the basic social-democratic demand, the welfare state.

Finally, in a large part of the Third World, regimes were the result of the rise of the national liberation movements that had managed to take power—sometimes through revolution and occasionally by other paths. In Latin America there existed openly populist and nationalist regimes that managed to develop among their inhabitants a series of sentiments based more or less on the belief that, finally, they had recuperated their national independence, thereby reinforcing the excitement of having reconquered Latin American independence.

Upon contemplating these processes from a more general perspective, we could say that in these years, from 1945 to 1968, the antisystemic movements as a whole had triumphed in terms of carrying out this first stage. But we could also ask ourselves what the results of these regimes were with respect to the tasks expected in the second stage and which of them managed to transform the world radically. The revolutionaries of 1968 began to complain that these regimes had not changed the world in a radical way at all. And they argued that the regimes had not changed it as promised, because we were still living in a capitalist world, there still existed a clear polarization between the countries of the North and the South, and the different *nomenklaturas* had remained in power in all countries on earth. This meant that, at root, these countries were not, and are not, genuinely democratic or truly egalitarian.

After 1968, the entire world began to realize that it was not possible to continue waiting for the radical transformation of the world and started to question the general idea of liberalism, which claimed that through state reforms—that is to say, through progressive reforms orchestrated by the state apparatus—it was possible to begin resolving, bit by bit, all the problems of present societies.

On this point, I should mention that the different antisystemic movements that developed throughout the twentieth century have said something very similar to this discourse of the liberal reformists. Because they have argued to the masses that if the latter stood by their side and supported them, when they managed to take power they would truly do all that the liberals had always promised them but never achieved. I believe that the hope in this future, which the antisystemic movements promised would be so bright, prevented these masses from adopting more radical positions. That is, they maintained moderate positions during these years. This situation was the true political foundation for the legitimation of the majority of these states within the world-economy throughout this stage in the history of the twentieth century. And this was also, in a manner of speaking, the secret of the political stability of the world-system during the whole phase prior to 1968.

But it was exactly 1968 that came to put all of these elements into question. From this date, the people began to say that they no longer believed the promises offered by these parties and even these antisystemic movements. And they began to think that perhaps they would continue to vote for such and such a party, but they wouldn't go out on the streets to jump for joy if they won, because they had lost faith that these parties would fulfill the promises that they made. So the people began to reflect and to ask themselves after 1968 if maybe there didn't exist other alternatives to those parties, and they lost faith in the very possibility of state action, which means that from 1968 the power and legitimacy of those states in general began to break down bit by bit.

This is reflected directly in the profound transformation of the geoculture, expressing itself as the end of the belief in centrist liberalism: people began to abandon the liberal idea that we are moving toward a bright and progressive future on a march that, although perhaps a bit slow, is nevertheless a certain and ineluctable one toward this better future. But we shouldn't forget that it was precisely this that guaranteed the survival of liberalism, and even at a given movement guaranteed the strength and even the existence of the antisystemic movements, which had also to a certain degree adopted that liberal position.

This is the change that 1968 provoked: the people had ceased to believe, or at least had begun to progressively disbelieve, this liberal point of view. I consider this to be the true transformation encouraged by the movements of 1968, and it doesn't have anything to do with the crisis and the end of United States hegemony. Because in reality, said crisis is a repetition of a normal process within the historical cycles of the world-system, of a sort that has existed before and has now repeated in the case of the United States.

CAAR: Do you believe that this crisis of the Old Left is linked to, or has to do directly with, the practically planetary rise of Maoism and the flourishing after 1968 of the various Maoisms that exist the world over?

IW: In effect, I believe that this crisis of the Old Left explains in large part the rise and popularity of Maoism. Because I believe that it is like a sort of first response, or a first reflection of a reaction faced with this crisis. To understand this, we need to recall two important elements that are present in 1968: on the one hand, the struggle against the hegemony of the United States and Soviet complicity and, on the other hand, the struggle against the Old Left. At that time it was said that the communist parties in general were the representatives of the Old Left, although they are not identical to this Soviet complicity with the United States. So a first response to this situation, given that the students of 1968 had denounced this Soviet collusion with the Americans, was to say that perhaps the problem lay in this Soviet leadership. So they reasoned that if this direction was abandoned, they could look for another new leader for the international communist movement, a purer and more revolutionary leader, which in this case would have been the Maoists.

On the other hand, we shouldn't forget a second element, one that I include within the whole of the movements that constituted the Chinese Cultural Revolution. I believe that this movement was extremely interesting. What occurred in this revolution? It happens that there was a character named Mao Zedong, who was the true leader of the revolution, but who did not have any official post, either in the party or in the state. And this character denounced the general secretary of the Chinese Communist Party and the president of the Republic, accusing them of being, as they said in those times, "followers of the capitalist road." This is something that seems truly unbelievable. If one reflected on this carefully, one would be surprised to see, all of a sudden, the leaders occupying the highest posts in a governing communist party denounced as both followers and promoters of capitalism. And who carried out this denunciation? Precisely Mao Zedong.

In many cases, the people argued that the new governments had promised an entire series of things and had in reality only passed from a situation of imperialist domination to another in which the new government didn't keep its promises either. In my opinion it must be kept in mind that as a general tendency there was, nearly everywhere, a great disillusionment of the people, which followed an equally significant euphoria, and this generalized disillusionment is in reality important from a psychological point of view in order to explain how the terrain was prepared on which the movement of 1968 would burst forth and prosper.

CAAR: You have described 1968 as a geocultural revolution. I wanted to ask if this term is equivalent to that of "cultural revolution," or if there is a shade of difference between the two and with what implications. I would also like to know your opinion regarding whether this shade of difference might be the reason you exclude the "counterculture" from the central elements of 1968. Why is this counterculture not associated with the creation of a space for the contestation of established knowledges and, as a result, with the present crisis of the social sciences that you have described?

IW: I haven't used the term "cultural revolution" much because I think it's very much linked to the phenomenon that I just mentioned, which occurred under the same name in China. On the other hand, I think that I have tried to be very precise in my terms; the phenomenon that I am discussing is not exactly the same as what is referred to by the term "cultural revolution" that we have mentioned.

But this isn't why I exclude counterculture from the elements of 1968. Regarding the latter, I think that while it is true that the counterculture was an element linked to the lives of young people in the years prior to and during 1968, to put this at the center would be to diminish enormously the political significance of those movements. I don't believe that we can consider as central to this revolution the personal desires of the people to affirm their liberty to take drugs, or their will to change their sexuality, or other similar things that are connected to this term "counterculture." So while it's true that this element was present, I don't think it was central at all.

To conclude, I would say that the global geography of 1968 is much more extensive and diffuse, and more extraordinary, than we are capable of imagining. And I think that in reality the impact of these movements is underestimated.

TOWARD THE REORGANIZATION OF THE CURRENT SOCIAL SCIENCES

CAAR: I was hoping to move on to the final part of our interview, which will be the briefest, in order to pose some questions regarding what I consider to be the third axis of your research: the subject of the total reorganization of the social sciences. In your book *Unthinking Social Science,* you argue that the objective is to surpass the limits of the paradigms inherited from the nineteenth century. But Marx was a thinker who lived in that century, if at the same time an acute critic of his world and his times. Could you go deeper into what you think is the critical side of Marx, as opposed to that side of his thought that corresponds to these nineteenth-century paradigms? And which of Marx's theses and theorems could be considered important to rescue within this enterprise of "unthinking" the present social sciences?

IW: I think that the response to these questions is simple, and I would say that insofar as Marx is a characteristically nineteenth-century thinker, it is necessary to go beyond him. But on the other hand, if we think that despite being a man of the nineteenth century he critiqued and surpassed the limits of his own century, then it seems that there's no doubt that he continues to be profoundly up-to-date. So I would insist on the idea of the two Marxes that I mentioned earlier and often repeat. There exists, without a doubt, a first Marx, who is a man of the Enlightenment, completely liberal, and also a political economist still very much in line with Adam Smith and David Ricardo. It is this Marx, one still trapped within the confines of the nineteenth century, who needs to be surpassed. But we also have a second Marx, who had seen the limits of all this and critiqued them radically and who had been able to imagine things otherwise, giving us an entire series of ways to analyze the world from a different perspective. It is this last Marx who continues to be valid.

I get the impression that it has been the first Marx in our understanding who was celebrated, taken up again, and recuperated between approximately 1880 and 1960. This liberal and Enlightenment Marx dominated throughout this entire period. It wasn't until the 1960s that the second Marx was rediscovered.

CAAR: Precisely as a result of the movements of 1968, right?

IW: Yes, partly as a result of 1968, but also due to other factors. Because if we wanted to reconstruct more carefully the intellectual history of this phenomenon of the "rediscovery" of the second Marx, we would need to go back to long before 1968 and consider other elements, among which, for example, a very important one would be the proposals and developments of the Frankfurt School, about which we spoke previously.

CAAR: I wanted to mention that the other thinker whom you recuperate in a central way in your book *Unthinking Social Science* is Fernand Braudel. Could you tell us, more generally, what essential theories, concepts, or proposals you recover from Braudel that allow us to unthink the social sciences? To what degree is your project of "unidisciplinarity" related to the Braudelian project of creating an "interscience," and what would be the possible coincidences and discrepancies between the two projects?

IW: I have already spoken of this problem in other parts of the interview, so I will just repeat that in my opinion, the three fundamental proposals of Braudel that I recover would be in the first place, the concept or theory of world-economies; in the second place, the proposal and the conception of multiple social temporalities; and, finally, the idea of monopoly as a central and permanent component of capitalism. I believe that these three are the pillars of Braudel's work, which will last a long time. And as to the second part of the question, I would refer you to the article that I wrote about Braudel's position with regard to this "interscience," which I presented in the Quintas Jornadas Braudelianas.[35]

CAAR: I wanted to remind you that since the appearance of *The Modern World-System* I in 1974, you have criticized "multidisciplinarity" and defended, on the other hand, a new "unidisciplinarity." Could you go more deeply into this critique of "inter-," "pluri-," "trans-," or "multidisciplinarity," today so in vogue, and explain why and in what aspects these differ from unidisciplinarity?

IW: In reality, we are talking about something that has today become almost something of a game. There are some who speak of interdisciplinarity, others who speak instead of pluridisciplinarity, still more who speak of transdisciplinarity, and finally others who speak of multidisciplinarity. But I don't think that any of these is clear on what the difference is between these distinct terms. Deep down, they all express the idea that some people have said that it is necessary to change certain things, but I don't think they are very serious about establishing the differences between all these variants or terms of inter-pluri-trans-multidisciplinarity. Against all this, when I speak of unidisciplinarity I refer to something about which I have been very explicit, that I have explained very clearly on several occasions.

What does it mean to speak of disciplines, to speak of a discipline? For me, a discipline is the claim of a relatively closed intellectual field, which implies the delimitation of a certain field of study with its specific theories and methods. So when I defend unidisciplinarity, I am affirming that the totality of the social sciences should not have more than one unified field of work, with only one methodology, since all of the realities that they study are governed by a single logic. Therefore, when it is necessary to specialize within this field, because it's clearly impossible for everyone to do absolutely everything within a discipline, I say that it's necessary to understand fully what one is doing, in theoretical and intellectual terms.

So when people speak of this multi-pluri-trans-interdisciplinarity and all this, it implies that one is recognizing the existence of various different disciplines, while I am trying to reject the idea that sociology, economics, history, and so forth constitute separate and different disciplines. This is the essence of my proposal with regard to unidisciplinarity, its nucleus.

CAAR: So, you would argue in favor of the unity of the social field as a whole. Would you also be in favor of the idea of going further still and proposing the unity of the entire field of human knowledges in general, beyond the purely social?

IW: No, I wouldn't go that far. Because I do believe, to the contrary, that there exist various disciplines within this field of general knowledges. Obviously,

I'm also against what has been deemed the regime of "the two cultures," and I ask myself very seriously if there exist perhaps various different epistemologies that provide the foundation for this regime. But if someone told me that there exist different fields of work, one that corresponds to the study and analysis of physical material, another aimed at analyzing biological phenomena, and a third dedicated instead to explaining the social, I would be inclined to accept such a claim. And I would also accept the idea that there exists a series of theorizations corresponding to these diverse fields.

I think we are dealing in essence with different levels of reality. So I don't want in any way to attempt to mix everything. But on the other hand, and on the basis of the recognition of these differences, I propose that on the specific plane of epistemology, all these realities can be embraced through one single epistemology. Since when we speak of the field of knowledges in general, from the exclusive point of view of knowledge, in my opinion we can indeed speak of the existence of a single type of epistemology. So yes, I would be for the unification of the natural sciences, the social sciences, and the humanities, but only from the epistemological point of view and without ceasing to recognize that we are dealing with different fields of study that correspond to different levels of reality. Now, where exactly do we draw the borders between these various fields of work? This can remain as a problem that is still under discussion.

CAAR: In several of your essays, you return to the analysis of the categories of time and space, which in my opinion are the basic elements of all possible Weltanschauungs. How has world-systems analysis helped to redefine these with respect to earlier perspectives? And what is the originality of this perspective compared to the contributions of authors like Fernand Braudel and Walter Benjamin, among others, who have taken up the same themes?

IW: To refer to the essential point, I think that in these problems of space and time I try to deepen and theorize Braudel's contributions on this point. And at the same time, I add a fifth time. Because Braudel spoke, as you know, of four times, and I propose adding a fifth time, one that refers to the space Braudel left empty concerning the problem of social change. In order to fill this space, I propose this fifth time, which would be *kairos,* that of the choosing of systems. As I explained before, I derived this idea from the work of Paul Tillich, and I think that with regard to this question, the crucial essay is the one I wrote for the meeting of the Royal Geographical Society.[36] In this essay I say that when we speak of different times, we refer not only to distinct temporalities but also to the fact that each of these corresponds to a different space, so in reality we should refer to various time-spaces, or space-times.

CAAR: Could you go a bit deeper into this time of *kairos*?

IW: I propose the time of *kairos* on the basis of the recovery of the Greek term *kairos,* which has gained a meaning within theological interpretations. This time means the moment in which it is necessary to make a profound, mental, and moral decision. This is a time that does not appear every day; nor does it appear easily. Rather it appears only in an exceptional manner.

CAAR: What you are saying about the concept of space-time is interesting, because someone else has repeated the idea that Braudel always intended to carry out, with respect to space, a reflection equivalent to what you argued in your article on *longue durée.* But I should also add that Braudel himself felt as though he never fulfilled this intention.

IW: I don't know what such theses about Braudel refer to exactly. But I have tried to argue with respect to the four times he mentions—short, medium, long, and very long time, or very *longue durée*—that these times correlate with different spaces, and so it isn't possible to have one of these temporalities linked with just any space, or vice versa, to have whichever of these spaces connected with just any temporality. Instead there is in effect a relation of correspondence between these different times and spaces. This is what I have tried to designate under the name space-time or time-space. And with regard to this question, I would refer you to the article that I mentioned a few minutes ago, which represents my most developed work on the subject.

CAAR: The next question has to do with the book you edited, *Open the Social Sciences,* which has had significant success the world over. There, you reconstruct the history of how the current "episteme," or mode of organization, of our contemporary social sciences was established, but very little is said regarding the possible paths to their reorganization. Could you discuss your personal ideas regarding the possible developments involved in such a restructuring and how we can move forward in the construction of the new "historical social science" that you defend and promote?

IW: I agree with you that this is the objective of the book. But why does it fail to discuss the paths for the future reorganization of the social sciences? This is due to various reasons. In the first place, I'm not sure that the whole Gulbenkian Commission, which wrote the book, would have been in agreement when it came to proposing these possible routes. But this isn't the main reason. The reason is that, upon beginning to write the final report, we determined that we had two possibilities: the first was to attempt to elaborate a very detailed report on the alternatives to this situation. In this case everyone would have very likely devoted themselves and their time to discussing these alternatives, concentrating on defining if it was best or wisest to do things in this or that manner, or not to do so, and so forth.

But we really wanted to draw attention to the fundamental problems, inducing and even forcing people to reflect on them. We didn't want them to discuss a proposed solution but rather to think around a problem, so that each of them might try to look for and elaborate a solution themselves. So in the end, we decided not to elaborate or include this detailed scheme of possible alternatives, with the explicit goal of having people focus on the discussion, on the one hand, of the history and the genesis of the problem and, on the other, on the present situation of the same. So this was the first option we rejected, that of developing this scheme in a very detailed manner.

The second option that we discarded was that of not saying anything at all about these alternatives. Because if we had chosen this second option, we would have run the risk of people thinking that we were a group who posed a problem but failed to indicate any possible way out because we had no idea how to resolve the situation. And as a result, they might conclude that this study was simply not worthwhile. So we agreed on a compromise solution between these two options, finally deciding that it would be best to develop only a few of these small suggestions. And I insist that we were speaking of small suggestions, which were only meant to function like a sort of first step on the path of these possible solutions to our dilemmas.

And even then, there have been people who took the book and, without paying attention to the argument at all, focused on these two final pages of small suggestions, discussing whether these were good ideas or in other cases arguing that they had already been doing what we proposed for a long time, and so forth. In the end, I think we bet right, and these reactions confirm for me that it was a wise choice not to enter into the development of these alternatives. This is in general terms, referring to the work of the Gulbenkian Commission as a whole.

As for myself, personally, I should say that I don't have a very clear view of how to orchestrate this reorganization of the social sciences either. I think that this will be the fruit of a long discussion among all of us, and I can tell you that regarding this point, my position is similar to that which I maintain on the political level: just as I support a plural alternative for the left, so too would I support the construction of a plural schema on the epistemological level for the reorganization of the social sciences. I would suggest therefore that we experiment a bit with our options, that we explore different paths and after a little while think carefully about the results of all these attempts, in order to try to recover those useful things obtained in them.

Perhaps after a long series of experiences, not necessarily general ones since these can also be local, we will begin to see a bit more clearly what might be the solution to the problem. In the meantime, we will continue discussing the fundamental epistemological and organizational questions, in the hope of constituting this new structure. In general, my opinion is that for the moment, this is the most useful alternative, and I also think this was the understanding of the Gulbenkian Commission.

CAAR: Could we say that the principal priority of your current intellectual efforts is the advancement of this line of work?

IW: No, I wouldn't say that. The idea of concentrating exclusively on a single problem conflicts fundamentally with my own method. Normally, I am always working various fronts at the same time, simultaneously.

CAAR: Perhaps I got this impression from the great impact that this final report of the Gulbenkian Commission had, but also from the fact that you have written a large quantity of articles in recent years on this subject of the reorganization of the social sciences.

IW: Yes, this could be the reason for the false impression. But I insist that alongside this work, I am continuing to work on other subjects all the time and simultaneously developing other research.

CAAR: Could we say then that you are always working along the three lines that have represented the axes of your intellectual production in general?

IW: Exactly. I have worked along these three lines: to one side the history of the world-system; in the second place the problem of what to do today and how to analyze the current situation, also united with utopistics, that is, the study of the possible future scenarios of this world-system; and, finally, the third line, which is this one that we are discussing regarding the reorganization of the world of knowledge.

CAAR: There is a topic that is sketched but not very developed in your articles and essays: that of the convergence of the exact sciences and the humanities with the social sciences. I would like to know if the "historical social sciences" that you propose would also include the current natural sciences and humanities. And in any case, what would be the new forms of linkage and how do you understand the reorganized spectrum of the coming system of knowledges?

IW: To respond to your question, I would say that when I speak of this convergence toward the social sciences, I do so above all from the epistemological point of view, in the sense that, for example, the new sciences of complexity might begin to use a language that approximates and is very similar to that of the social sciences. On the other hand, those cultural studies developed in the field of the humanities might also begin to utilize a language very close to, very characteristic of and similar to, the language of the social sciences. In my opinion, perhaps we are witnessing the development of a process of, in a manner of speaking, the social scientization of knowledge structures, that is, an impregnation of the whole of the knowledge structures by what has been the mode of proceeding characteristic of the various perspectives of analysis of the social sciences.

And perhaps one of the effects of this "social scientization" might be that in the future all of these different knowledges will come to combine with each other even more. It could be, but the truth is that I don't know very well; I'm not sure that this will be the case. We can ask ourselves, might a biologist who works in the field of genetics begin to combine within her activity, on the one hand, elements rooted in chemistry and, on the other, elements related to the social organization of populations and to incorporate both of these into her everyday work? I don't know, but it's an open possibility. And I think that once epistemological divisions are overcome, the path is open to all sorts of combinations that are difficult to imagine in the present. I try, then, to leave these questions open: I don't want to try to foresee how this will develop because, moreover, I think that it is fundamentally impossible to do so.

So, just as Ilya Prigogine says, I am deeply convinced that we are only at the beginning of the development of the sciences and not, to the contrary, at the end of this development. I believe therefore that the human sciences will flourish enormously in the future if they are able to overcome their current limitations. And what will become of the relation between the social sciences on the one hand, the natural sciences on the other, and the arts and humanities? I'm not in any way certain of what could happen. All sorts of things are possible. It's even the case that today they are discussing, for example, if the argument of a historian is different from that of a novelist: in reality, I don't know. As for myself, yes, I do believe that there is a clear difference between the two. But I think that whatever the form, this will continue to be an open problem.

CAAR: I seem to remember that in a speech you said that fifty years ago or slightly more, the social sciences were like the Cinderella of the story, the "poor relative" within the system of knowledges, and that now, on the other hand, they constitute its center, its nucleus.

IW: Yes. And I would even go further and say that perhaps within fifty years, if we are correct, it is possible that the social sciences will come to be the "queen of the sciences" and at the pinnacle of these sciences. It's possible. We'll see.

CAAR: The second to last question—no doubt coinciding with your critique of the current parceled-out and specialized "episteme" of the social sciences—is whether, in your opinion, some elements developed in the last hundred years of the social sciences could be or should be recovered within the new structure of the historical social sciences, and if this is the case, which elements are these and how would they be eventually redefined and restructured within this structure.

IW: My response to your question would be the following: in general, yes. Yes, there will be elements that can be recovered. But don't ask me exactly which ones. And I say this because I think that in the past 100 or 150 years, in the field of the social sciences, we have simultaneously learned so much and also incredibly little. So, I would tell you that, for example, when I read books written a hundred years ago, they occasionally seem very weak to me in the sense that their authors don't say some things that I think are obvious, while they assert other things that just seem silly today. So, I would say that when we try to take the general balance of everything that has been done during these past 150 years, our general conclusion is that very little has been done. And I have written an article in which I use a metaphor to explain this situation, saying that it has been like a sort of enormous black hole into which light enters but from which it generally never, or almost never, leaves.

So if within 150 years, for example, people try to take a balance of what we have done, I think that they will also come to the same conclusion, and they will say that very little was done during this period. And above all, I would say that this will be the case with respect to what subsequent generations are going to accomplish and materialize in the next 150 years. Because at the same time that I live with this heritage and always use it, it is reflected in everything that I write. Because it's obvious that one can't start from zero. And there is a whole series of things that seem clear to me, but if you ask me why this is, I would respond that it's because such and such an author showed it to be the case at a certain moment.

CAAR: The last question: you have indicated that perhaps the greatest difficulty in moving beyond the paradigms of the nineteenth century is of ceasing to think within the classic division of the economic, the political, and the sociocultural. Could you go a bit deeper into these difficulties and, above all, into how you foresee another possible way of confronting social phenomena, exemplifying this with a specific example, if possible?

IW: I would say that this division is rooted in our modes of thinking to such a degree that it will be difficult to eradicate in practice. So, you can see that, for myself, even though I explicitly struggle against this division, when I begin to speak to someone, I return to the same sort of distinction between the economic, the political, and the sociocultural. To not go any further, I have done so more than once during this very interview. If you or the reader were to reread the whole of this text, you would notice the number of times that I have returned to such a distinction. And deep down, I am very disappointed with myself for not having been able to find and develop a language that would allow me to eliminate this distinction. So, when I say that this is the biggest difficulty to be overcome of the paradigms inherited from the nineteenth century, perhaps I say so because, for me as an individual, it is the most difficult. Perhaps we are dealing with a personal problem, but I should say that frankly I doubt it.

And I believe that it's important that we ask ourselves why this is the greatest difficulty to be overcome. Because I think that if we were capable of responding, then we would have the key to carrying out this very process of overcoming. So this is a problem whose resolution would merit a special prize indeed. I don't know if you are aware that mathematicians, since several centuries ago, at least five hundred years if not a bit more, have organized prizes saying, here is a mathematical problem; those capable of solving it will receive a prize. And only recently, someone has begun to claim that after five hundred years, they have finally managed to solve Fermat's theorem. I think that this problem we are discussing is more or less similar and would merit the creation of a prize for whoever is capable of eliminating the use of this distinction between the economic, the political, and the sociocultural. And perhaps then, if this prize is instituted, we will finally manage to overcome those modes of thinking inherited from the nineteenth century and based on this distinction. Perhaps then we will be able to advance a bit beyond this enormous and fundamental difficulty.

NOTES

1. Immanuel Wallerstein, "McCarthyism and the Conservative" (master's thesis, Columbia University, New York, 1954). This thesis remains unpublished up to the present.

2. The acronym "WASP" refers to White Anglo-Saxon Protestants, a higher social stratum in the United States, who until very recently occupied all the influential positions within the spaces of general social life.

3. Immanuel Wallerstein, "Revolution and Order," *Federalist Opinion* 1, no. 7 (Chicago) (May 1951) (translated into Dutch and published in *Orbis Terrarum* 5, no. 25 in October 1951).

4. Theodor W. Adorno, Else Frenkel-Brunswik, Daniel Levinson, and Nevitt Sanford, *The Authoritarian Personality* (New York: Harper and Row, 1950).

5. Immanuel Wallerstein, introduction to *The Essential Wallerstein* (New York: The New Press, 2000).

6. Raymond F. Bulman, "Discerning Major Shifts in the World-System: Some Help from Theology?," *Review* 19, no. 4 (1996).

7. Robert S. Lynd and Helen M. Lynd, *Middletown: A Study in Modern American Culture* (New York: Harcourt, Brace, and Company, 1929).

8. *Knowledge for What? The Place of the Social Sciences in American Culture,* (Princeton, NJ: Princeton University Press, 1939).

9. *Africa: The Politics of Independence* (New York: Random House, 1961), and *Africa: The Politics of Unity* (New York: Random House, 1967). The former was republished in 1971 with a new introduction.

10. "African Unity Reassessed," *Africa Report* 11, no. 4 (April 1966).

11. The oral testimony is an interview conducted on May 17, 1968, by Chet di Mauro for the Oral History Research Office at Columbia University, a testimony of slightly more than 150 pages. There is also a second interview, conducted in mid-June 1968, by Robert Friedman and Andrew Crane, of approximately 110 pages. Both remain unpublished but can be consulted with some restrictions in the Columbia University library. The book mentioned was written by a collective of journalists from the *Columbia University Spectator*: Jerry L. Avorn, *Up Against the Ivy Wall: A History of the Columbia Crisis* (New York: Atheneum, 1969).

12. Immanuel Wallerstein, *University in Turmoil: The Politics of Change* (New York: Atheneum, 1969). See also Immanuel Wallerstein and Paul Starr, eds., *The University Crisis Reader* (New York: Vintage Books, 1971).

13. "1968: Revolution in the Geoculture of the World-System? Theses and Questions," *Theory and Society* 18, no. 4 (July 1989): 431–449.

14. Wallerstein, *Unthinking Social Science,* part 4, "Revisiting Marx."

15. Wallerstein, *Historical Capitalism,* 9.

16. Some of the essays that Wallerstein refers to include his "Hold the Tiller Firm: On Method and the Unit of Analysis," *Comparative Civilizations Review,* no. 30 (spring 1994); "World-System," *A Dictionary of Marxist Thought,* 2nd ed. (Oxford: Blackwell, 1991); "An Agenda for World-Systems Analysis," *Contending Approaches to World-Systems Analysis* (Beverly Hills: Sage, 1983); "World-Systems Analysis," *Encyclopedia of Political Economy* (London: Routledge, 1999); and several of the articles included in Wallerstein's *Unthinking Social Science: The Limits of Nineteenth-Century Paradigms* (Cambridge: Polity Press, 1991); *The Capitalist World-Economy* (Cambridge: Cambridge University Press and Maison des Sciences de l'Homme, 1991); *The Politics of the World-Economy* (Cambridge: Cambridge University Press and Maison des Sciences de l'Homme, 1984);

Geopolitics and Geoculture: Essays on the Changing World-System (Cambridge: Cambridge University Press and Maison de Sciences de l'Homme, 1991); and *The End of the World as We Know It.*

17. Immanuel Wallerstein, *Report on an Intellectual Project: The Fernand Braudel Center, 1976–1991* (Binghamton, NY: Fernand Braudel Center, State University of New York, 1991).

18. These conferences have been held annually since 1977 in various American cities, organized by the Political Economy of the World-System Section of the American Sociological Association.

19. Wallerstein, "Hold the Tiller Firm."

20. Immanuel Wallerstein, Samir Amin, Giovanni Arrighi, and André Gunder Frank, *Dynamics of Global Crisis* (New York: Monthly Review Press, 1982).

21. Immanuel Wallerstein, "Semiperipheral Countries and the Contemporary World Crisis," in *The Capitalist World-Economy* (Cambridge: Cambridge University Press and Maison des Sciences de l'Homme, 1991).

22. "El fin de las certidumbres en ciencias sociales," talk given on October 16, 1998, and published as a pamphlet by the Centro de Investigaciones Interdisciplinarias en Ciencia y Humanidades of the Universidad Nacional Autónoma de México, 1999.

23. "Time and Duration: The Unexcluded Middle, or Reflections on Braudel and Prigogine," *Thesis Eleven,* no. 59 (August 1998): 79–87.

24. "Crisis: The World-Economy, the Movements, and the Ideologies," in *Crisis in the World-System,* ed. Albert Bergsen (Beverly Hills: Sage, 1983).

25. *Unthinking Social Science,* especially part 4, "Revisiting Marx": "Marx and Underdevelopment," and "Marxisms as Utopias: Ideologies in the Process of Evolution."

26. "The West, Capitalism, and the Modern World-System," *Review* 15, no. 4 (fall 1992).

27. "The End of What Modernity?," in Wallerstein, *After Liberalism.*

28. Bruno Latour, *We Have Never Been Modern* (Cambridge, MA: Harvard University Press, 1993).

29. This book was written in 1962 and was published in 1963 under the title *Le monde actuel,* as part of a larger book used as a manual for students in their final year of French secondary school; it was republished independently in 1987 under the title *Grammaire des civilisations.*

30. "Historical Systems as Complex Systems," *European Journal of Operational Research* 30, no. 2 (1987), later included in Wallerstein, *Unthinking Social Science.*

31. "The Three Instances of Hegemony in the History of the Capitalist World Economy," in Wallerstein, *The Politics of the World-Economy.*

32. "La crisis como transición," *Dinámica de la crisis global* (Mexico City: Siglo XXI, 1987).

33. "The Crisis as Transition," in S. Amin et al., *Dynamics of Global Crisis,* New York: Monthly Review Press, 1982.

34. See *The Politics of the World-Economy* and *Geopolitics and Geoculture.*

35. "Braudel and Interscience: A Preacher to Empty Pews?" (paper presented by Immanuel Wallerstein at the Quintas Jornadas Braudelianas organized by the Fernand Braudel Center, Binghamton, New York, October 1–2, 1999). This paper has been

published in the proceedings of these Quintas Jornadas in *Review* 24, no. 1 (2001). It is also available online from the Fernand Braudel Center.

36. "The Inventions of TimeSpace Realities: Towards an Understanding of our Historical Systems," in Wallerstein, *Unthinking Social Science,* part 3, "Concepts of Time and Space."

Chapter Two

A Discussion of the Itinerary of World-Systems Analysis and Its Uncertainties

Immanuel Wallerstein and Charles Lemert[1]

CHARLES LEMERT: One question we've previously discussed was, how might the elements of world-systems analysis have changed if, say, you had been a student of South Asia instead of Africa? Your response has often been, "Well, if I'd done India, it would have amounted to the same thing; it'd come out of the same place, with India instead of Africa." But, if I may, I would press the point. In the years leading up to *The Modern World-System* I (1974), the South Asian situation was vastly different both internally and globally than Africa was. Both broke with colonizing rule (though the African colonies, of course, at different times, later). By, say, 1968 and certainly by 1974, when the first volume of *The Modern World-System* appeared, India especially was, if not a solid member of the semiperiphery, at least a good candidate. Regarding the former colonies in Africa—especially in the sub-Saharan zone but also in the north, where the colonial arrangements broke very much later—the region was near a pure instance of stateless vulnerability to core exploitation.

I wonder if maybe you've thought about it since and whether you could talk a bit more about Africa's relation to the European cores as your pure analytic model.

IMMANUEL WALLERSTEIN: I'm not sure what I can say. India always fascinated me. I first went there in 1954, and I've been there at least a dozen times. For a week, for a month, for various lengths of time, and I've been all over India. So, it isn't sort of an unknown zone in the world, right? Even today, most recently, I was there in 2004. So, 1954 to 2004, a fifty-year range in India, and in Africa I have the same fifty-year range. First time, that was 1952. When was the last time? I don't know, a year ago.

CL: So that first trip to India was shortly after the end of the British rule in 1947.

IW: Yes, right, right. It was.

CL: Even in the colonial period, even relative to other Asian countries with colonial pasts, India was always a more independent and stably formed nation-state, even after the partition, than other postcolonial powers (Vietnam and Korea, for example). I'm thinking of this visually in a way and of at least sub-Saharan Africa (except for Rhodesia and the Union of South Africa) as a metaphor—a metonym, really—for the very idea of periphery: resource rich, regionally organized, weak states. Parts of Africa are peripheral in the way you describe the world-system. Certainly parts of South and East Asia fit the model—Bangladesh and rural China, for example)—but if we can speak of Asia and Africa as comparable, Africa seems to be the more powerful instance of the world-system as you describe it. I'm not sure Asia is—but, I admit, I don't know if this is a particularly important point, but ...

IW: But now you're talking about the difference between a zone that had been a world empire, which had a so-called world religion that had a big bureaucratic structure, that had a lingua franca literature. And most of Africa is a different phenomenon. The nearest thing to it in Africa would be Ethiopia, but other than that?

CL: In part because in Africa, what tribal and traditional civilizations there were had been overwhelmed in the colonial period in a way that they weren't in India.

IW: Well, right.

CL: I think the more important implication for your intellectual biography—perhaps viewed as a kind of virtual history in the manner of Niall Ferguson,

Chuck Tilly, and others.[2] But the connection that comes to mind is Wally Goldfrank's statement that you are a prophet. Indeed, I cannot think of anyone among sociologists or other social scientists who both called out what happened in 1989–1991 and then interpreted it without missing a beat. What I am stressing is that, on the one hand, the thought and the work to that point were evidently the basis for that prophetic vision, if you want to call it that. On the other hand, one could wonder what would have happened had you developed the scheme even slightly differently, had you started out working on South Asia (or some other region) instead of Ghana.

IW: Well, I think the answer is there if you look at the origin of world-systems analysis and the whole link intellectually with dependency theory. Dependency theory was developed in Latin America. There is a kind of parallel literature in India.

Then there is the Arab world in Africa. So I'm working in Africa. Giovanni Arrighi[3] is working in Africa. People are moving in that same intellectual direction from many geographical loci. So I'm not sure it would've been that different. Though the immediate impetus to—I mean, there are all sorts of accidents as a result of the Africa connection. I don't know that I would've gotten to Braudel[4] through India and so forth. I can't say that what was important about Africa, I think, for me but then also not unique, I think, is the ability to move as an intellectual, as a sort of scholar in contact with all kinds of political figures all the time. To see them quite often, to know a lot of them personally well, and so forth. Get in the middle of their frames of thinking and then of kind of all levels from the top to sort of different category levels and so forth. So that was the illuminating part.

CL: That in itself is an interesting point. You mention Gandhi, but of course Gandhi in several senses was not available, and there were no other leaders of comparable prominence in the decolonizing struggle in India. You have to contrast that with the situation in Africa where there were a good many salient intellectual leaders—Frantz Fanon, Aimé Césaire, Patrice Lumumba, Kwame Nkrumah, among many others.

IW: A lot of them were most interesting thinkers. I can't say that's different from India. I mean Gandhi with all that time not only in London, but in South Africa, Nehru. Most of the Indian intellectuals have been through a British university experience, and I'm not sure if that's terribly different from Africa, where many passed through French universities. You take someone like Amilcar Cabral. He was by training an agronomist. He studied at the university in Lisbon, and so did most of the Portuguese African leaders. The

French ones were all in Paris. Fanon was in Paris for many years. They're all pretty cosmopolitan types.

CL: Let's switch topics now. By 1974, when *The Modern World-System* I appeared, and in the years before that when you were developing that first volume, how intent were you on explicitly criticizing modernization theory, which had been so well fixed in place since at least 1960.

IW: Oh, yes. In 1975 there was a session at the American Sociological Association (ASA) meetings on—I forget what the title was, something like modernization theory. I was on the program, and so was Alex Inkeles. The third person, sort of, didn't play a big role. And so, Alex Inkeles gave his talk on modernization standard stuff. And I gave a talk called "Modernization: R.I.P. (Rest in Peace)." And so it was a very direct, explicit denunciation of modernization theory in 1975. As early as 1966, when I wanted to give a course at Columbia on what was, in effect, the beginnings of the whole business of world-systems analysis, I called it "Social Change: Modernization." By 1970–1971, when I'm writing the book, modernization theory was already under attack. I think 1968 killed modernization theory definitively in my mind.

CL: And, elsewhere in the social sciences, not to mention geopolitics at the time?

IW: Well, you know, what conclusions do you draw from this? The conclusion is getting increasingly radical. In 1980 Thierry Paquot comes to me in Paris and asks if I would I write a book for a little series—one called *Capitalism*. And I said, "Well, if you call it *Historical Capitalism*, I will." And then, shortly after that, I get a letter from the University of Hawaii asking me to do a series of three lectures, so I say, "Okay, that's terrific. I'll give the lectures." That is the spring of 1982, and I write them up as the book for Paquot, *Historical Capitalism.*[5] Now, if you read that book, you will see that, first of all, there are three lectures plus a fourth chapter, which is the consequence of public reaction to the first three lectures. And you will see there is a section in there that I added because it's the subject that came up in the "questions." It has to do with progress. So I'm writing this in 1982–1983, approximately, and I say, "I wish to defend one Marxist proposition which even orthodox Marxists tend to bury in shame—the thesis of the absolute, not relative, immiseration of the proletariat." I hear the friendly whispers. "Surely, you can't be serious. Surely you mean relative immiseration." And so, this attack on progress, I'm only daring to make it in 1982–1983 at a time when I feel this is a very radical proposition. If I made that today, half the audience would say, "Ho hum."

CL: Half of *your* audiences?

IW: Yeah, alright.

CL: I've been participating in a seminar at the Council on Foreign Relations. They will talk on about Francis Fukuyama or Sam Huntington—both at least de facto modernization theorists—but when I mention your ideas on the global situation, it is clear that they are familiar with them, but, well, for them they don't count, at least not in public.

IW: Yeah, I understand. But anyway, the point is, I draw increasingly strong conclusions from my basic position, but the shift out of modernization theory comes in the middle of the 1960s, I'm sure. By the time I write the book, I'm out of that; I'm into something else.

CL: Was that more politics than intellectual work—or both?

IW: It's both because it just didn't make sense intellectually and with the politics, sure.

CL: Where does the expression "World Revolution of 1968" come from?

IW: I invented it.

CL: I am sure you invented it. Is it singular or plural?

IW: Well, it's singular. It's the World Revolution of 1968. It comes from, first of all, a simple observation that it's worldwide in scope, partly at the same time, and, I argue, the same basic underlying themes everywhere despite the multitude of different situations. I start with that. Then, I say later, yes, the same thing happened in 1848. That was a world revolution. That is, to contrast with the so-called French Revolution and the Russian Revolution, which are the ones that are traditionally looked at, which in many ways had less of an impact. They didn't change the geocultures, as I keep calling it in another of my books. I have a lot of terminological inventions, which have caught on. "Geoculture" is another.

CL: And unlike Bob Merton, you didn't devote the last thirty years of your life tracing them.

CL: Right. So back to the World Revolution of 1848. But did you have in mind 1852 as well—the failure?

IW: Yeah, I mean my point about both—1848 and 1968—is that in terms of their political and economic objectives, they were both like phoenixes. They blew up, and they were extinguished, and then they failed—almost everywhere. But, culturally, in terms of the geoculture, they transformed the situation.

CL: So, in the one case, republicanism ...

IW: No, what I really argue is that, as a result of 1848, what happened was the crystallization of the three ideologies and the centrality of liberalism. Not merely was it the center, but it was central. So a whole series of changes result that lead to the creation of antisystemic organizations and so forth and so on. And 1968 is the end of this era. It's the destruction of the automatic centricity of liberalism as the only legitimate ideology and the resurgence of a true conservatism, which we can see all around us these days. And it was the release of the Left from its independence on centrist liberalism.

CL: This must be in the geoculture book?

IW: Well, where is it? It's in various places. Well, I tell you. It's called "Three Ideologies or One? The Pseudo-Battle of Modernity," and it is reprinted here in ...

CL: There is also a version in the book you did for André Schifrin and the little one that appeared about the same time as the short book.[6]

IW: Three or four years later.

CL: *Utopistics*—that's the other one.[7]

IW: That's another term I invented.

CL: Yeah, but it hasn't caught on as the others have.

IW: Well, I've got a lot of terms: "antisystemic movements," "semiperipheral," "world-economy" (hyphenated), "world-system" (hyphenated). I think some-one once drew up a long list of all these terms.

CL: The one thing that is surprising when you list your sources ... your three influences ... At least in one place, you say, well, of course, Marx, Freud, and Schumpeter, and I forget who the fourth was.

IW: A Hungarian.

CL: Lukács?

IW: No. Karl Polanyi.

CL: Right. Upon reflection, somehow Marx seems more important. And I also have the impression that Marx has sort of resurfaced in your thinking in the last twenty years. What do you think of that?

IW: Well, I think yes. I do in fact say in the beginning of the antisystemic movements piece[8] ... I definitely say [reading], "Finally, let me say a word about Karl Marx. He was a monumental figure.... He has bequeathed us a great legacy that is conceptually rich and morally inspiring.... He knew ... he was a man of the nineteenth century whose vision was inevitably circumscribed by that social reality.... Let us therefore use his writing in the only sensible way—that of a comrade in the struggle who knew as much as he knew." He's more important than these others in the sense that he had more to say, but a number of things that the others say, which he didn't, are part of the things that I weave together. So, already back in 1975–1976, a Dutch political scientist interviewed me. This is right after *The Modern World-System* I came out. He wrote a big thing in a major Dutch newspaper which was entitled the "New Marx," referring to me. I don't have any trouble acknowledging the big of role of Marx.

CL: No reason you should. It is striking, in the first volume, I think, you may even say somewhere "the evolution of class." You couldn't miss it. And yet, in fact, I think the early criticism was that world-systems analysis was all functionalist.

IW: I have a standard line. I always get the question sooner or later from a large audience. "How would you situate yourself in relation to Marx?" And my standard answer is that there are four views in the world about me and Marx. One is he is a Marxist, and that is a good thing. Second is he is a Marxist, and that is a bad thing. The third is that he is not a Marxist, and that's a good thing. The fourth thing is he's not a Marxist, and that's a bad thing. Obviously, I'm not what is called an orthodox Marxist—meaning a Marxist of the party. In that sense, I get criticized all the time.

CL: We Midwesterners have a great advantage over you who grew up in New York. We were completely innocent of all these various tendencies in the 1930s and 1940s in New York.

IW: In the 1930s and 1940s in New York, in the circles I grew up in, you were either a social democrat or a communist.

CL: Then there's all this business with Daniel Bell, who is ten years older? He was more active in the 1930s.

IW: He started at twelve years old ... on Union Square. And Dan Bell, one has to say, remained consistent since he was twelve years old. He was a social democrat then; he is a social democrat now. He hasn't moved to the left; he hasn't moved to the right. He is on the left economically, center politically, and right culturally.[9] That's of course the standard social-democratic line—traditionally, the real social-democratic position. That was the position of the 1930s, of any good member of the social-democratic movement in the United States. And he's still there.

CL: There are several reasons I'm pursuing this. One of them is Foucault's line on this in a different but related kind of situation of Paris in the 1960s, with all of this Althusser and Stalinist business. Foucault was once asked if he was a Marxist. Essentially his answer was, "Look, you can't write history today without being Marxist anymore than you could do physics without being Newtonian"—a snide answer in a certain sense. But then he said, "Let the bureaucrats worry about my credentials." So, it was kind of a putting-off move. He was trying to create something different at a time when, for one, he was identified with his teacher, Althusser—not a happy identification at the time. Relatedly, you mentioned last time that in your youth, fascism was the issue. You also were developing all of this thought early in school during the 1950s during the Red Scare. In many ways, the surprising and, if I may say so, the wonderful thing about what you did, and are doing, is that you came to it with a Marxist sensibility of some kind at a time when it was not on the table anywhere in American social science. The story of Al Gouldner is so striking. Before he died, Al made a pilgrimage to visit Bob Merton. And he took great pride in being Bob's student. This radical from the Bronx who was a Marxist who in the 1950s goes to Buffalo, which was the only center for some kind of Marxism, and he writes this Weberian study of industrial bureaucracy, which had been his thesis for Bob.[10] Then fifteen years later, he went to Washington University, where he would name his chair the Max Weber chair. Gouldner is another you would have expected to be more out as to his Marxism and was not until the decade before his death, beginning with *Coming Crisis of Western Sociology* in 1970. And you were doing this before that. Why? Was it your experience in Europe?

IW: There's a sense in which ... well, somebody who is in a left political organization said about me, "He has the best understanding of the thinking of the
Right of any man on the Left." There is a sense in which I have always tried
to hold tight to my position but express it in language that is not doctrinaire.
And I still in my writings try to do that. Indeed, I try to persuade reasonable
intellectuals of more conservative views of the correctness, utility, or worth of
my views. I didn't feel I had to fling Marx in anybody's face. But I remember
once, in my early days as an Africanist, I wrote an article—I guess it was
published around 1964—called "Class and Tribe in West Africa."[11] In politics,
nobody was using the term "class." What I did—I remember it now—I took
a whole series of analyses of what people had been writing about particular
situations in West Africa and showing how usually (but without saying it in so
many words) they were talking about class. I was sort of bringing to the front
what had been hidden. All these people like Gouldner were talking about it
but not quite saying it.

CL: Talking about it, believing in it, knowing it very well ... being closeted
in respect to it.

IW: They were hiding it in other terminology.

CL: Still in the United States by the 1960s and even into the 1970s, it wasn't
as dangerous. Still, for younger people with interests in a professional career,
it was felt one must avoid being labeled a Marxist. This was like, in another
time, being called "postmodernist." It was kind of a vulgar dismissal. Now I
wonder if you would agree that your European relations were both a source
of your boldness and a kind of safe passage.

IW: Yes, that's certainly true. Certainly, I mean, one of the attractions of
Europe was these kinds of, should we say euphemisms, of American social
science weren't necessary. One could talk about class or Marx or things like
that quite openly. And lots of people did, even people who weren't on the left.
Even Bob Merton, when he was young, was a Marxist or close to that.

CL: Well, I actually have written, and believe it to be true, that Bob's famous 1938 article "Social Structure and Anomie" is the first really serious
structural sociology in America. It, of course, paled in comparison to what
the Europeans were doing, but it was a very serious piece. I don't know
how anyone could read Durkheim and not see that what was missing was
class—jobs and income. Merton saw that but with no mention of Marx—
much the same sort of cover-up as Gouldner in the early years. But, getting

back, is it fair to say, in regard to those outside your sphere of intellectual commitments, that you were willing to go as far as you could without giving up the central principles? Is it possible—this is a general question—to hold principles such as yours, intellectual as well as political ones, and not face that conundrum? That is to say, whether to give up the principles or give up being a certain kind of influence?

IW: Is it possible when?

CL: Well, I mean people who came to this work in the 1960s as opposed to the 1950s. We are rather close in age, but for a number of reasons I came to the work nearly a generation later.

IW: Well, look. First of all it depends exactly what decade we're talking about. Also, what universities you're in.

CL: Well, in the 1960s there were, like, Todd Gitlin and Alan Wolfe, for just two examples, who did (and professed) all this leftish work (and ideas) and now are acclaimed as public intellectuals and even sociologists. But in Gitlin's case, at least, he is hardly a scholar in any usual sense of the word. Russell Jacoby is another who comes to mind. You mentioned Dan Bell, who on the crucial values remained much the same. People like these, of the 1960s generation, which I'd claimed as my own, have tended to go very soft, even centrist if not rightist. Dick Flacks is one the few who comes to mind of a 1960s activist who has remained true to principle and devoted to a serious academic life. People of the 1960s are inclined either to stay with it and get lost or go over to the other side. Then there are these people today, good people many of them, who suddenly discover public sociology and the importance of the 1960s, while most of them spent the 1960s in high school or university carrels.

IW: I always realized the political consequences of x and y and z and always wanted to protect my back in terms of ... but that's what tenure is for. And that's what good universities are for. That's what good relations are for, being respected intellectually by establishment figures. So, I always worked hard at being a good scholar. The idea of just sort of writing denunciations all the time never struck me as very useful.

CL: I agree with that.

IW: I mean ... it gets applauded and read by a certain number of people. It doesn't persuade people who will not be persuaded.

CL: Going back to policy ... so you had what was in effect an argument by accident with Inkeles and certainly others. But there's then the wider question of modernization theory and global policy and social policy and the World Bank; then there's W. W. Rostow in particular. Of course, they're the ones who have been the movers and shakers and have applied modernization theory—I think to disastrous results. You look at Sam Huntington. I don't know if you've ever bothered to read any of that stuff.

IW: I've read the latest one.[12]

CL: It's horrible.

IW: It's horrible, I agree. Most of that stuff in fact I don't read. You're quite right. If I wanted to be Zbigniew Brzezinski I could've been. I was at Columbia; he was at Columbia. I could've attached myself to various liberal political figures. This kind of thing.

CL: I may have told you this story. You are responsible for me getting kicked out of the Council on Foreign Relations.

IW: Oh, no. You haven't told me *this* story.

CL: Well, it's not a very dramatic story, but the point of it applies. In that seminar there was a discussion about the world situation, Iraq and all of that. And somebody was framing this debate in which the key figures were, again, Fukuyama and Huntington. They may have gone so far as to mention Stanley Hoffman, who as you know has put forth a rather biting criticism of the whole thing in "Clash of Globalizations."[13] Then I said, "Listen, there's at least a third view here." I mentioned your name and said something about the crucial difference. They were, so far as one could tell, quite familiar with the argument but would not talk about it. I was not invited back. There is some sense in which—I wonder if you aware of it—the so-called foreign policy establishment has to be aware that they are on shaky grounds.

IW: Not the neocons, but the whole Council on Foreign Relations establishment, which goes from relatively conservative to sort of Clintonian liberals. They are aware that they are on shaky grounds.

CL: Did you know Arthur Schlesinger?

IW: No.

CL: He was in this seminar. This is beside the point, but in some ways you wonder about how the ground washed out from under the liberal, the vital center notion. Anyway, going back to the Marxism question in the 1950s: you said in a previous conversation about your own family and political background that the most important thing was fascism. In New York and on the East Coast, fascism already by the 1930s was bound up with communism, in the sense of the revelations of Stalin's atrocities. I wrote you last year about Eric Hobsbawm's memoir.[14] It's sort of astonishing how open a communist he remained for so long. Now that was very different in Britain. And I guess my question is, how did the uniquely American politics in those early years of the 1960s and 1970s affect you? And did you ever wish you had packed your bags and gone abroad?

IW: Yeah, well, that had occurred to me at various points, but in the end, no. In American politics, in New York, we had the American Labor Party (ALP) and the Liberal Party. Then, when I went to Columbia, as a freshman, the most vital, the most interesting, most exciting organization on campus was the American Veterans Committee (AVC), whose meetings I attended regularly though I wasn't a veteran. But they were big meetings; they were always fighting. The American Veterans Committee had three factions. One was sort of an ALP faction; there was a Liberal Party faction, and then there was a group in between, who were trying to call those two factions together and find some middle road. So from these meetings, AVC disintegrates, as a result of all of this. But my sympathy was always with the middle faction. And I said from the beginning, and I say it now—I said it somewhere in my writing—I always agreed with everything the social democrats said about the communists. But I also always agreed with everything the communists said about the social democrats. So I was not going to link myself with either. Then I found myself sympathetic to all those in France and Italy and Britain and so forth who drew parallel positions.

CL: Were you ever at risk of being dismissed or attacked?

IW: No. Well, I certainly was at risk in that sense. I'm sure that this entered into people's thinking about me at various points. In terms of appointments and so forth, I don't know.

CL: Did you ever think during the Binghamton years that it was not quite a proper place for you—so far from the city, rural countryside and all that?

IW: Well, the answer is, I went to Binghamton because I could have the world there. It provided the department I liked and could construct; an administration that could be sympathetic and give me as much as they had, which was very little, and so forth. And then, it became a kind of self-sustaining enterprise. I couldn't drop it because there was no real alternative.

I'll tell you where I made a choice which was fateful, in 1974 or 1975. I was teaching at McGill. I had a sabbatical coming up, and I arranged to go to Paris for a year. At that point, Dan Bell, who liked me very much when I was at Columbia, was at Harvard, wrote me a letter to ask if I would come to Harvard—but as a visiting professor for 1975–1976. So now I had to choose between visiting professor at Harvard, which at that time basically meant they looked you over. So I probably could've ended up at Harvard. I decided I wanted to go to Paris. And of course, this created the strong link to Braudel.

CL: You've been very clear on globalization. I've heard you say that globalization is nothing more than modernization theory writ large. To what extent was there, going back even to Marx, ever any possibility of a sociology without at least implicit global theory. This is an open question about ...

IW: And I in fact wrote on that. It's an essay reprinted in *Unthinking Social Science*; there's a section called "Revisiting Marx,"[15] which includes "Marx and Underdevelopment," which was originally a paper I gave in Italy to the Istituto Gramsci. Well, anyway, I try to answer all of the Marxist critiques of my work—that I don't think enough of class, that I'm not enough of a productionist, and so forth and so on. I'm showing them they hadn't read Marx carefully. In "Marx and Underdevelopment," I put together everything that he wrote to show there is a different Marx, but it's perfectly true that there are other parts of Marx that lend themselves to the orthodox Marxist view, which is a theory of progress, which is the later-countries-who-will-copy-the-earlier-countries kind of view, and there is a strain in Marx of that. And then if you look at the second essay in that section, "Marxism as Utopia," which I gave in an ASA meeting at a big session on utopians—there is where I argue that there are three Marxisms: the Marx of Marx, the Marx of the parties, and the Marx of the Marxism of the postparty era. How did I get into this?

CL: Globalization and Marxism and ...

IW: So you can derive from Marxism, what's his name that guy in England? ... Bill Warren wrote a whole book showing you how Marxism leads you straight into modernization theory.[16] He was trying to answer all these people like me. You can find the quotes, and then you can find the logic that'll lead you straight into modernization theory, which is, after all, nothing. Modernization theory was preached in the Soviet Union in the 1950s and 1960s, but this wasn't called modernization theory.

CL: Well, Talcott Parsons was always on a plane to Moscow.... The question is striking to me. I would say that you've remained surprisingly loyal to sociology. I don't mean institutionally so much but intellectually. You still deal with its institutions and often speak in its terms, and you could've bailed out at any point intellectually as well as professionally if you wanted. And yet, sociology has really struggled on issues like this one on modernization and world realities. But now sociologists you'd never have associated with the topic are writing on globalization (myself included). But all the predicate of disciplinary sociology was the nation-state as society, the bounded nation-state.

IW: Sociology wasn't better or worse than the others. So too were all the predicates in political science and economics. So, that's the point. If I stayed loyal, it was because there was no point in shifting. I went into sociology originally. All through college, I couldn't figure out whether I wanted to be in economics, political science, philosophy, history, sociology. And I decided on sociology on the grounds that it gave me the most space. That was the criterion. And I could, more or less, do what I wanted in sociology to a degree that I couldn't in any of the other disciplines. And I don't think that has been historically wrong.

CL: Would you estimate that your influence has been greater on the periphery of sociology than in sociology? I meet people all over the world who have studied with you.

IW: Again, you have to talk about when and where. Okay. I think only recently has my influence been great within American sociology. That begins somewhere in the mid-1990s, I think. It's sort of creeping in. So now, I'm always amazed to see that I'm a big figure because I never thought of myself as a big figure in American sociology. And it's perfectly true that, if you just take the United States, I was maybe more read by geographers, by certain kinds of historians, certain kinds of political scientists, and only then by sociologists. And, international relations people read me, but they don't like me. I'm always struck, in France, absolutely always, if someone writes a little blurb on me in the back of a book or in a newspaper article or anything, they will call me usually something like this: Immanuel Wallerstein (and the order of these words varies), sociologist, historian, economist. Or economist, historian, sociologist. The first book of mine that The New Press put out called it political science. They didn't put sociology on it at all. So, yeah, certainly I have a bigger reputation earlier elsewhere in the world than in the United States, but I think it's all catching up. I'm a patient fellow [chuckles].

CL: How do you feel about the future?

IW: I don't worry about it actually.

CL: You just don't think about it?

IW: No, it's not that. I think that the politics of my intellectual life is to just keep plowing ahead. There's actually a marvelous review of *The Modern World-System* III in *American Anthropologist*. The author said something like this: "Well, Wallerstein has written two volumes already and it's been subjected to this critique and that critique, but he just plows on." He said it sort of admiringly. In a sense that catches it. That's true. If critiques are sensible, I bend with them or take them into account. I do just plow on.

CL: Has there been any criticism more telling and either helpful or disturbing?

IW: Most of the criticisms are of three kinds. First, there are those who refuse the premises, which I have rejected—that is, they invert and go back to whatever they were already thinking. Then there are the people who attack a particular book or a particular article because that's all they've read, who complain, "He doesn't say *x*," when I do say *x* somewhere else. And then there are people who make the critiques who think that I haven't gotten around to or haven't taken into sufficient account some issue. There's no question that I ignored culture, which I thought was wrong from the beginning but was just the same on the surface challenging. And so I started to write more on this. And sometimes I don't even remember what I'd done that upsets somebody. An interesting young fellow who is kind of a geographer/sociologist and is into ecology says, "Wallerstein has been attacked for not really taking ecology into account but reread volume 1 of *The Modern World-System*, chapters 1 and 2." I didn't even realize all this stuff was there. To show that in 1974, there I was, taking ecology into account without using the word.

CL: You could hardly have been influenced by Braudel and not have something to say on that.

IW: I'm occasionally surprised at how early some of the things that I think I only said later, I actually said much earlier. For example, the whole business about the unidisciplinarity, history of the disciplines, somebody said to me, "You were telling me all of this stuff in the 1960s at Columbia." I said, "I was?" I certainly didn't remember that. I reread something that I'd written in the late 1960s, and there it was. I had the stuff there, unelaborated. In some sense, it's like an unfolding, bit by bit, of the argument. It is also true of our work on cultures. Terry Hopkins said sometime in the mid-1970s that culture is the one domain that we have not elaborated, and it is essential to elaborate it and so forth and so on.

CL: That early?

IW: Yes, probably in the essay Terry and I did together in *Review,* in 1977, "Patterns of Development in the Modern World-System."[17] But there's also something that he and I wrote together published in 1980, called "The Future of the World-Economy" in *Processes of the World-System.* There was a great deal of talk between us about how culture is the big thing that needs to be filled in that we haven't filled in this exposition.

CL: It would be interesting again, not to spend a lot of time on it, to ponder at least what changes there have been in the social study of culture. In the 1960s and 1970s, the culture criticism of almost anybody was really very nineteenth century. You know, this sort of Hegel-versus-Marx, ideal-versus-material theme. Since then, culture has become a much more complex concept.

IW: Well, 1968 made culture a concept because what 1968 did was force people to see that economic arguments that were standard Marxism just missed this one. Also, the political conclusions missed a lot of them. What has been put in, obviously, is that culture itself comes in but also multiculturalism. It comes in postmodernism, and it is all a political and intellectual conclusion out of the crisis of 1968.

CL: You link 1968 to 1848. What is the link between, let's say, 1947 and the beginning of decolonization and the events of 1989–1991? I'm sure you write about this somewhere. Do you see them linked that way? In particular, would 1968 have been possible without the decolonizing movements?

IW: No, of course not. That's absolutely true. But it's also a reaction against those movements as well. That's very important. Do you know the essay that Terry Hopkins, Giovanni Arrighi, and I wrote called "1989: The Continuation of 1968?"[18] There we say essentially that what happened—it's a very nice analysis of why what happened in 1989 was so much like the last aftershocks (I don't think we use that phrase) of 1968.

CL: In that sense, since the implications were enormous, 1968 was more of a success than 1848—more than just having introduced culture.

IW: It was certainly more than just having introduced culture—more of a success, I mean. Because of 1848, we have socialist and labor movements, the national liberation movements—all that grows from 1848 … we have the welfare state. All of this logically emerges out of the Revolution of 1848. However, 1968 brings that to an end. That's the era of the triumph of liberalism. At least, that's my view. And now, it's the beginning of an absolutely new era.

CL: So FDR in 1932 was just America catching up.

IW: Yeah, kind of. You know, in many ways, America in the 1930s did more, if you look at more than just the installation of … it's catching up in some ways, and in others it's actually jumping to the head of the line because the role of the social democrats in the New Deal was social democracy. It was stronger in the United States than it was in most West European countries in the 1930s. But anyway, it certainly is part of the catching up. Well, the welfare state is a kind of complicated accretion, and one of the good things FDR did was to show that the post–Civil War was all the welfare state.

*   *   *

CL: You said last time we talked here that your major influences were Marx, Freud, Braudel, and Polanyi. But in this you must be referring to the earliest, perhaps formative influences. Then, more recently, you have provided another intriguing list, which again, and obviously, includes Braudel, but now also Frantz Fanon, whom you met in the 1950s, and most interesting of all, the physicist Ilya Prigogine. Could you say something about the differences in the two lists, including what may have been unique and distinctive about Prigogine? The relation to Fanon is one thing that seems obvious and quite early. But I wonder about the interplay with Braudel and Prigogine—that's interesting.

IW: Now I did write an essay on that. You saw that.

CL: Well, I know "Itinerary of World-Systems Analysis."[19]

IW: No, there's an essay on Braudel and Prigogine.[20] ... In either case, I met Prigogine at some event in Europe. I said something on the occasion about a similarity between Braudel and him, which amused Prigogine. Braudel, of course, was dead by this point, and it amused Prigogine no end to discover that I thought that he had some things in common with Braudel.

CL: Oh, he was familiar with Braudel? Or was it ...

IW: I don't know that he was *really* familiar with Braudel ...

CL: But this was—you met Prigogine in the early 1990s, right?

IW: I met him—no, no, I'll tell you exactly how I met him. I met him in 1981.

CL: Oh, it was that early?

IW: And what happened was, here I was sitting in Paris with these two young French business guys, professors at the business school, and they said, "Look, you know, there is this big conference every year which we run and bring together middle-level people from around the world to sort of get them to think about intellectual issues. And ... would you come? And just sort of be there? We'll pay you." And I said, "Fine." And when I got there, they said, "Look, the guy who was supposed to give a talk fell through. Would you give a talk? We'll pay you even more." "Fine. Okay. I'll give a talk." Before I talked, Prigogine talked. Now, I had heard of Prigogine, you know, and he blew my mind because I said, "My God, he's saying all these things which I've always thought, but he's a Nobel Prize–winning chemist." So I introduced myself to him, and I persuaded him to come to my talk, which he did, and that was it. I mean, I started reading him. And he had this conference coming up. The next year—I guess the next meeting was a conference in Texas. Then I was invited back to another conference in Brussels. Prigogine invited me to that, and so on. ... We kept meeting at conferences. It was a relationship that developed over the years, but it was absolutely fortuitous. ...

CL: Well, how then did Prigogine change your thinking?

IW: I say somewhere along the line—you know, here I am brought up in sociology, that all these quantitative guys are constantly telling me that they've got to imitate the physicists. And here are the physicists and chemists like Prigogine saying, "Everything is changing, and in effect, we've got to imitate sociology, so to speak." He was very well educated. First of all, he hesitated as a student between history and hard science, and he had a lifelong interest in art. He was an art collector. So he was a cultivated man of culture. And he was always in contact with philosophers and so forth; in fact, we went to this conference in Italy that he arranged, and it was arranged around him, but it was sponsored by the departments of physics and either history or philosophy. It was called "Beyond the Two Cultures."

CL: So how did things develop with him and his ideas?

IW: So he was always bringing everybody together like that. After I met him, he was always there in my thinking. And I read virtually everything. He had written in book form quite a bit, some for a general reader like *The End of Certainty* (1998). In fact, once, toward the end of his life, there was a conference in New Mexico that he was supposed to go to, and at the last minute, he couldn't go because he was ill. And he sent this young physicist from Texas named Dean Greenberg, whom I had met before, in his place. Oh, I know what it was—that's right, we were both getting honorary degrees, and he couldn't make it, so Dean Greenberg accepted for him. And then I gave a talk there and—which dealt with Prigogine. After, Greenberg said I really was one of the few people who really understood Prigogine. So, I think you know, Prigogine wrote very well for nonscientists, but every once in a while he gives one equation too much, where I get a bit lost.

CL: So you've got a good math background?

IW: Not really. I mean, I was very good at math in high school, but it ended there.

CL: Well, let me ask, then, this question, which came to me in kind of thinking about that. Actually, it came to me yesterday when I was lecturing on William Julius Wilson on the disappearance of jobs, and going back to Elliot Liebow, and they were looking at this very particular question about the impoverished urban Black man, and they'd already read some of you. And I said, "Now let's go back and realize that when you talk about the core exploiting the periphery, doesn't that in effect, in this situation, create a periphery within the core?" And I did a little thing on what's long since happened in American cities, and I said, "You've got to think about this"—I may have even used the word "complexity," but some word like that about the dynamic system—and that's my way of asking the question. In one sense, you can look at the Braudel part and say, "Well, that sort of special-izes time, and by categorizing time, it sets it in its place in historical time."

Complexity studies is entirely different, and I suppose there are those, I may have even thought of myself, who would say, "The original formulation you made was too static, too Braudelian." Do you see what I'm driving at? It's the question of how in the work ...

IW: Right, that essay I just gave you.[21]

CL: Yeah, how in the work the complexity studies specifically—

IW: Well, the point is—I make the point here somewhere that they come from opposite ends.

CL: I do remember that from somewhere else, but keep going.

IW: That Braudel is looking for duration and that because historians only deal with time and he's dealing with the duration, and Prigogine is coming from duration, he's looking for time. And they kind of meet in the middle because they both end up with this very carefully formulated middle position in which they basically don't like either of the ends so—they didn't know it, but they arrived at the same point from absolutely opposite parting points, and that's how I pulled them together, so it's absolutely true that Braudel gets critiqued because he emphasizes duration, which lots of people don't like, and Prigogine sits on the arrow of time.

CL: So to speak. Where did that come from—the phrase?

IW: Oh yes, it's not his own phrase; it belongs to Arthur Eddington, a scientist from the beginning of the twentieth century, who invented it. But Prigogine made it something everybody talked about: "Yes, well, the arrow of time." And the whole point is, everything has an arrow of time; he added that so do certain universes. And everything is a consequence of this temporal development. There's nothing timeless. That's the whole critique of certainty.[22]

CL: So, in French, I wonder if the better term would be the "trajectory of time."

IW: No, no, he says *la flèche du temps.*

CL: Really? Interesting. And this was in Brussels. When did—it slipped my mind—when did volume 2 appear, that was ...?

IW: 1980.

CL: 1980. So this is about when you met Prigogine.

IW: No, Prigogine comes after that. Prigogine is—if you want to see his influence, it's more in the later stuff, like *Utopistics*. It's a whole discussion of transition, when things move far from equilibrium and the bifurcation, and I used all that—that's all Prigogine's language.

CL: Well, how about jumping ahead to everything after 1991—or at least that—well, *Utopistics* comes in there too. But I think that the very first essay I saw in *Theory and Society* was certainly prophetic.

IW: Which one was that?

CL: I was on the editorial board in those days, and I know that they had the manuscript possibly as early as 1990, well beyond even 1989 had played itself out fully. The name slips my mind right now.

IW: I know what you mean; you mean "America and the World Today"[23]?

CL: But one can say—at least as an outsider, I would—that there you were then talking about a collapse of a system, as obviously you are now. But I'm trying to ask the question of the theoretical, how these tied together.

IW: Braudel deals with the system, the structure—it begins, it ends, it isn't eternal. But he never really deals with how the system collapses. He does—at the end of his life, he was giving a couple of interviews and writing some articles in 1972, after the economic crisis of 1973, because he sees things happening in the world. But it's not in his books; it's not anywhere. Whereas Prigogine lends himself completely to that because he is concerned with chaos, deterministic chaos, and therefore bifurcation and transformation.

CL: Well, chemical structures do collapse.

IW: Well, of course he's a chemist, but the point is, you see, the second law of . . .

CL: Thermodynamics?

IW: Thermodynamics, which is the heart of chemistry, is regarded by physicists historically as the result of ignorance—we don't know enough. So, because we don't know enough . . .

CL: To prevent maximum entropy . . .

IW: Someday, we'll know enough, and then we can do away with this. In other words, chemistry will disappear, and it will dissolve into pure physics because this is the result of ignorance, and Prigogine is fighting ignorance of this kind all his life—it's a turf battle in some sense—but anyway, he's saying, "No, no, no, no, this is not accidental. It's inherent. It's an emergent characteristic ... And I'm now going to show you it's the other way around. I'm going to go into physics, and I am going to show you that it works like chemistry rather than chemistry works like physics." In fact, his ambition, secretly, was to win a second Nobel Prize in physics.

CL: Wow. Now isn't that something? But you know, the other—and this a little bit to the side and before Prigogine, but it's very interesting. Around then—I don't know if you ever read Norbert Wiener or any of those early cybernetic theorists, but that was roughly in that year, I don't remember. I think Wiener was earlier.[24] But they, too, played on this second law of thermodynamics. There was, you might say, an interesting bifurcation in that tradition that allowed some after Wiener to take cybernetics toward artificial intelligence and a sort of destabilizing view of, essentially, communication reality, while others essentially revert it to a systems theory. But, in the former, there arises the question from artificial intelligence theory, is the instability built in?

Anyway, there is the question of the unstable global cleavages that you write about now. You can trace each of those, I think, back, but certainly they continue to be a factor—United States versus East Asia and West Germany, Davos versus Porto Alegre, North-South, and the rest.[25] But could you say a little bit about that? Do you see what I'm saying? Once the system was formed in the long sixteenth century, what would you identify as the structural instabilities that were there before they became obvious after 1968 or 1989?

IW: I think what you have to say is that the system tries to hold them in check. My model is that the system holds them in check by resolving the problem in the short run—or in the middle run. Then middle-run problems create long-run problems—so the system, in this sense, is always going toward crisis. So you solve a problem, which gets the system working again, but you do it in a way that increases something along an upward curve, which is going to hit sometime later.

CL: Okay, but if you don't mind just for this occasion, could you give an example of the trends?

IW: The business of wage levels and of ecological costs and so forth.[26] You solve the problem, you solve the problem, and then you can't solve it anymore, and the system breaks because of these tensions that are the structural contradictions of the system. But the system is a system precisely because it can handle that for a while. Otherwise, it wouldn't hold it together and would not be a system.

CL: Would you say that's true of all systems? All structures?

IW: Prigogine would say it was true of all systems.

CL: And you?

IW: I'm not competent to argue with physicists about this. He's persuasive, but I …

CL: Well, you've engaged in a good bit of philosophical writing, and philosophers deal with the difference between concepts and realities. Are you critiquing here a concept or reality? And I suppose it's more the latter.

IW: No, no. Absolutely reality. And it raises all kinds of questions about cosmology, the big bang, where does that come from? And is the big bang just—is the universe just one of many universes? Is it the result of bifurcation in the system?

CL: Where do you think, if I may say it this way, "we" are now? I mean, is there another structure arising somewhere?

IW: I normally say we're in a transition. It's shaky, it's chaotic, but it's a process that plays itself out, and … well, the cleavages as between Davos and Porto Alegre are not the issue of process but of what new systems we can create as a result of the fact that the system has to go in one direction or the other. There are two possible paths, and it's not yet decided. And that's the model Prigogine suggests. You have this line, and it has a certain arrow in his word, or line of movement, and do you go on this path or that path? It's impossible to predict in advance; it's not determined, but it will go in one direction or another.

CL: Well, do you reckon on the possibility of utter collapse? I don't even know what that would mean in social history, but …

IW: I think we're in a collapse right now. That is to say, what does a collapse mean? It means that the oscillation of the system, the fluctuations, are fairly wild as opposed to fairly controlled. It goes like that [motioning as if to draw a bifurcation], and the stuff that pulls it back—the equilibrium is fairly weak, and the stuff that pulls it back is fairly strong, and I think we're in that kind of time. We're in that right now. So, if you say to me, "What's going to happen in five years or ten years?" I say, "Who knows?" There are so many different possibilities that all I can tell you is that this isn't working.

CL: Well, people would have said that in 1848, and certainly 1968, but in fact, you didn't in 1968, I don't think. And you haven't said it about 1848. In fact, you viewed both as world revolutions because they reconsolidated—

IW: That's right, exactly. And that kind of thing is said to me all the time, you know, that this concept of the collapse is an old one, and it never happens, and that's perfectly true, but those weren't crises. And so, I mean, the difference between my view of a collapse and the traditional view of a collapse is that the traditional view of a collapse said that they knew what the outcome of the collapse would be. And I'm saying, there's absolutely no way to know what the outcome of the collapse would be. It's absolutely unpredictable, and I've ended seven books this way. It might be better; it might be worse.

CL: Actually, we covered this in that material that I hope I can retrieve, but let me go back to it. What is your thought on whether 1968 was really—led to 1989–1991. That is to say, that 1968 was the consolidation of the decolonizing revolts that began, say, in 1947–1949 with India and China—that the world revolution was actually there from the beginning ...

IW: Well, right, I think I told you, but if I didn't, I should—which is that Hopkins and I wrote the last of our joint articles, the one that appeared after the book *Antisystemic Movements,* which is called, "1989: The Culmination of 1968," or something.[27]

CL: Alright. So, then again, just to stay with this point. One could say that your basic view about 1848 is that it consolidated potentially, the liberal—

IW: Well, that's right, after 1848 the liberals saw themselves now as the center, and they put forth their scheme, and they became the dominant force, yes.

CL: And so then, in 1989.

IW: 1968 undoes that; 1989 is simply the continuation of 1968. It didn't, you know—it was the final sort of ...

CL: Okay, that's what I'm getting at. So, this is a way of saying that it is not a great mystery that liberalism, at the point of its full achievement, was already fated.

IW: That's right. That's why I can call my book, which comes out in 1991 or so, *After Liberalism*.[28]

CL: You once said that acting and the theater had been important to you in your youth. Do you ever find yourself applying or attempting sort of theatrical notions like tragedy or comedy or farce? You know, Marx used farce famously ...

IW: No, I—how should I say? That turns me into the playwright, and I'm the actor.

CL: You're not interested. You just do the play.

IW: I know, but so the acting is very useful in training you how to handle situations politically and also how to speak publicly, and these are its two legacies for me.

CL: So you never wanted to think in terms of tragedy, or ...

IW: No, I'm a little—yeah, I have—everything is tragedy. I don't—it's not a metaphor that I employ very often.

CL: You see, I ask it because, in many ways since 1968, the—in the core, at least, and beyond now—the so-called cultural wars were really about how one views changes in the world. Everyone on the writing Left knew something had happened; they had different theories of it. And, of course, the Right viewed it as this grand tragedy because of the collapse of the values.

IW: And of all respect for authority.

CL: The liberal program, the individual, the mother of history, and all of that. And, of course, you can say that the problem with the Left, at least in the United States and much of Western Europe, is it couldn't make up its mind what it really thought and sort of celebrated it without knowing really what the hell the view was.

I guess that brings me back to the little discussion we had another time: I wanted to put two parts together from the question of how you responded to criticism, and you said, "Well, I just plow ahead." And, but, there's also all of this characterization of you as the prophet. To what extent do you think—you know, character issue or not a character issue—the plowing ahead is what allowed you to make the discoveries that were in many ways prophetic? I mean, you don't write of discovery—I don't even know that you use that word—but you do signal a number of crucial discoveries, like back in the 1960s that Fanon helped you see that you were really being a modernization theorist without wanting to be. Could you say a little bit more about the plowing ahead? I mean, it's an impressive quality of character, but it seems, you know, to be key to your ability to see what was coming into recognition.

IW: Well, I suppose in part it's arrogance. In part it's, sure, basically being on the right track and staying with it. But it's also a political judgment. A political judgment is—if you want to push ahead on what you think of the paths that other people aren't going down, if you think it's important to do it, you don't want to spend your energy answering critics on their grounds. I mean, it just—it's such a waste of your time; it's inefficacious; you don't persuade people. And it stops you from doing your work because you have to say, "No, look, your premise is wrong, and I didn't say that, and … " So I have chosen very carefully the times that I'm actually willing to engage anyone. I have—the half a dozen times in which I've actually engaged, it was for a particular political reason. When somebody wrote an article—Steve Stern wrote an article in *The American Star* review, late 1970s or early 1980s. He's a Latin American historian, and he said I got it wrong. And I said, "Okay." And they invited me to reply, and I said to myself, "Well, it's a big audience. Okay, good. I'll pick him apart." I did his show, and what he said about Latin America, he was confirming my usual tactic, attack. And so I did that. And I answered Patty O'Brien in the *Economic History Review.* You know, he was saying, "Well, periphery didn't really contribute that much to the core, it was *only* seven percent." And I said, "Only seven percent? Seven percent is a hell of a lot." And I tried to show all the circumstances in which seven percent really mattered usually. So, okay, so I picked occasions, but most of the time I was sure that most of this stuff was feigned, and what was important to me was to consolidate the point of view that I was pursuing and also to get a lot of empirical evidence for it.

CL: Well, there are several levels. I mean, this is, I think, a very mature, correct attitude toward critics. But there's also—I asked the question poorly, because I have this hunch. You know, scientists put all the emphasis on discovery and a kind of almost mystical notion that one discovers truths and believes them to be true. It's a very Enlightenment principle because, as Weber might have put it, the light dawns when it dawns—and on this Weber is very clear in "Science as a Vocation." But the plowman is more the one whom you don't see who just keeps at it day after day, row by row—I'm talking about the day-to-day practice of science now. I'm trying to get to the . . .

IW: Alright, well, I think of myself as discovering . . . The idea of seeing the world-system was for me a discovery. It wasn't one that was always there, although I look back on it, and I always talked about the world context. But nonetheless I—in the early writings even in the method of the standard comparative state histories—I thought in terms of world relations. So world-system was a discovery, and it was a moment of discovery to me; I can remember it clearly. And when I was writing volume 1 [of *The Modern World-System*], it hit me one day that what was going on in Latin America was the same thing as what was going on in Eastern Europe. At that time, I was only reading about Eastern Europe, and I didn't know anything about Latin America, and I don't remember why it just hit me. Sometime early on, I asked a Latin American historian, "Tell me what I should read." And I started reading about Latin America, which hadn't been on my program at all, so of course it was a discovery, and I remember years later learning that a great Hungarian economic historian said it was a breakthrough for him; he should have discovered it himself. I mean, the idea that this is the same thing. So I can—yes, I can think of myself as having moments in which I suddenly have an "aha" experience.

CL: Well, you seem to have had—maybe it was around the same time when you talk about Fanon and realizing you shared his rebuke of modernization. But if you had to do it over again now, and this were—if, that is, 1974 were now—would you still use "system," given the history of systems theory, which turned out to be quite another matter? Because what you just described is exceptionally counterintuitive. The idea that these two very different locutions . . .

IW: Yeah, but you see—yes, I would, because when I tie it all together, what social scientists deal with are historical *systems,* because they're both systemic and historical simultaneously. And if you just—if you drop one or the other end of this, you get what we had, and it doesn't work.

CL: I'm thinking, though, about Braudel's terms in regard to time and historical structures because even the conjunctural—which is, in many ways, of these three categories, the one that had the influence in France with Althusser and others, and . . . It's the longer-enduring history that many don't illuminate—or some people took the Annales shift as the end of event history, which is fundamentally not possible, and they fail to locate the historical time aspect to each other. And maybe this is the connection: what I'm searching for is in Prigogine, that Prigogine reintroduced that dynamism of the three layers—or four, I suppose—specifically in Braudel. But the system has this—I think again because it was taken over by the systems theory people and turned into this really kind of all-too-neat conceptual scheme—even Parsons, I think, is guilty of this, though he was clearly the best of that lot. He at least had a concept of environmental effects from outside on a system and thus allowed for any given system not being entirely closed.

IW: Well, you know, I am comfortable—most people are not—I am comfortable with a lot of fuzziness, so sure, you know ... Systems are never perfectly closed, but they're substantially closed. And I mean, you know, that doesn't bother me. And everything is open, and I said everything was connected with everything else up to a point, but ... So, yeah, I have to deal with that when I—already in volume 1 [of *The Modern World-System*] when I talk of the external areas. There are these phenomena that are there, but they're external to the world-systems of a given time. And I distinguish the external area.

CL: Well, somewhere—maybe you alluded to it at the end of the first volume when you seem to set the Soviet Union in the external—

IW: No, no, no. I insist, in fact, that the Soviet Union—and that was, that used to outrage people in the assembly—I insisted that the Soviet Union was in the capitalist world economy and could be described perhaps as in a semiperipheral zone based on the description. And it was closed off in many ways, but that was not unusual. Other zones closed off. But they said, "But it's communist, it's socialist." And I said, "No, no no ... It's part of the capitalist world economy." And it drove people wild. It drove conservatives wild; it drove Marxists wild—

CL: Well, after the fact, it could not be more obvious.

IW: After 1989, yes. But anyway, that I was always clear of from the beginning....

CL: But do you think that the semiperiphery has gotten its due? I don't mean from you, but it's—it's so tempting for people to reduce this to core, periphery, and then just leave the rest unless you're doing—

IW: Yeah, well, of course that was—you know, core/periphery—I certainly didn't invent; I borrowed it. And I threw in the semiperiphery, and that bothered people too. It still does, but it's gotten accepted.

CL: But without the semiperiphery, you don't have that same dynamic quality.

IW: Exactly, I agree.

CL: But they make this issue of the long sixteenth century. As it played out, Latin America and Eastern Europe were . . .

IW: Were growing. The idea was to think of—you know, of Spain and Portugal becoming the semiperiphery at this point, and . . .

CL: Lapsing back into a secondary relation, yeah . . .

IW: The rise into it or the descent—

CL: So, when you talk in the "Cleavage"[29] essay about the triad—United States, Europe, East Asia—there are implications for the core, right?

IW: Because there's a triad—it *is* the core. And the semiperipheral powers play a clear political role right now—you know, there's the G20. And the semiperipheral powers operated in a new World Trade Organization, as we saw quite clearly. And everybody does it; in fact the semiperiphery is stronger than in some and weaker in other arrangements, but it is the same language, but it's the same idea.

CL: Going back to that, I wanted to get at the three parts there. It's pretty clear that the North-South cleavage and even the trilateral core, as you say— you can trace those back in certain ways to the beginning of the system. But then the Davos/Porto Alegre cleavage is something else. That whole World Social Forum to which you attribute a considerable importance but—you know, some would say it's a little more on the culture side, political culture. And what strikes me in reading the World Social Forum sites is the question of what would happen if they had to go face-to-face, on the streets with the Davos people. Against, say, Bono and Bill Clinton, all the World Social Forum talk seems rather too programmatic. I don't know how much you follow it; I know you've been there.

IW: Yeah, but now you're talking about the actual people at Davos and the level of their analyses and so forth, and I am using it—

CL: You said metaphorically.

IW: Metaphorically and symbolically, but also as political forces. The fact is that the people in Porto Alegre would like to transform the world in a certain direction, and they're not very clear how to do it, and they certainly have no unified strategy—but that's the whole point of the structure of the actual world. But I'm not sure that Bill Clinton could talk them to death because in fact, the last couple of years, the people who literally have dazzled us in the past have been tongue-tied. They haven't known how to handle the situation. They're no longer self-confident.

CL: That's true. That's very true. Well, they've got Bono there, and these other people ...

IW: Well, exactly, but that's a sign of weakness. And they've got all their sort of reformers now from [George] Soros to [Paul] Krugman to ... what's his name ... the guy with the World Bank ... Joseph Stiglitz?[30]

Jeffrey Sachs is another one of those. But anyway, I mean this whole thrust of people saying that, you know, there are limits to the market and so forth. These are signs of unclarity as to what they want to do or think now.

CL: When do you suppose—I guess it's a little more on the cultural side, but there's a structural element—that the idea as well as the reality of markets entered in the long sixteenth century? I mean, you had this long sort of lead-up period—the market.

IW: Well, I think the reality enters ... the idea—I think the whole point of my discussion of the geoculture in the nineteenth century is the invention of it and that they didn't have the language in the sixteenth, seventeenth, and eighteenth centuries to talk about the reality, and they were still trying to use out-of-date language in the speaking about the economic world and what was going on, and so there was no sort of dominant—and, finally, "market" breaks through. And I think the French Revolution had a lot to do with its breaking through. But the point is—and that's why people insist that the sixteenth, seventeenth, and eighteenth centuries were premodern, preindustrial, pre-this, pre-that. It's perfectly true that they're still talking about the divine right of kings and had to be pretentious about their work and so forth; they wouldn't be in the twenty-first century, but they were there. So we have a kind of geocultural lag. You get the political and economic reality of the capitalist world-system without the cultural reality dominating for a good long while.

CL: Is that a bit of vulgar Marxism there that the materialism always leads? I'm playing with you here, but ...

IW: I'm not sure because—

CL: The reason I ask is 1848—I mean, if you look at it another way, 1789 was not a world revolution. But then, as with this other discussion, maybe one could say 1848 was a consolidation in that it led to an institutional structure, the liberal state that solidified then, you could say that was sort of the cultural coming together of terms, the point in which both the dual revolution solidified, but you don't really have the modern world-system as we would talk about it in the subsequent hundred years in full maturity, full blossom until then.

IW: You don't have it in full blossom, I think, until 1945.

CL: Okay, even better.

IW: But it's the *only* system. In other words, it does not fully blossom in the sense of self-conscious presentation of what it is, but the fact is that you already way back then have it operating in terms of the primacy of the accumulation of capital. So the people who don't put that element primary in their operation lose out.

CL: How would you ... ? You probably wouldn't like this very much, but ... One could say that from Nagasaki in August 1945 to George Kennan's long telegram on deterrence in February 1946—that's the history of the consciousness of the system, and therefore was a fantasy. You know what I'm saying? There was a very short moment in there before the rise of the Soviet Union, American power and its market, then soon enough the United States was in Korea, and cultural adolescence continues, but you know, the perfect core didn't last more than a couple of years.

IW: I'd give it twenty-five years.

CL: Twenty-five years? You'd give it until what, 1968? Really ... A lot of those twenty-five years, they were struggling. Did you have this in mind in Columbia in 1968?

IW: No.

CL: So you didn't view that in any global way at that time ...

IW: Well, I viewed it in a global way from the beginning, but I didn't have all this worked out in Columbia.

CL: One interesting side point is that I've been reading your master's thesis and found a section that had been withdrawn ...

IW: Herb Hyman[31] wouldn't let me put it in a short section on the Caine Mutiny Court-Martial.

CL: You want to hear an amusing Herb Hyman story? Herb, when we were together at Wesleyan, knew of my relation with Al Gouldner, and he was doing his research for this last book on the history of measurement. He had checked out some very rarified text by—it may have been—well, I don't know who it was, but somebody that you would expect Hyman to be interested in, and he showed me the signatures from the Columbia Library thesis collection and the only other person who'd read that was Gouldner. Anyway, he found that quite amusing, but I knew that Al, in spite of what most thought, knew quite a bit about social statistics.

By the way did you remember that I have both your master's thesis at Columbia and the transcript of the Columbia Oral History?[32]

IW: No.

CL: Well, they are safe, and I can return them any time. In either case, the thesis itself with its strong point about the tensions between McCarthyism and the conservative movement in the United States and a remarkably similar situation today. Where are we now?

IW: That was fifty-five years ago.

CL: And now the right wing is so different from the categories you used then. I suppose the question is, what are your thoughts on the right today and the disappearance from party and movement of the ... ?

IW: Sophisticated, internationalists ... they're gone from the Republican Party, but they're not gone.

CL: Right, they're not gone. But I mean what you called the official right wing is gone, and the other one was ...

IW: Well ... the practical Right. Those were terms that C. Wright Mills had invented. Maybe it was in *The New Men of Power*. But yeah, I took those terms from Mills.

CL: But they certainly don't apply to the situation today. And yet this complaint about Barack Obama and socialism lingers on. Amazing though, maybe, maybe not.

IW: I think that, you know, the Sarah Palin right is preparing for civil war.

CL: Really?

IW: Oh yeah. They're storing guns; they consider the center traitors. I'm waiting to for them to denounce George W. Bush because he sold out his last two years by allowing Condoleezza Rice to be more important than Dick Cheney. It took years before Cheney admitted that Reagan had dubious policies from their point of view. He came close to admitting it two years ago. Now the thing is, of course, that they are passionate; they will get out their vote; they will try to purge everybody from the Republican Party.... Reagan made this point if somebody agrees with me 80 percent of the time, he's not my enemy, he's my friend, OK? So they grabbed hold of that and came to the Republican National Committee, and they said, here are ten things ... if somebody disagrees with three of them, then he's not a conservative. Well, then, a while back, there was that one Senate seat the Republicans hoped to win in Delaware. They had this very strong candidate, Mike Castle, who won elections all the time, and the Democrats were in a little bit of trouble, and so forth. Well, it turns out Mike Castle is only a 70 percenter; there were three other cases like this ... So this illustrates the problem: will they actually now learn how to succeed? So, on the other hand, the kind of withdrawal by the Democrats, the extra voters that Obama got out are going back into the woodwork, the young, the Blacks, and also, of course, he tends to lose some of the independent workers. So how this turns out remains to be seen.

CL: Yeah, who were on the fence to begin with.

IW: With all their problems, the Republicans can do better than they ought to—given the fact that they are shrinking in size.

CL: But on the, how to put it, larger scale. You've got these two things ... a willingness to self-destruct or at least make stupid moves on the right that may or may not correspond to their attitudes toward America's wars abroad. What thoughts do you have about whether this is what happens in the declining core, in the bowel of uncertainty, that may be in the system at large.

IW: You know, I don't want to ... I'm not sure there was a comparable phenomenon in Britain, but what I would say is that, you know ... the United States ... well, the Brits found it very difficult to admit that they were no longer the top dog, but in a sense they finally accepted the fact that ... at least it was the United States in the core position and that they would have this special relationship and God knows what else; they still talk of the special relationship till this day. But American public opinion is going to find it very, very difficult to swallow the reality of a declining standard of living, declining power in the world, declining everything! So a lot of people are buying into treachery, sellouts, God knows what else ...

CL: Well, there are several issues in the decline of greatness matter—the decline of a core, the emergence of another, and the decline of a system ...

IW: People aren't aware of the decline of the system. I mean that's not a widespread consciousness.

CL: No, I'm sure not. And not these people.

IW: And certainly not these people. These people don't even know really what they stand for. I mean, they claim they stand for free enterprise ... But really, they stand for ... a kind of militarism and imposing their values on everybody else, and they're against the elite, so it really is a populist movement, you know. I have no doubt about that.

CL: Looked at one way, it's these four people, one of whom, Joe Lieberman, seems to have just lost his mind, although I think his ... should be subsidized by Hartford.

IW: He has nothing to lose. That's A. I don't know if he thinks if he has a political future at all.

CL: He's just mad.

IW: Just mad, and he really is on the military stuff, passionate. And then the Israel stuff, he's passionate.

CL: And he always has been.... Somewhat relatedly on another global aspect of militarism. I've spent a lot of time in, well, a fair amount of time last year, in Central Asia, in Kyrgyzstan, where you do see an often overlooked region where there is a lingering effect of years of Soviet rule. Kyrgyzstan, until the latest semirevolt in 2010, was run by a series of quite absurdly politically illiterate governments, mostly, in spite of a revolution in 2005, in a Soviet style. Kurmanbek Bakeiv, who came to power in 2005, had long tried to get rid of the American Air Force base outside Bishkek, but he couldn't do it. Then there is Turkmenistan, which is even worse. And you see there, in some sense, the kind of underbelly of what Putin is covering up in Russia, I think. So you do have somewhere in the dregs of the old Cold War this kind of unthinking violent right wing. And I guess I might be making something out of nothing, but when the system suddenly collapses ...

IW: Well, you have a small group who grab hold of the state. They don't stand for anything in the Central Asian countries. But if we lose control, we get killed, and somebody else takes over, so it's an all-or-nothing proposition, and they can get very vicious with any perceived threatening group. But I don't see that as Cold War; I see that as a kind of mafia-like group that have taken over ... and are living high off the hog but know that, if they lose control, (a) some other mafia takes over, and (b) they're dead.

CL: So it may not be a better game, just another game ... Well, I've written something in a book on globalization[33] about this André Gunder Frank[34] thing. I said that basically you were more right than anyone else, including him, on the Asia issue. Still, what remains unexplored is the question of where—to the extent that the world-system was the first systematic globalizing movement, which I assume is the position that you still hold—there were still some of these imperial impulses that had a systematizing if accidental consequence.... But the Frank claim that only Asia was a world-system sort of keeps coming into play, especially today with the rise of East and South Asia. Frank made a strong, absurdly aggressive argument—that was his way—against you. A vast area of the then globe, Alexander earlier sort of drawn into that, the beginnings of the Silk Road and all these tensions, it does suggest that there was something like a world-system, and I'm certainly not taking Frank's position.

IW: I said everything I think in that article in the interview.

CL: This was the one responding to him ... Oh yeah, this is the one in *Review* in 1999.[35]

IW: Yeah, my position on that, I haven't changed it. Aside from the accuracy of his empirical statements, the question of—in the end he throws capitalism out as a category entirely. It's the only way he can ... well, three of us objected to that centrally in his analysis and then, you know, any links between, any place where *a* and *b* touch each other is, for him, already a system, and I try to be more careful. So that's why I have the whole concept of the external area and try to argue the theoretical differences in the trade and so forth and so on. He throws that all out, and he feeds on a sense of downward Eurocentrism, hitching it to China, the rising star.

CL: Yeah, that was a little quaint. I mean that line and not necessarily the argument. But the dismissal of capitalism or the slighting of it ... ?

IW: No, the dismissal.

CL: The dismissal. Is that just capitalism, or to what extent is it the element in your view that is the rationalizing of capital accumulation and, of course, it's true that the whole Asian synthesis was a lot rational accumulation.

IW: Well, Frank in the end didn't know what capitalism is. It's not a category worth having in his view. Nothing has changed in the economic structures of the world for five thousand years, and, of course, that is the classical nature ...

CL: Closet neocapitalism, you mean neoliberal?

IW: Well, it takes the same theoretical position that ... the economics of the world have not changed for five or ten thousand years because of these universal rules and in a sense ... analysis was a protest precisely against that, and he was part of that protest until the mid-1980s, and he pulled away.

CL: The question of the enduring nature of certain of these right-wing ideologies, from which it is easier to see the decline. Are you shocked in any way that the neoliberal, at least even the more sophisticated versions, modernization theory, I mean it is diplomatic in its geopolitical form. I guess it's almost impossible to distinguish it from neoliberalization and such, but it seems to have this incredible staying power.

IW: Yes.

CL: And you almost feel, well, what the hell is Obama going to say, because he couldn't in the campaign or even now say anything about markets.

IW: It's not a question of market; what the staying power of modernization theory really is, is the sense that we want to improve our economic situation. We are the people of a state, and that means the state has to do x or y or z, and you can argue whether this is more social-democratic stuff or more pure-market stuff. That doesn't matter; the state has to ensure that we even maintain our position or improve our position. And if you take that away from people, they say, well, what are we fighting for? because their nationalism is so strong everywhere. And it's hard to make progress with the argument that everybody will not become Denmark within the framework of a capitalist economy, and pushing for it is counterproductive, but then people say, what are we supposed to be fighting for?

CL: *The Economist* got very excited about Botswana not so long ago—as a development story.

IW: Botswana?

CL: It has pretty good numbers, and they controlled AIDS and their growth rate ...

IW: And diamonds ... Diamonds and a small population. And also, nobody is taking them over.

CL: Well, that is one point; they concede that they had the British and in the end didn't care at all, so they had a free hand. But in some ways, maybe the answer is obvious; the way you formulated it sounds right to me that the state—it's a formulation of a kind of slippage also—the state, that has much debate, from the state being the defender of the global market, of last resort, that's the ideology in fact of the first resort, now the state, at least that's what you hear, the state must defend the nation at a distance with only the vaguest— I need to talk about vague relations between a and b. Iraq is one, and now so is Afghanistan. The thing is to mean exactly the same thing. I mean it's a different theory of the state; it's more entrenched.

IW: I mean everybody in a capitalist system depends on the state, even if the official ideology is that they don't. What does a freedman want? He wants the state to make sure that there are tariffs and barriers; he wants the state to maintain a certain policy on monetarism, and so forth. So in force, what he wants, he is turning to the state to do it, and the social democrats are turning to the state in a different way. But they're all turning to the state; it's all state oriented.

CL: Well, there is the health-care debate this year [2011] where it's not too long a jump to the argument that this kind of attempt at destroying Obama by destroying health care really has the effect of destroying what remains of the American market position globally and maybe even destroying the state. We talk about the shift in what the state is and the questions ... like you mentioned earlier, the war aspect ... is there any credence to that? People like Cheney, they try to do it inside the government and did to a large extent, and now they want to carry on outside.

IW: I think they have made a decision that the politics of dealing with Democrats, especially now that Obama's in, is simply to vote no, no, no, no. So they make sure everybody votes right. They do it by basically menacing people with local fights for nomination—if you don't vote my way, you'll just go in as they did in the First District in New York, the one that they lost, which was a Republican district, always had been, but it was a moderate Republican district for social reasons, and the right-wingers said not on your life, so they were willing to lose the seat. Well, you know, they were right in the sense that they might not have lost the seat had they started this earlier.

CL: And then lose the election.

IW: And then lose the election.

CL: So this leaves the corporations standing in ...

IW: And this is why, by and large, for the time being [2010–2011], they're throwing their support to the Democrats. They're getting from the Democrats, from the Obama administration, more or less what they want, and the Republicans are not giving them what they want. And the only thing the Republicans will offer them is no increase in taxes. They do want that, yes, but they want the state to be viable, and they know a certain amount of taxes is necessary.

CL: Well, Obama again, there are early indications that he's made his decision on Afghanistan.

IW: Yeah, I think it's quite clear.

CL: But he hasn't said it yet.... I don't know if you recall it but one of the seminars you gave at Wesleyan was within weeks of what turned out to be the start of the Iraq thing, and you called that within days. I suppose I have two questions there: How do you see that war in particular now so long after it began? The inability to just say that whole thing has moved geographically into areas we can't deal with and the inability to let it go, or at least apparently seriously consider letting it go.

IW: I mean letting it go in the case of Afghanistan, if you read my thing about two weeks ago on Afghanistan ...

CL: Your blog?[36]

IW: Yeah, my blog ... I said that—no matter what Obama does—he loses. And could he, even if he wanted to, which I don't think he does, really pull out? He might get away with a full pullout. Just the other day William Polk wrote a very long analysis on Afghanistan, which he knows quite well and in detail, as to why a pullout is the only thing that makes sense. He did it in terms of analyzing exactly what goes on in Afghanistan but this ...

CL: This is the behind-the-scenes guy in the embassy? Is that who it is?

IW: He, no

CL: Somebody, was it initial resistance to General McCrystal ... ?

IW: No, no, that's the ambassador; that's Ikenberry.

CL: Oh, that's John Ikenberry.

IW: Ikenberry, who is an interesting character himself, PhD, speaks Chinese fluently because his father was a missionary.

CL: He's also the guy who writes in *Foreign Affairs* that the current structure of things economically won't fail precisely because of all the Internet and other connections that have been developed since, which is a bit of a stretch, and of course Afghanistan belies that.

IW: But anyway, I think Obama is trapped on this; if he had grabbed the bull by the horns immediately after election, it might have been otherwise. But he had already undone his position before the election. Remember, he *promised*? He said, look, this was the bad war in Iraq. Afghanistan is the good war. I'm going to put my troops there.

CL: It had to do with Hillary Clinton and the 2008 election campaign.

IW: Whatever it is, I want to distinguish what may be his real views—who knows what his real views are, a lot of debate on that. What he says publicly has got him in this impossible position, where he can't win, in the Middle East, at all, nowhere, and its all going to come crashing down. Now, if he can get the health bill through, which he may be able to do—I don't doubt it at all—it may balance a little bit what's going to look like a terrible situation. The economy is going to get worse, not better, more job loss, more collapse of the dollar, and so forth, and it's all going to be blamed on him.

CL: Sure. But this may be the early indicators of long periods of uncertainty and of the inability of a system to right itself—in measurable economic terms ... but isn't this the way it plays out? These kinds of impossible-to-anticipate political consequences, forced decisions that just make things worse. Do you have any further thoughts about the uncertainty itself?

IW: I think it will last, I've said, twenty to thirty to forty years, and I still think that. I think we are in a chaotic fluctuation situation in which everything is unpredictable. When it's unpredictable, it means that it's unpredictable. That means you don't know what to do, because anything you do may be wrong, politically, economically, like where you want to put your money.

CL: The answer is TIAA-CREF. I lost only 15 percent, and I got almost all of it back. I don't know if you have any with them, but they're great. But you know guys our age, it's a little late to play around too much. But again, no reason for you to remember it, but I've several times asked you about it: uncertainty is one thing, and you've been very clear about how this evolved, but where do you really stand now on the question of whether any sort of system can reassert itself? Is all lost?

IW: When you mean any kind of system, you mean a sort of revised capitalism?

CL: Whatever it would be.

IW: I think there will be a new system because I also believe that chaos doesn't last forever. Some water comes out, all I'm saying is some predictable, which water, could be worse, could be better, but something will stabilize, which will be systemic in some way, and we'll be in for another couple hundred years, who knows, of another system. The only thing I say that is sure, is that the present system can't survive, that one thing that's absolutely unpredictable is what we'll succeed in.

CL: But you believe—well, of course, you allow for the possibility—that what could succeed is something really terrible and not at all rationalized.

IW: Yeah, I think it could be an early top-down autocratic system. One might want to call it fascism. I just don't like to use those words because they bring up particular images, which may or may not be correct but may be much worse.

CL: But it would be capitalist in some recognizable sense?

IW: No, it wouldn't be capitalist. It would be hierarchical, polarizing, exploitative, but not capitalist. Capitalism is a particular kind of system, works in a particular way, but you can have other systems that can have those features. We did historically have all those kind of systems and came up with new ones, but it won't be capitalism. I still hold on to the idea that capitalism is a particular kind of system; it's rare. It was created once, was difficult to create, has thrived for a long time. It's no longer thriving, and that's it, and I don't think we had capitalism before that, and I don't think we'll have capitalism after that. I don't know what will happen after that, whether it's a better or worse system.

CL: You were braced by the fact that there are now twenty years since 1989. So, in how many generations . . . we could be halfway through the uncertainty. But the question that comes to mind is that it has taken all this time to even begin to clear the decks, and they're not very well cleared. I forget when you first wrote the global cleavages piece—that's about ten years, maybe about 2000—and it's interesting how that sort of holds up except for Japan, which probably now, I suppose, would have to be a generic East Asia.

IW: I was just reading today an article in . . . which validates my hypothesis of Western Europe and Russia getting together.

CL: Wasn't that? What's his name? Dominique [Moïsi]? He's married to an American, a major French foreign policy advisor. But there's a lot of names for this, but there you have these sort of three different axes of cleavage, and they're all becoming more and more aggravated, so I do wonder how you feel about that. We talk about multipolarity and even granted a high degree of capital, political, and even military interdependence, the idea of system somehow just doesn't . . . you see . . .

IW: I mean why not? System doesn't depend on everybody being, you know, how shall we say it, calm in relations with each other.

CL: No, no, not at all. But it does assume—I was looking back over earlier conversations we had where we touched briefly on the systems-analysis people, including Talcott Parsons. The idea I seem to hold on to is that the history of the core implies, perhaps requires, an integrating core much as Parsons and others thought of culture or, that terrible expression he used, the pattern maintenance function. In some sense, if the core is itself unstable or is just more than interactive in any conflict over forces, this is beyond Cold War, but in some kind of a death grip—you might even say that's a little extreme—with other major powers. In the *Financial Times,* they recently had a big moan-and-groan day on the whole issue of Europe trying to be a dominant player in the system.

IW: Oh, they were worried about the election. I saw it all, but I think, I don't take that seriously. What really happened there is first of all that until 2007 Tony Blair thought he had it sewed up, and there was a real rebellion against him, not merely by "the smaller countries," but then France and Germany both turned against him, and I interpreted that as another way of pulling away from the United States. They saw him as, you know, what you call it in the *Iliad*...

CL: The Trojan horse!

IW: So they got rid of him in June 2007; then they had to figure out who, and actually the younker from the Luxemburg might have been the alternative, posed himself as the anti-Blair, and they turned to a guy who is really exceptionally competent in pulling all the pieces together. I don't think that was a bad decision actually; in fact, I think it was a very good one.

CL: But the *Financial Times* is always moaning: look we need all this, we need the military, we need to stop being...

IW: I usually like the *Financial Times,* but I thought that one was off base, and then I thought also with this woman, she turns out to be not so bad at all, and nobody has ever heard of her, that's true, but she's been in this other job for a year, which is also a foreign policy job, and she's done exceptionally well at it. And I think again, the present guy, the Spaniard, got too linked in with the United States, so at the same time it was a bone for the British, but I thought the choices weren't bad. I think Europe came out of it quite well. They finally got the damn Lisbon treaty, overcame not only the Irish but this Czech ultra ... Klaus Havel ... who is more neoliberal than the most neoliberal. But his arm was twisted hard enough—I don't know quite how—then he said, OK, I got to sign this, though I think it's a bad idea.

CL: Well, you see, that's the other thing: resistance in the United States that's got a history and that makes sense. Do you detect that also—yes, United States—but more importantly resistance to neoliberalism?

IW: Well, you know, I think they're all—whatever the official line is—they're all social democrats in Europe. Even Sarkozy ... basically they still have the ideology of thirty, forty, fifty years ago that you've got to buy off the working class and keep them quiet, and that's the only way you can do it, and they've never bought into the ... what's been going on in the United States since the 1970s.

CL: What an irony for Sarkozy because he ran in the first election on this social program retrenchment for a forty-hour workweek and all that.

IW: Of course, but, you know, you've got to say something to get into power.

CL: It's like Obama.

IW: Yeah, I don't know if you noticed, but just yesterday or the day before, the, the British Conservative backed down, he ... what's his name?

CL: Cameron.

IW: Cameron has been pushing the line for two years now at least, well, when we get into power, frankly it's not going to be nice, because we have to tighten our belts, and we got to do all these things, cut all these things, and so forth and so on, and, you know, cut taxes and cut benefits. And I'm being honest with you, I'm running on this platform, and he's got this number two, the economist ... he's even stronger on this.

CL: Cameron's Gordon Brown, I guess. Is that how it is?

IW: Yeah, yeah. And what happened is a couple of things, what's the Gordon Brown one in, let's see, in Scotland, and, secondly, what's happened is that the public opinion polls, they were maybe twelve, fifteen points ahead of the Labor six months ago, and now they're sort of like six points ahead.

CL: Do you think the Tories could lose this? On social policy?

IW: Yes, and he thinks so too. So he made a speech in which he didn't quite come out and say it, but in effect he said, we don't really mean it totally;

we're not going to cut everything. And that may lose him even more because now they're being seen as terribly inconsistent and not standing for anything. Because they had a clear line, and he's pulled back from it. But you see he's pulled back already, in advance, because he's worried that he's only within five or six points. Within five or six points, you can't win an absolute majority, and he might even get less. People do these calculations, and he comes out with a few seats more than Labor.

CL: So then he has to have a government with the Liberals.

IW: But not only that, it's only that he has a few seats more. Should it turn out that he has a few seats less than the Liberal leader has already said that he's going to go with the guy who has the most seats.

CL: Very interesting. But Tony Giddens did something clever there. I mean, he was ... Tony Blair's guru and all that business, probably was on the third way program ... but when he talks about Europe, it's really interesting, because he has been very strong on the EU as the new postnational form of social democracy on two points: one of them is social benefits, and the other one is experience with real democracy and its worth in the face of Europe's experience with the Holocaust. So Giddens is really against the EU Constitution, and he opposed Habermas, who, it seems, made Derrida on his death bed in effect sign a statement he wrote on the constitution.... Anyhow, speaking of these people more or less of our generation, and to change the topic, do you find anybody out there who's new and coming along in social thought and world-systems ... anyone in the many fields who's daring enough to take this particular moment by the horns, as you did?

IW: There are people who dare to take it by various horns. I'm going to a meeting in Porto Alegre in late January. They have convened sort of, I don't know, about fifteen or twenty leading people who have been involved for a kind of public think tank session—it will be open to the public.

CL: It's going to be a summit meeting of sorts.

IW: Debating about the future of the World Social Forum and internal struggles within it and so forth, and I'm actually looking forward to seeing where things really stand. There's some real movement. Today Hugo Chávez was involved with a meeting of left movements in Latin America. They invited a lot of different people, and he announced that we should create a Fifth International. He used that phrase: the Fifth International. The third got caught in Stalinism, and the fourth has fallen apart. We need a fifth one, which will include all the governments he likes in Latin America and maybe some others; he doesn't really spell it out. So it will be an international that will be made up of the governing parties of these various states, plus these other movements. And he's already run into at least two major communist parties who said they thought that was a terrible idea because there is still a structure of a world meeting of communist parties. They just had one in New Delhi, and the next one is going to be in South Africa.

CL: From where you just came back.

IW: Right. The South African communist party is in itself an interesting locus of debate both internally and then externally, it's in a big fight now with the ANC Youth League. It's kind of complicated. I don't want to get into South African politics. This idea of the Fifth International is of course one of the debates in the World Social Forum because a lot of people are very strongly against the idea, very strongly.

CL: Well, the original statement called for only more than NGOs but ideological. But do you see that Chávez is trying either on the one hand to co-opt the World Social Forum or at least is being drawn into it because it won't go away, or is he intelligent enough to see that?

IW: He wants to stay in the center of things, and it's a real question of how other people regard him. The Cubans don't want him to lose power, but I'm not sure that they're always that happy with him.

CL: Well, there's a joke, I guess in Caracas, that when Castro dies, Caracas will be the next capital of Cuba, mostly because of Chávez's oil funding of Cuba.

IW: Yeah, and the Bolivians have a very different position in—what do they call it?—the plurinational state. Got a lot of problems with their indigenous people. So there's a lot of conflict there, within all these structures. I don't see that the Fifth International is going to come into existence, but it's part of Chávez's grand plan, and Brazil is of course still trying to pull him in. They may get the Brazilian parliament now to ratify—it's coming close to being able to do it—ratify Venezuela being part of the Summit of the Americas ... which, in Brazil's point of view, is pulling Chávez back into their domain. Of course, he sees it the other way. There's a friendly or not so friendly tension there. Brazilians are certainly trying to make sure that they are the unquestioned leader of South America.

CL: Well, they've gotten good press on their economic growth. But you look at the—2010 growth figures, and leapt from near zero to over 7 percent, and you have Vietnam still at 6, and India at 6.8, China backing that up. Now growth rate isn't everything, but it is very striking to look at the economic map. I mean, Europe is just no place—I think Poland has a 2.1. There's just not that kind of economic growth there. I certainly don't hold the view that Brazil or East Asia or South Asia has the answer. But those numbers are pretty remarkable in the disparity, and maybe the question is, what are we going to conclude about real economic growth? What does it measure? I mean there are a lot of surprises with growth. Martin Wolf at the *Financial Times,* whom Paul Krugman has called the smartest guy writing about economics today, says China's big problem is not just consumer reinvestment; it's stable investment and durable capital, of which they have very little. I mean, do you have a view on that—at least, the sort of tremendous imbalance?

IW: Yeah, but it's really dependent, heavily, on the ability of the United States, and to a lesser extent some other countries, to buy their stuff. Growth figures are cyclical. Mind you that the best figures in the 1950s and early 1960s were those of the Soviet Union. Strongest. Much higher than the United States.

CL: Wasn't that mostly technology and defense spending?

IW: Well, no; the standard of living went up ... they were doing better.

CL: So Nixon was wrong in 1958, the kitchen debate.

IW: Well, they still didn't have the standard of living in the United States.

CL: Right, certainly. I don't want to get too far from the World Social Forum[37] because of the question of politics. You've written several things that have tried to say what kind of politics we must have in this uncertainty period, and there were two or three, I don't remember which one is which, but a lot of the points seem to conform to the stated principles of the World Social Forum and trying to come to terms with democratic politics as best as you can. Some would say, in the present situation, that Obama was maybe the best possible outcome. What do you say to young people or anyone about what politics should we have? Let's assume the worst happens with Obama—that he gets deeper into Afghanistan, and it all goes downhill from there, which is likely. What's to be said? What is a Left, if you can even use that term, to do? Because a lot of even the World Social Forum principles, well, maybe, you're going to tell everybody in Porto Alegre what the answer is.

IW: Well, I don't know, or I may hear the answer when I'm there.

CL: Well, there's also the question of your meetings with Subcommandante Marcos[38] in Chiapas. I've often held out the thought that he's a kind of model, neither inside nor outside, neither visible nor invisible. You still look at that kind of thing?

IW: I think he's not quite sure what to do at this point. But he certainly hasn't changed his basic line.

CL: Well, he's sort of changed from that period as an invisible something, the masked man. But he gave that up for the national elections. Since this is a question you explore in detail toward the end of your interview with Carlos [elsewhere in this book], it seems that we've closed a circle of sorts, coming to a good place to end for the time being.

NOTES

1. The conversations were held at Yale at various times in the mid- to late 2000s. They have been edited to remove extraneous chatter. Otherwise, the conversational style is retained, with incomplete sentences. Lemert, working with transcripts generated immediately after the meetings, backed and filled as best he could. Wallerstein then edited and added as he saw fit. A subsequent conversation (the last in this series) was recorded in the autumn of 2010. The document therefore can be viewed as a work over several years, 2005 to 2010, with periods of silence in the middle as we waited for the translation of the earlier discussions made in Mexico of the Spanish-language interviews and texts.

2. Niall Ferguson, *Virtual History: Alternatives and Counterfactuals* (New York: Macmillan, 1997); Charles Tilly, "Future Social Science," in *Roads from Past to Future* (Lanham, MD: Rowman & Littlefield, 1997).

3. Richard Lee is a longtime colleague at Binghamton and successor to Wallerstein as director of the Fernand Braudel Center.

4. Fernand Braudel, France's most influential modern historian, is one of the most important influences on Wallerstein, in particular for his famous criticism of event-history for which Braudel proposed and used a more subtle method that included the concept of historical time as long-enduring—in effect as geological time.

5. Immanuel Wallerstein, *Historical Capitalism with Capitalist Civilization* (London: Verso, 1983).

6. Immanuel Wallerstein, *After Liberalism* (New York: The New Press, 1995), and *Utopistics: Or Historical Choices of the Twenty-First Century* (New York: The New Press, 1998).

7. Wallerstein, *Utopistics*.

8. Immanuel Wallerstein (with G. Arrighi and T. K. Hopkins), "Dilemmas of Anti-systemic Movements," *Social Research* 53, no. 1 (spring 1986): 185–206; see Immanuel

Wallerstein, Giovanni Arrighi, and Terence K. Hopkins, *Antisystemic Movements* (London: Verso, 1989).

9. The original transcript read, "I am on the left economically ... " I quoted that line in a public seminar as made by Wallerstein in reference to his own views. He objected, saying that he was referring to Dan Bell. I offer this note not to dispute him but to illustrate his remarkable ability to recall details. At the time of the seminar, it was several years after the conversation, and Wallerstein had the source of the misattributed statement exactly right.—CL.

10. Alvin W. Gouldner, *Patterns of Industrial Bureaucracy* (New York: The Free Press, 1954).

11. "Class and Tribe in West Africa" appeared in the proceedings of the Fifth World Congress of Sociology, Vol. 3.

12. Samuel Huntington, *Clash of Civilizations and the Remaking of World Order* (New York: Simon & Schuster, 1996).

13. Stanley Hoffman, "Clash of Globalizations," *Foreign Affairs* 81 (August 2002).

14. E. J. Hobsbawm, *Interesting Times: A Twentieth Century Life* (New York: Pantheon, 2003).

15. Immanuel Wallerstein, *Unthinking Social Science: The Limits of Nineteenth-Century Paradigms* (Cambridge: Polity Press, 1991), part 4.

16. Bill Warren, *Imperialism: Pioneer of Capitalism* (London: Verso, 1980).

17. Immanuel Wallerstein and T. K. Hopkins, "Patterns of Development of the Modern World-System," *Review* 1 (fall 1977).

18. Immanuel Wallerstein (with G. Arrighi and T. Hopkins), "1989, the Continuation of 1968," *Review* 15, no. 2 (spring 1992): 221–42.

19. Immanuel Wallerstein, "The Itinerary of World-Systems Analysis, or How to Resist Becoming a Theory," in *The Uncertainties of Knowledge* (Philadelphia: Temple University Press, 2004), ch. 6.

20. Immanuel Wallerstein, "Time and Duration: The Unexcluded Middle, or Reflections on Braudel and Prigogine," *Thesis Eleven* 54 (August 1998): 79–87; also reprinted in Wallerstein, *The Uncertainties of Knowledge*.

21. Wallerstein, "Time and Duration."

22. Ilya Prigogine, *The End of Certainty: Time, Chaos, and the New Laws of Nature* (New York: The Free Press, 1997).

23. The article was Immanuel Wallerstein, "America and the World: Today, Yesterday, and Tomorrow," *Theory and Society* 21, no. 1 (February 1991): 1–21; reprinted in Wallerstein, *After Liberalism*.

24. Norbert Wiener, *Cybernetics: Or Control and Communication in the Animal and the Machine* (Cambridge: MIT Press, 1948).

25. Immanuel Wallerstein, "Global Cleavages of the Twenty-First Century: What Future for the World," in *The Decline of American Power* (New York: The New Press, 2003), ch. 13.

26. Among many other places, see Immanuel Wallerstein, *World-System Analysis* (Durham, NC: Duke University Press, 2004), ch. 5; more specifically on the environment, see Immanuel Wallerstein, "Ecology and Capitalist Costs of Production: No Exit," in *Ecology and the World System,* ed. Walter Goldfrank et al. (Westport, CT: Greenwood Press, 1999), 3–11; reprinted in Immanuel Wallerstein, *The End of the World as We*

Know It: Social Science for the Twenty-First Century (Minneapolis: University of Minnesota Press, 1999), ch. 5.

27. Wallerstein (with Arrighi and Hopkins), "1989, the Continuation of 1968," 221–42.

28. Wallerstein, *After Liberalism.*

29. Wallerstein, "Global Cleavages of the Twenty-First Century"

30. The name we, at that moment, could not come up with was, of course, Joseph Stiglitz, onetime chief economist at the World Bank, Nobel Prize winner in economics, and author of *Making Globalization Work* (2006), among other works.

31. Herbert H. Hyman was one-time chair of the Department of Sociology at Columbia and a notable political sociologist who supervised the thesis.

32. The master's thesis in political science, "McCarthyism and the Conservative" (1954), was written and submitted at the most heated period of Senator Joseph McCarthy's reign of terror, which ended abruptly with his censure by the U.S. Senate on December 2, 1954. The oral history transcript, "Columbia Crisis," is dated 1969 (Oral History Research Office, Columbia University) but was recorded June 1968. Its subject was the crisis centered on the Columbia campus in late April 1968.

33. Charles Lemert et al., *Globalization* (London: Routledge, 2010).

34. André Gunder Frank, *Reorient* (Berkeley: University of California Press, 1998).

35. "Frank Proves the European Miracle," *Review* 22:3 (1999): 355–371.

36. Wallerstein posts periodic commentaries on current global events, many of which can be found at www.iwallerstein.com/commentaries. Concerning Afghanistan, a recent commentary is "Limping Out of Afghanistan," April 15, 2012, http://www.iwallerstein.com/limping-afghanistan.

37. The World Social Forum is a loose federation of nongovernmental groups aligned with the global Left and more or less explicitly in direct opposition to the World Economic Forum's neoliberal approach to the global political economy. It was first organized in 2001 in São Paulo and held its famous international meeting in 2002 in Porto Alegre, from which the World Social Forum gained its secondary, informal name.

38. Marcos is a Mexican leftist and spokesman for the Zapatista Liberation Army who is famous for creating a veil of mystery as to his whereabouts in Chiapas by, among other transformations, wearing an identity-shrouding mask in the early days of his movement.

Chapter Three

Wallerstein and the Uncertain Worlds

Charles Lemert

More than once, in various venues, I have been present at a public event featuring Immanuel Wallerstein. Never once was there less than a standing room audience. Yet, though at least one hip-hop lyric out there features his name, he is not a star of that or any similar genre. He gives no sign of wanting to be. He sent me the hip-hop lyrics because, he said, I was the only person he knew who might understand them. I was charmed. He can be charming in a wry sort of way. But he is not preoccupied with this sort of thing.

What is, indeed, charming about Wallerstein is the way he simply plows ahead with his work on several fronts at once—with complete confidence that whatever he does will go down well. It usually does. When he had agreed to come to speak at my university on the occasion of a memorial lecture held annually to remember the life of a young person in the community, he proposed a lecture topic I feared would not go well. I knew that the boy's mother and a number of her friends, none of them sociologists, not even remotely, would be there. I wanted them at least to feel that what was being said by a man they had never heard of would honor their then still-ripe pain. I obliquely suggested that Immanuel might consider another of his papers, one I knew to be more accessible (at least to the extent that it did not get into the finer points of Ilya Prigogine's scientific theories of uncertainty). Wallerstein wrote back instantly (he answers e-mail almost immediately), "Don't worry. They'll enjoy it."

On the night of the event, the room was indeed overflowing such that, it being early winter, with the windows shut and the heat on, the room soon

151

reached sauna-level temperatures. Wallerstein was introduced warmly by the dean, himself a prominent academic. Immanuel rose to the podium, paper in hand. He must have said thank you. I don't remember. But he started right off on the paper. He reads his papers—reads them well. They read well because they are so well written, and they are no doubt well written because Wallerstein works at his use of the language—probably a carry-over from his youthful days in the theater. Like his personal manner, his writing and reading are never overdone, never done for effect. They are plain and compelling—composed to convey ideas he believes in on good evidential grounds under the reasonable assumption that others will enjoy them as he does.

After the better part of an hour, I feared that students and old people would flee the room for the cool night air. If they did, I didn't notice because of the attention his paper demanded and demanded in spite of the fact that I'd read it several times before. At the end, not to be rushed, the packed house stayed on for Q&A. Eventually, in what I considered (perhaps mistakenly) to be an act of mercy, I excused the house. Afterward, only the mother of the child memorialized by the lecture series, herself one of wry humor, said something passively negative, on the order of, "Whatever ... but it seemed important."

What is this charm that defies the standards of a sitcom culture? There is no laugh track accompanying Wallerstein's public work. It just is what it is, and what it is is plenty good enough. But what is it?

It has been said reasonably enough that he is a prophet. If, instead of this essay, I were writing an ode to the man, in a major key, I might use that line. It is true that no sociologist of his prominence has ever quite grasped a world-changing event as Wallerstein did so soon after 1989, which he recognized as the coming end of the enduring structure he, more than anyone, had named and explained in the first place. If, indeed, the fall of the Berlin Wall turns out to be the end of the modern world-system, his 1992 paper in *Theory and Society,* "America and the World Today,"[1] was written with the events of 1989–1991 in mind. The Soviets did not finally give it up until Christmas Day 1991. The paper, I know for a fact, had been sent to *Theory and Society* not later than late 1991 in mind. Its touch was just right. The Cold War had ended. What now of America? And in respect to the American core, what will be the tomorrow of the modern world-system? His answer was sharp to his point. The American global hegemony that began effectively in 1945 had ended in 1990. America had begun its decline, which, he said, would also be the decline of the capitalist world-system itself. The date he put was 1990. By the time 1991 had come to its denouement, nearly everyone else not of the thoughtful Left was predicting the final triumph of the American century. The big idea in those days was Francis Fukuyama's "The End of History"—a 1989 essay that became a best-selling book in 1992. These were the days of George

H. W. Bush's end of the Vietnam Syndrome. Wallerstein stood virtually alone in seeing the end of the American era and, effectively, a dramatic uncertainty in the capitalist system America had dominated for a near half century. Prophetic? Yes. But does "prophet" do justice to whatever Wallerstein is?

More down to earth—and, in my view, more to the point—would be to describe him as steady, focused, undeterred. Though he is an admirer of Max Weber and certainly a Weber scholar, I do not mean to suggest that Wallerstein is purely and simply a disciplined entrepreneur imbued with the spirit of capitalism. This he may be, as are many of us. Still, few are as steady in their pursuit of the work. For one thing, over the years he has been subjected to a steady stream of criticisms, some worthy, some overwrought. His attitude toward them all has been, roughly, to ignore the ones that don't matter and respond sparsely to the ones that do. In the early years, mostly in the 1980s, the fashionable attack was that world-systems analysis ignored culture. I confess to having held such a thought myself upon first reading of *The Modern World-System* but had the good sense or lack of conviction not to write the idea down for publication; or if I did, I don't remember and certainly now realize that it was a weak criticism.

Wallerstein is clear that he responds only rarely to criticisms and only when doing so serves some intellectual purpose. At the same time, he recognizes what others say. In respect to the culturalist critics, he is, first of all, able to identify the more responsible ones, of which he singles out Stanley Aronowitz.[2] More importantly, in time he set out to develop and clarify his theory of the culture of the modern world-system, beginning notably with *Geopolitics and Geoculture* (1991), but also that same year *Unthinking Social Science* (1991), then, in the years following, *After Liberalism* (1995) and *The Uncertainties of Knowledge* (2004).[3] Otherwise, he is, in his way, courteous toward his critics, even when they behave badly toward him. Of these latter, the most striking case is that of André Gunder Frank, whose last book, *ReOrient: Global Economy in the Asian Age* (1998), was a stunning "reversal" (Wallerstein's word) of views Frank and Wallerstein shared in the 1970s. Frank's *ReOrient*, like most of his books, is a work of careful scholarship undergirding what can only be called a pointed rebuke of Wallerstein's thinking. I have pressed him several times on his views of Frank (who died in 2005), but try as I might, I could not extract from him a bad word about Frank. The worst he would say about *ReOrient: Global Economy in the Asian Age* was to the effect that somehow "André just lost his interest in capitalism," which says a lot about Wallerstein—his refusal to be drawn into pointless arguments, but also his dogged approach to what *some* would call their life's work. I say some because I cannot really imagine Immanuel referring to his work as a life's work, an expression that edges toward pomposity. In either case, whatever he would call it, the work over a good half century so far has, needless to say, been prodigious; more importantly, he keeps at it.

When he is in town, Wallerstein is at his desk at Yale usually by eight in the morning. He reads online for the most part a good half dozen newspapers in several languages. He answers e-mail—never at length, always to the point, always seriously, if occasionally sardonically, if mutedly so. But soon he is bent over a special computer system that allows him to peer down to a screen situated just above floor level. The idea is to relieve strain on the back. When he installed a new one of these, he very kindly gave me the one he'd used for many years. I couldn't quite figure out how to get used to it. Then again, not many bend over their work, relaxed but steady, as he does until well into the afternoon, when often Beatrice is there to meet him for dinner out or a musical event in New Haven. Some of those close to him call him a workaholic. I suppose this arises from the desire to have him around more. Yet, those who have passed social evenings with him know that he is a gracious host and, needless to say, an engaging conversationalist. As to his good sense of humor, I once took my then five-year-old daughter over for dinner. She was notably rude in the way children sometimes are, so I asked if she could watch some TV. Immanuel was kind enough to go with her and try to find some kid channel she wanted. She kept demanding such and such a program. She was beyond baby stuff, and this was before Hannah Montana. I was lost; so was he, but he kept at it until she was satisfied.

It may be, of course, that when home he works so assiduously because he travels so much—to all parts of world, and I should say not always on a direct line of flight. Apart from their keeping up the habit of living in Paris from late December through April, he keeps a long list of global commitments. Once, a few years ago, I was trying to arrange something minor with him, and he told me, "Well, I have to go back to Paris, then to Korea [or was it Chiapas?], but I have a talk in Dallas in between, so I'll try to get back to you then." (He did, by the way.)

He lives a full life, apparently without visible drama. He just keeps at the books and articles and talks (some of which are written out) and, usually in the Paris months, completed work on the fourth volume of *The Modern World-System*. That fact alone is important, and not because it illustrates the man's determination but because Wallerstein's truly great invention is the discovery of the drama of the modern era.

HISTORICAL METHOD AND DRAMA

Among sociologists and others in related fields, methodology is often a loathsome subject. In sociology, methodology is at least a troubled topic because it is so fraught with silly debates that come to nothing. Of these, none is more futile than the claim that at the highest (or is it the lowest?) levels, there are two kinds of methods: *quantitative,* in which statistically certified mathematical explanations are put forth, and *qualitative,* in which deep, closely gathered observations of local gatherings are collected, then put into (sometimes) well-written accounts that propose to demonstrate just how the locals studied represent a general phenomenon of the same or similar kind.

Those who do either kind are often proud and arrogant to the point of calling the other names of a supposedly devastating sort. The latter, for example, are overheard dismissing the former as mere "quantoids"—as if quantitative methods turn those who deploy them into machinelike expellers of numeric waste. Not all qualitoid name callers are aware that in some quarters "toid" is a euphemism for "turd," even when they consider the work of quantoids to be the virtual equivalent of, pardon the expression, shit. On the other hand, quantitative sociologists consider themselves superior to these others and thereby take a high-minded approach to their disdain, calling qualitative sociologists, often, mere storytellers, which bears the meaning of the old saw that the plural of "anecdote" is not "data." The weight of the criticism of qualitative methods is that general explanations cannot be represented without mathematical tests of their validity beyond the local populations from which the observations and stories were gathered. At most, it is sometimes said, storytelling can support theories, not explanations.

Thus, theory is the tertium quid in this not-so-enlightening argument. Many quantitatives object to theory without realizing that, when all is said and done, theory is at best storytelling of a well-intended kind. When it is merely a local story, skeptical quantoids are not quite so far wrong in their claim that theory shorn of quantitative evidence is no more than words about the words other theorists have uttered. Then again, read a piece of quantitative sociology, and you will see that even that sort of work must tell a story, even if it is told arithmetically.

These debates, still around today, were rife in the 1960s and 1970s, when Wallerstein was beginning his work. He did not engage them as such, in part because after his student days at Columbia's Department of Sociology, he had, perhaps it might be said, seen enough of it all. Those were the days, as is well-known, when the debate came to a head in the tandem of Paul Lazarsfeld, the quantitative sociologist than whom, then, none was greater, and Robert K. Merton, the theorist who, by inventing the phrase "middle-range theory," meant simultaneously to bring theory down from Parsonsian heights toward testable propositions and to limit if not eradicate the poetic license of mere anecdotal sociology. Wallerstein was trained at Columbia in the 1950s, then taught there in the 1960s, when this tandem was at the height of its powers. Somewhere in that experience, he obviously determined to seek another method that was immune to this sad argument that still preoccupies the field more than it should.

More importantly, it was then that he resolved to refrain from calling his work "theory." As a result, we have world-systems *analysis*. I have personally, on several occasions, attempted to get him to concede that, at least in the long run, people have come to use world-systems analysis as a theory of how the world as such works. He would not yield an inch, which, by the way, is quite another matter from his own willingness to use and engage theories in his analytic work, of which one notable instance is the conclusion to *The Modern World-System* I: "Theoretical Reprise." At Columbia, he had, as I say, seen enough of (my words) small theories and weak categories for social scientific analysis. These attitudes, long typical of American sociology, were not, however, simply a rejection of his teachers at Columbia. So far as he let on to me, at least, Wallerstein had good relations with all quarters of the Columbia faculty without being drawn into one or another sector. His master's thesis was written in 1955 under Herbert Hyman, who was, yes, an early pioneer of political sociology but also, and even more, a cofounder of survey research in the post–World War II era in the United States and a close ally of Lazarsfeld. Wallerstein is not, so far as I can tell, a joiner of parochial causes. He goes his own way, thinking independently and inventing new solutions to old problems.

Among Wallerstein's methodological inventions, none has proven more influential and lastingly important than his clarification of the basic unit proper to social research. Whereas from the beginning of sociology, in particular, "society" had been assumed to be that basic unit, Wallerstein argued (and still does) that from the beginning of the modern world, with its array of societal and national states, the actual unit that made the separate national cultures possible was the world-system. Hence, world-systems analysis— "world" to denote global, "systems" (plural) to denote the variety of system dispensations in the emergence of the modern world-system from circa 1500 through the long sixteenth century, down through the centuries, until late in the 1900s on the eve of the 2000s.

To begin with a unit like the modern world-system is to commit oneself not to a theory of it but to its history over the good half millennium of its coherence. Today, the better part of a half century after the publication of *The Modern World-System* I (1974), there are technologies that afford relative ease in gathering (or, as some younger techies call it, "tracking") global trends. These are good, and one thing we know, even if we do not regularly use digital tools this way, is that to track anything of human social importance—wealth, poverty, inequality, diseases, well-being, and so on—is to track global trends. Disease and capital have always been global phenomena. The illusion created by the idea of the nation-state that had its elementary forms at the beginning of the modern world in Europe is that these and all other human trends occur within an illusory and lesser unit—namely, society (which, when it was analyzed at all, was in effect the social things said to be provincial to a given nation-state).

One of the reasons that, in so many fields, methodology is a dull game is that, so often, the techniques by which data are collected get in the way of the stories the data might eventually tell. In recent years, what some people call the narrative method has emerged among sociologists, and some of that is interesting.[4] But to consider storytelling as somehow new and original these days is to have missed the point of all the traditional stories. All data, of whichever kind, make no sense unless they are lodged in a story—related to a literature, written with assurance that the story told is well founded in reality, and formed with some sense of drama. That the drama may not always be apparent in a given scholarly article or book does not mean it is not there. In short, the story told is what theory is, and there is no theory worth a damn without evidence, which is what data are for. It makes no difference which kind of data apply, except insofar as they support the dramatic story. Call it an argument or even a proof, but either way the point of social science is to engage something new and something important. These are the twin towers of good stories—telling it freshly and revealing its urgency.

I digress in order not to digress. Wallerstein has said, more than once, that his background in his youth was in theater. When I pressed him on this, he denied that he was ever more than an actor and said he never meant to be a playwright. That is fair enough, referring to the abandoned career as an actor, but, if I may say so, not fair in reference to his own quite honest and dramatic way of gathering evidence and telling the story it allows to be told. And this is nowhere more in evidence, in my view, than in the, so far, four volumes of *The Modern World-System.*

I realize that first-time readers of these books, who may not already be medieval or early-modern historians, will find this claim difficult to trust. Yet, I dare to advance it because I believe it to be true, whether or not Wallerstein himself does—and it is true in a way that illustrates his social scientific method of analysis of the modern world-system.

At the most general level, his method is that of social and economic history—at least that seems a good enough way to put it in respect to the illustrative text I choose for the present purposes: *The Modern World-System: Capitalist Agriculture and the Origins of the European World-Economy in the Sixteenth Century.* The subtitle alone suggests the extent to which, here, economic history is foundational, and to the extent that there is social history (as the term has come to be used today), it is really just as much political history. Thus, the political economy of the early forms of the modern world-system, a social unit of global proportions that arose out of the social, political, and economic fate of early Europe in the long sixteenth century from roughly 1450 to 1650, or from the rise of Portugal as the first explorer state, but then a relatively weak state formation, to the English and Dutch revolutions, those states that would surface as the strong capitalist states, for different reasons, but ones sufficient to fix the core states of the world-economy for a good three centuries, give or take, after the sixteenth. Even this utterly abstract summary of the book hints at the drama within—again, to repeat, the drama may not be theatrical in nature, but it is there.

Wallerstein's idea of the modern world-system exposes a history of changing, unstable, fluctuating, conflictual systems over time. It does so while set in the language of a global unit (the system itself) with boundaries and structured elements within, as well as competing forces both inside and out (including external arenas or other systems, such as the East Asian world-economy until 1800). Analysis is applied to (as opposed to theory derived from) them. Wallerstein's debt to Karl Marx notwithstanding, one does not hear him tell of dialectical materialism (a formal method of its own kind). Rather he more often speaks concretely of the rise and fall of states, prices, trade routes, the European division of labor, the French slipping away, the Dutch and English rising, and so on and so forth—or, in the key phrase, of uneven development.

Read the book, and you will feel the drama of the story told, which in brief (still all too briefly) is this:

> In the medieval prelude to the sixteenth century, conditions—notably a long history of technological innovations in agricultural production [52–53]— were established that led the modern capitalist world-economy: "an expansion in the geographical size of the world in question, the development of variegated methods of labor control from different products and different zones of the world-economy, and the development of relatively strong state machineries in what would become the core states of this capitalist world economy" [38]; in other words (1) overseas colonization and settlement (at first the Americas), (2) a new modern division of labor (of which a bourgeoisified yeoman class was crucial), and (3) a modern state able to control by rational means (Holland, then England).
>
> The first state to emerge as the core of the new system was the least probable, Portugal—which, because it was poor in geography, found overseas expansion necessary, for which it benefitted from Venetian capital investments to further capitalize its proximity to the African slave trade and its geographic advantage of jutting well into the southern Atlantic, hence closer than the rest of Europe to the Americas [50–51]. Soon Spain followed, but

neither would hold the core for long because, precisely, they were weak states. Spain, though powerful on the seas, began to decline after the defeat of its armada in 1588.

Yet, even in the years between, say, 1492 and 1588, as Spain eclipsed Portugal, the two settled into a division of global labor: Portugal had free rein in Brazil then South and Southeast Asia; Spain dominated the rest of the Latin Americas as far north as California and the Philippines. In the Americas, Spain implanted a new method of organizing agricultural labor in the *encomienda* system in its colonies, while, in Europe, a new division of labor developed among serfs, tenant farmers, and again yeomen farmers in northwestern Europe [116] on the socioeconomic level as, at the level of states, the first signs of a continental and global division of labor were apparent. The new system exploited the money-wage system of payment as means to control labor. Eastern Europe came to the fore as the breadbasket for all of Europe in the system, leaving the New World as a source of precious metals, including bullion, spices, and eventually sugar and cotton, which would close the three angles of the Atlantic slave trade triangle that generated more capital surplus in Europe and eventually North America [86–88, 99].

By the seventeenth century, revolution in Holland spelt the decline of the Spanish Empire and the appearance of a bourgeois capital class bent on capital accumulation throughout the new world-economy. The Dutch revolution was the first true example of a national liberation movement [206–7] that unified Holland under a strong, rationalized state. Meanwhile, between France and England, the superiority of French technology and mercantile practices proved futile under a relatively weak, overly extended, and indebted state. The strong English monarchy, combined with its insular peculiarities and advantages, gradually was set, after its revolution, to emerge in the Elizabethan era as the next core state to be. In England, administrative efficiencies allowed, as they were required by, the coordination of capital. London then emerged as a "strong capital city and economic unifying force" [232–33] for the global colonial system that would dominate in the eighteenth and nineteenth centuries until 1914, when war in Europe would undermine British control of the system, opening the way for the Americans to assume the core after 1945.

Thus, an intentionally understated story of the dramas of what would become the modern capitalist world-system.

To be sure, a first-time reader of the story's telling may well be put off by the twists and turns—not to mention Wallerstein's copious footnotes and nuances. Even the expert may balk, as some have, at the fact that in his sources, secondary historical accounts predominate over original archival research. The purist would ask, surely, what kind of method is this? Even one familiar with the influences might ask, why, if Fernand Braudel's enormous *The Mediterranean and the Mediterranean World in the Age of Philip II* was drawn largely from the archives, could not Wallerstein's just as ambitious work have been? The easy answer is that Braudel was a historian; Wallerstein is a sociologist. A slightly less easy answer is that Wallerstein, being a sociologist, was free, if not totally free, to stand on the shoulders of giants—and Braudel and the Annales School were chief among the giants on whose shoulders Wallerstein stood. Sociologists, since Weber, have tended to be consumers of the work of historians—not all, to be sure, but there is ample precedent and good reason for the practice.

But these reasons, though good in their way, are not sufficient. I think it is far better to consider that Wallerstein, influenced though he was by Braudel, was up to something quite different—something that was, when it first appeared in 1974, original by being, however understatedly, both a literary and a sociological method. Here again is my unruly claim that Wallerstein—his denials notwithstanding—had the touch of a playwright. In this he surpasses—or, better perhaps, diverges from—Braudel, whose *The Mediterranean* overlaps the time of *The Modern World-System* I and II. Wallerstein's books are, of course, true to Braudel's intent of being a historian of the long-enduring world from which, indeed, the modern world-system emerged. Yet, Braudel, ever the archivist, divides his story into chunks—environment, economies, empires and societies, politics and people—each in turn further subdivided into its proper analytic parts. Braudel's literary achievements are real, but they are at the level of the word and the locution. Some of his sentences, especially in the occasional and collected essays, are beautiful beyond measure. Among them are the sentences with which Braudel opens the conclusion to *Capitalism and Material Life, 1400–1800*:

> A very old bell struck the hour in the small Lorraine village where I grew up as a child: the village pond drove an old mill wheel; a stone path, as old as the world, plunged down like a torrent in front of my house; the house itself had been rebuilt in 1806, the year of Jena, and flax used to be retted in the stream at the bottom of the meadows. I only have to think of these things and this book opens out for me afresh.

Braudel stirs the soul, but his literary brilliance is of the stories of material and social things and their environments and times. His is more a literary nonfiction, while, I claim, Wallerstein's is more the work of the dramatist he claims he is not.

Just read any particular passage in *The Modern World-System* I, and you are unlikely to be stirred by childhood memories; rather, the writing draws the reader into the writer's world. Where Braudel lets his childhood world be what it was for him, as an inspiration for the book he opens up for those who would read it, Wallerstein tells, actually, the story of what other storytellers have told of the worlds he is creating—or discovering may be better—out of the record. No question about it: Wallerstein, whatever may have been his immersion in primary archives, works with secondary sources. And he works with them as few other writers of the kind have.

On the surface, I agree, *The Modern World-System* is a series of diagnostic representations of what others have said in respect to elements in the story of the emergence of Iberia, its decline, and the rise of strong core states beginning with Holland. Read it on the surface alone, and you can be bewildered. But the bewilderment—usually a sense of awe at the author's vast and discriminating learning—can be set aside under closer scrutiny. Wallerstein is telling a story—his story—but telling it on the ground, nothing less, of what is known about his subject. Let me illustrate with a passage of particular virtue, I think. It occurs late in *The Modern World-System* I, where Wallerstein comes to account for an irony in the rise of the Dutch and the fall of Seville after the defeat of its Armada. The irony is that, though bullion imports fell, prices did not—the value of capital remained constant in spite of the political and economic decline in the trade of coin of the world-economy. Just then Wallerstein introduces a dramatic insistence: "Here for the first time the existence of a single world-economy of uneven national development made a crucial difference" [271]. Experts will recognize immediately the technical concepts this statement is built upon (single world-economy, uneven development), but Wallerstein does not fail to satisfy them with the finer details some may demand. He continues,

The countries of northwest Europe devalued far less than those of southern, central, and eastern Europe. These are of course the bullion prices. René Baehrel has a very brilliant excursus in which he demonstrates that shifts in bullion prices bear no necessary relationship to shifts in prices and that men make their real economic decisions primarily in terms of the latter. It is significant, however, that he does this in a book devoted to discussing the economy of the seventeenth and eighteenth centuries. A. D. Lubinskaya makes the point that what distinguishes the seventeenth from the sixteenth century is precisely the fact that, after 1615 for the first time, there is "an *independent* movement of prices, *not* dependent on the influx of gold and silver." She insists that this fact defines the end of the "price revolution." [271]

Still, I repeat, on the surface a now somewhat less skeptical reader may say something on the order of "okay," as if getting the drift but without yet being enchanted. But to resist at this point is to resist the occurrence, in one paragraph, of two firsts in history: uneven development in a world economy, and now the freeing of prices and thus capital from its material backing in gold and silver. Even the skeptic, at this late point in Wallerstein's minidrama, must at least grant that the language itself is—as it always is with him, in the form of short, pithy, declarative sentences—linked nicely into an argument (dare I say, a story line) of his own composition.

But to be serious in reading this sort of paragraph for its literary method, it is important to grant that, against and with respect for the sources he uses, Wallerstein is constantly bobbing and weaving: a tender punch of disagreement or correction here, an affirmation there. In this case René Baehrel's references to a later period are brought back to bear on the sixteenth century, the subject of the book.

But there is more still than meets the eye. The footnotes. The countless, small-print footnotes that one is inclined to skip over as the reader in a rush often does. But you cannot read this book against a deadline. The footnotes count, and they are usually composed with the same pungent grace that inhabits the page text. For example, footnote 210 [still referring to page 271] cites René Baehrel's work but then goes on to explain the attribution as "very brilliant":

> See Baehrel, *Une Coissance* in ibid. [Cambridge Modern History, IV]; also René Baehrel, "Economie and histoire à propos de prix," in *Eventail de l'histoire vivante: hommage à Lucien Febvre* (Paris: Lib. Aramd Colin, 1953) I, 287–310. Baehrel concludes this article "Pay attention to 'social screens,' Marc Bloch recommended. Must we also speak of 'economic screens?' Lucien Febvre taught me once that Luther's objection to the indulgences was that they provided a false security. Can we say as much about bullion prices?" [still note 210]

At this point, one need not bother with what the skeptic says if he won't yield the point. Here is Wallerstein, the text and the note, doing as his sources do (in this case René Baehrel)—digging deep into the material in order to (if I may borrow Braudel's phrase from his village scene) "open up" the book as a whole. I find this drama of a special sort. I took me a good quarter century of reading these books to get the point—to be drawn in, but then I may be slow.

In a word, the drama of the origins of the European world-economy, as of the world-system itself, is in the details into which the dramatist bores, deeper and deeper, until he comes to a series of "first times" and "by the ways" that bring the reader up for air. Perhaps it is because my own training was first in the biological sciences, then in biblical exegesis, that I am particularly drawn to this sort of thing. Weber, you'll recall, once said that politics was the boring of hard boards. His view of science was much the same. The problem with Weber, if one dares say so, is that he seldom bored in ways that called the reader into the depths. In his most accessible work, *The Protestant Ethic and the Spirit of Capitalism,* the countless notes lead the reader away even when they mean to explain the concepts or movements to which Weber alludes. Wallerstein draws the reader in, if he will be thus drawn. Not every reader, I suppose. But those who get the larger drama of the rises and falls that form the substantial history of the modern world will want to go with him into the details. It may take a number of readings, but it *should* take time for this sort of thing.

Still, the time taken, more or less, is not the essence of the method. However one gets to the essential dramatic line of the history of the modern world-system, the drama surfaces all the more when Wallerstein's historical analysis is compared to its principal rival.

THE MODERNIZING WORLD: TRAGIC FLAT LINE OR FARCICAL INEQUALITIES?

At the least, it would be hard to argue, however skeptical some might remain, that Wallerstein's historical analysis of the rise of the modern world-system is, if not a drama as such, vastly more dramatic than the still dominant alternative: modernization theory.

Modernization theory purports to be a historical account of the stages of growth in the modern world. I say *purports* because, unlike Wallerstein's approach, modernization theory is, whatever name its proponents may prefer, a theory pure and simple, and one based on scant actual historical evidence. Yet, in its manifold deployments throughout the councils of global social and economic policy makers, modernization theory is very much alive in spite of the fact that the theory itself is deadly—hence, a flat-line theory. Or, to keep the comparison with world-systems analysis, modernization theory, as theory, is without tensions or surprises—hence, without honest drama of any sort, a tragic sitcom, if you will, lacking only the laugh track.

Too strong? I think not, at least not when reference is made to the classical and still current formulations of modernization theory as a formula for economic development. Though some would argue that Joseph A. Schumpeter's *Theory of Economic Development* (1934) is the key document in the theory of economic development, it is surely W. W. Rostow's *Stages of Economic Growth:*

A Non-Communist Manifesto (1960) that had become the most influential since mid-twentieth century. Leaving aside for the moment the ideological tip-off in Rostow's subtitle, key to both Schumpeter's and Rostow's statements of development theory is the entrepreneur—whom Schumpeter said was the "fundamental phenomenon of economic development."[5] Despite Rostow's giving Schumpeter but one footnote, the latter's influence is clear in that both, though to varying degrees, rank the rise of an entrepreneurial class alongside new modes of production and capital surplus available for credit as the central factors in historical cases of modernizing development.

Rostow's version of modernization theory is famous, most of all, for the four important stages of growth out of economic traditionalism: *preconditions* for take-off, the *take-off* of development, the *drive to economic maturity,* and the age of *high mass consumption.* Where Schumpeter is brilliant in diagnosing the social psychology of the new entrepreneur of the industrial era, Rostow is more vague, a difference due in part to the fact that Schumpeter was an economic historian while Rostow (who held positions as an economic historian) came to be, after 1960, the general (and generalizing) economist turned policy theorist—even ideologue, as the book's subtitle (*A Non-Communist Manifesto*) illustrates. One curious difference between the two, thus, is that Rostow was oddly deaf when it comes to historical realities (as opposed to economic facts, of which many), and no place more so than on the question of Max Weber's contribution to the history of the capitalist entrepreneur.

> It is increasingly [this was 1960] conventional for economists to pay their respects to the Protestant ethic. The historian should not be ungrateful for this light on the grey horizon of formal growth models. But the known cases of economic growth which theory must seek to explain take us beyond the orbit of Protestantism. In a world where Samurai, Parsees, Jews, North Italians, Turkish, Russian, and Chinese civil servants (as well as Huguenots, Scotsmen, and British north-countrymen) have played the role of a leading élite in economic growth, John Calvin should not be made to bear quite this weight.[6]

It is apparent in this passage that Rostow had little appreciation for the historical claim Weber was making (that Calvin's influence was deferred by a good three centuries). More importantly, Rostow thought solely in terms of historical time as a flat, forward-moving line. For Rostow, the modern world *was* progress—irreversible, stable, incapable of spilling over into the traditional pasts of differing historical times. Hence, in both senses, Weber's history was unthinkable to Rostow in the sense that (and keeping the contrast to world-systems analysis in mind), in historical time, what may have begun in a sixteenth-century religious movement in regions of the West could grow secular, then come to dominate the geoculture such that the spirit of capitalism (hence, by implication, capitalism itself) might, in that time, act back (especially from the British core) upon the less mature, capitalist developing areas or the still traditional and underdeveloped parts of the world it dominated.

There could hardly be a more shocking symptom of the historical flatness of modernization theory than these, admittedly offhand, remarks by one of its codifiers. Rostow may have taught economic history, but the history he taught was that of a certain—and, in real-world terms, limiting—historical time that moved flatly without dimension or disturbance on an upward plane. Or, if not the time of economic progress, Rostow's and modernization theory's time was no time at all—the time of traditionalism, which is effectively dead time from the modern point of view.

The effect on Rostow's theory is between the lines. Like Schumpeter, and notwithstanding Rostow's disregard of Weber, he considers the entrepreneur fundamental to development, but one reads Rostow's manifesto for anything approaching serious historical judgment and finds, instead, hesitations and qualifications:

> Although an elite entrepreneurial class *appears* to be required for take-off, without significant power over aggregate income flows and industrial investment decisions, *most* take-offs have been preceded or accompanied by radical change in agricultural techniques and market organization. *By and large* the agricultural entrepreneur has been the individual land-owning farmer.... A small purposeful élite *can go a long way* in initiating economic growth.[7]

In defense of Rostow, one might claim that this book is, after all, a manifesto and thus might be excused from the usual scholarly declamations. Still, a manifesto, one would suppose, would be precisely when and where one would want to assert without qualification the particulars of the theory.

By contrast, compare the following from another manifesto-like text, one by Wallerstein that could have been titled *Historical Capitalism: A Left but Non-Liberal Manifesto*:

> A first elementary *contradiction* in the [capitalist] system [was that] while the interest of all capitalists, taken as a class, *seemed* to be to reduce all costs of production, these reductions *in fact* frequently favoured particular capitalists against others, and some therefore preferred to increase their share of a smaller global margin rather than accept a smaller share of a large global margin. *Furthermore*, there was a second *contradiction* in the system. As more and more capital was accumulated, and more and more commodities

produced, one of the key requirements to maintain the flow was that there be more and more purchasers. However, *at the same time,* efforts to reduce the cost of production often reduced the flow and distribution of money, and thus inhibited the steady expansion of purchasers needed to complete the process of accumulation. *On the other hand,* redistributions of global profit in ways that could have expanded the networker of purchasers often reduced the global margin of profit. *Hence* individual entrepreneurs found themselves *pushing in one direction* for their own enterprises (for example, by reducing their own labour costs), while *simultaneously* pushing (as members of a collective class) to increase the overall network of purchaser (which inevitably involved, for some producers at least, an increase in labour costs).... Historical capitalism is, thus, that concrete, time-bounded, space-bounded integrated locus of productive activities within which the endless accumulation of capital has been the economic objective or "law" that has governed or prevailed in fundamental economic activity.[8]

This, evidently, is Wallerstein writing, here in *Historical Capitalism* (1983), which, while not quite a manifesto in tone, is a much shorter book than Rostow's manifesto and one that aims to put forth the key features of capitalism's historical role in modernization. Notice, in the comparison, that Wallerstein qualifies rarely, and when he does, it is to open one side of the key concept, or in the passage: contradiction. For Rostow the qualifications are hedges against the evidence; for Wallerstein they are part of the narrative line. Here, there are no notes; but here everything is concrete, without wavering, definite to the main point that capitalism is a bundle of elegant contradictions.

What is the truth of the matter? Is it that modernization theory is inherently vague and ideological, while world-systems analysis is concretely historical? Though many have accused Wallerstein of being either too Marxist or not Marxist enough—thus, an ideologue of his own kind—the fact remains that Wallerstein has history on his side, and modernization theory is at best a pseudohistory that freezes or kills historical actors in artificial stages of growth.

By contrast, though expressed in oftentimes straightforward historical language, or (like the quote here) even in conceptual terms, Wallerstein's method obeys the first rule of dramatic tension: things are never what they seem to be. "What was remarkable about capitalism as an historical system was the way in which ... unequal exchange could be hidden; indeed so well hidden that it is only after five hundred years of the operation of this mechanism that even the avowed opponents of the system have begun to unveil it systematically."[9] Capitalists profess growth as the liberal good for all, while hiding the costs they impose on society and labor in order to rake in accumulated capital for themselves. Or, in the earlier example, a drop in bullion imports ought to mean a drop in price and economic disaster; in fact, the level of bullion imports in the sixteenth century (and seemingly ever since) is not significantly related to prices and economic growth—hence the illusory progress forward in the history of the world-system. On the surface the capitalist entrepreneur, whether an individual or a firm, remains an actor, but one whose actions are always in a certain tension with other players in an arena—where states and prices and labor and costs are indefinitely indeterminate tensions with one another. That, we know, is how history and life work. By contrast, modernization theory, in either its classical expression by Rostow or its adumbrations in global banking and foreign policies, is a false history because, first, its facts are synchronic (GDP rates in selected developed countries, or well-being comparisons between underdeveloped, developing, and developed economies). Second, modernization theory relies on a periodization of economic history that is hinged on both ends by empty categories. On one end, traditionalism, the category to which Weber, its inventor, gave definitional clarity, is a historical stage defined all too simply by the lack of modern virtues (agricultural efficiencies, capital, an entrepreneurial class, a dynamic mode of production). At the other end lies awaiting a penultimate stage of mass consumption, and even beyond that is a kind of postmodern stage, "beyond consumption"[10]—both of which are just as empty in that they represent, in effect, the collapse or end of modernizing values and efficiencies. In between, modernization theory gives pride of historical place to take-off, drive to maturity, and maturity, or to early developing, developing, and developed economies. There are few tensions in such a theory. One need only look at the comparative economic data to find that Rwanda, ranked #141 in GDP (2011) is, whatever else, a failed United States at #1 or that China (#2) in 2011 is what Japan (fallen to #3) was thought to have been in the 1980s and India (#11 and rising fast) might become in 2020, and so forth.[11] Whatever the modernization scheme is (and it is important to say that it is not nothing), it is not historical drama. Each economic arena has its own stage, and the attainment of a stage is explained in purely descriptive terms by a scheme that allows only failures of location and character. Rostow's history is only always a drive toward maturity—or a failure to drive.

Plus which, there is no serious allowance in modernization theory for dynamic reversals, of which in world-systems analysis the most basic is that the core, in cahoots with its semiperiphery, exploits the impoverished periphery for its natural and cheap labor resources. The terms themselves were invented in the heyday of modernization (1945–1970) by the United Nations Economic Commission for Latin America, which also coined the expression "dependency theory." Wallerstein and world-systems analysis thus describe the underdeveloped periphery in terms that depict anything but the moral and economic failure of the poor. "The key element distinguishing core-like from peripheral processes is the degree to which they are monopolized and therefore profitable."[12] The core, thus, in the famous expression, develops underdevelopment in the periphery. It is the dishonesty (or hidden secrets) of the capitalist core that accounts for vast regions of global impoverishment. The periphery is unstable and economically peripheral because the core states and their allies extract the wealth to the benefit of the wealthy corporations and nations in which they are based worldwide.

In modernization theory—which it should be said is the cultural apparatus of highly dedicated and compassionate liberals in the U.S. State Department, the World Bank, the International Monetary Fund, the European Commission for Economic Development, and others—history is a false triumph covering an underlying tragedy. Underdevelopment is, in effect, the moral failure to become economically disciplined enough to rise out of the traditions. World-system analysis is, if any sort of drama, perhaps a farce or an irony in that the poor are always waiting for their Godot, who was there all along in the colonizers and the bankers and corrupt weak-state officials who grew wealthy dealing with the core and semiperiphery. This may seem harsh, given that without doubt such institutions as the World Bank have surely done good in the world. Still:

> The World Bank is a vital source of financial and technical assistance to developing countries around the world. Our mission is to fight poverty with passion and professionalism for lasting results and to help people help themselves and their environment by providing resources, sharing knowledge, building capacity and forging partnerships in the public and private sectors.[13]

Nothing wrong with this. But what is between the lines? "Knowledge for Development offers policy advice to client countries on the four pillars of a knowledge economy: economic and institutional regimes, education, innovation, and information and communication technologies to help clients make the transition to a knowledge economy." Faint are the shadows of Rostow's ideology, but they are there, in the language of development theory, in the commitment to "transition." It is not that there are no benefits for developing countries in these programs, but the premise is that their greatest need is to make the transition to modernity—and this, remember, is from the self-defined principles of of the most benevolent institutions of the core nations. Imagine how much more deeply the same principles are embedded in the clandestine chambers of the intelligence, military, and foreign ministry establishments of the modernized nations where, no doubt, modernization theory does its work ever closer to hard global realities.

Modernization, viewed from the critical point of view of its professed cultural and political principles, is a farce that betrays the tragedy of the global poor, who, far from failing at entrepreneurial (and related) games, have seldom ever been in the game the core plays with its wealth. The story told by world-systems analysis is not, in the end, very funny at all.

LIBERAL TIME VERSUS GLOBAL TIMESPACE

Whether tragedy or farce, the triumph of liberalism in 1848 conjured up, in one and the same instant, the deadly ghosts of modern social thought and political practice that had the effect, if not the intention, of confirming modernity's theory of itself as the heart of all things historical. Thus, from 1789, when the nineteenth century began in earnest with revolution (and Immanuel Kant's second critique), modern liberal thought was forced to overburden the ideal of practical reason as the local sign of the essence of human action. Hence, the great divide of the high modern era was aggravated by Hegel, Kant, and Marx—all of whom trusted that knowledge could be salvaged after the death of the gods, who were remade into the dialectic of universal consciousness, the moral imperative, and the utopian vision of a new socialist state—all of which were to be found, if at all, outside history in a final synthesis, or the starry skies above and the social impulse within, or in a variety of communisms in nineteenth-century sectarian movements and twentieth-century socialisms, nationalisms, and labor movements. None was able to stand up to the demands of the real contradictions of modern history.

If there is a decisively fatal flaw in the long narrative of liberal geoculture, it would be its implausible, if implicit, theory of its own time. No other globally dominant culture even dared to consider the prideful idea that the time of the modern era, beginning in the long sixteenth century, was the time of humanity itself, from which it deduced, without evidence or logic on its side, that the modern European diaspora was inherently and self-evidently progressive. Modern time, thus conceived and imposed on global culture, was the time of the ever new, ever renewable advance of modern economic, social, and technical change for the better. One of the modern global culture's most common rhetorical gestures was the stipulation that the time of human bondage was in the past. The past was primitive, elemental, tradition-bound—thus a prison house in which the true soul of the human was held captive. The modern was reason itself, hence inclined toward growth, complexity, and change—thus a temporal field of free-play on which, in principle, there were none other than technical limits on human freedom.

When it comes to time, the question whether human time is a prison house or a playground is always open. Thus, it is surprising that it took so very long for those occupied with the study of the social history of human being to put the question that exposed the now more obvious third alternative. Against the straitjacket of historical time as either absolute prison or pure liberty, now stands the idea that modern history is *the* time, neither the one nor the other. Rather the history of modern culture is an elaborate scheme whereby humanity itself, in the ideological sense, came to be the carceral form that confined time, thus the human, in a pure implausible absurdity. Man, as the ideology puts it, is at the least, and without reservation, naked before his constructions of life itself as somehow split between the time of his animal nature and the progressive time of his progress. In our day, in the 2010s, the author best known for calling this out is Giorgio Agamben.[14] But, as he would be the first to say, the possibility arose, first, with Michel Foucault in the 1970s and, shortly after, along a different line of inquiry, with Gilles Deleuze and Felix Guattari. In 1975, in *Discipline and Punish*, Foucault began the series of studies of biopolitics, then to speak of the "carceral texture of society," by which he meant to say that modern politics are the politics of life in service of the creation of docile populations. Thus, they are the politics of a global social mechanism in which the institutions of society were carceral institutions that stripped human life of its allegedly sacred nature, exposing the human animal to death, the ultimate prison house.

Foucault's idea of the carceral society is today justly well-known. Those preoccupied with Foucault and others of his day in Paris understand less well that at the same time, also in Paris, another theory of the modern was taking shape. This alternative did not use the language of imprisonment, but it was just as historical as Foucault's own thing and, at a certain remove, also indebted to the French school of historical studies by which the particular event, hence the historical individual, was called into question and, thereby, the idea of historical time as an open trajectory in a field of free play.

In his analytic of the modern world-system, Wallerstein, more than any one to that point or since, codified and elaborated the critique of the modern system as itself a kind of carceral of social and economic underdevelopment. He used different, more measured language, but his critique amounted to much the same thing by stipulating, on good and generous historical evidence, that the modern system of domineering European core states economically and legally enslaved an impoverished periphery of underdeveloped regions.

Among others, two aspects distinguish Wallerstein's approach as oddly similar to, yet different from, Foucault's. One is that, as time went by, Wallerstein developed a specific philosophical position toward time, hence toward history itself. Foucault, by contrast, had a theory of time and history but never one so fully articulated as Wallerstein's. The other distinguishing aspect of Wallerstein's thinking was that it avoided the trap of becoming a doctrine. Thus, more than anyone else among social scientists, he both anticipated and explained the decline of the modern era into a deep and prolonged period of uncertainty. One supposes, in passing, that Foucault, had he lived, might well have done much the same. But the fact remains that Wallerstein's work, while far from being above criticism, has led the way out from under the limiting features of so much of modern social thought (and most especially radical thought overly indebted to Marx)—hence the justification for this attempt to assess its origins and continuing importance to the prospect that the modern system, if not exactly a prison house, was at least more trouble than progress for the species.

* * *

Whether the structures of the modern world-system are uncertain in a deep structural sense remains controversial well after the events of 1989–1991 appear to have changed global things in ways hard to define but impossible to ignore. Still, if there is room for responsible inquiry into the possibility that modern structures have fallen into disequilibrium, then there must be a corresponding inquiry as to the whither of historical time in the decline of a temporal order so rigidly linear and spatial as that of the modern world-system.

Time in its modern formulation is ultimately historical time—generally conceived as a measure of movement in space along a definable if imaginary trajectory. This is liberal time—what Wallerstein and, before him, Braudel and others have identified as event—or, properly, episodic—history. *L'histoire événementielle* is, of course, a formula so loaded as to press the idea of history down to its narrowest and least enduring units—an analytic hypostasis that reduces the wider and larger structures of social time to a downright arbitrary. Episodic history fabricates the uniqueness of allegedly decisive events selected according to the prominence of (usually) some political figure or event as if the ordinary nuances that abide in the larger structures of conjunctural and enduring structures were mere background noise. Hence, Waterloo on June 18, 1815, is taken as a decisive event in Napoleon's political and military career that turned Napoleon (the figure) into a metonym for France in a certain period of its history and, thus, by extension, synecdochical for the early history of modernity. The figure of speech thus allows no signifying room for the geographic features of the battleground outside Brussels, not to mention the long-building and complex structure of Britain's superior naval power, advantaged by Britain's insular geography that, with much else, codetermined the range of possibilities for the Waterloo episode itself. Waterloo was indeed an event on an interior plain, but the structural advantages and disadvantages were, as such things always are, complex, inscrutable, and distant in time's space. They began, if structural forces have a beginning, with Wellington's hold on the higher ground and continued in the rain the night before the battle, but rains and much else go back to the seas from which England's navy could limit an enemy's approaches, while supplying its own forces with relatively little interference. Plus, even to move to these levels of historical time is only to touch on the long-enduring structures of climate and geography that, always without exception, shape the episodes comprising events in history.

Wallerstein's theory of time's space is of course drawn from his most fundamental direct influence, Braudel, and thus appears very early in his writings, prominently even in *The Modern World-System* I in 1974. Yet, it is striking that his deeper reflections on his analytic time begin only after the encounter with Ilya Prigogine early in the 1980s and become most explicit in the years just before and after 1991—notably in "The Inventions of SpaceTime Realities: Towards an Understanding of Our Historical Systems" (1988)[15] to "SpaceTime as the Basis of Knowledge" (1997)[16] and "Time and Duration: The Unexcluded Middle, or Reflections on Braudel and Prigogine" (1998).[17] More interesting still is that two of these texts and others related to the general theme of historical times are collected in three books wherein Wallerstein offers his most sustained and challenging interpretations of the limits and possibilities of social thought (including social epistemology): *Unthinking Social Science* (1991), *The End of the World as We Know It: Social Science for the Twenty-First Century* (1999), and *The Uncertainties of Knowledge* (2004).[18]

Though it is at best allegorical to name texts as indices of a turn of mind reflecting on the changing times, Wallerstein's other writings of the 1990s and since are well-known to have been serious reflections on the theme of the endings of the system he, more than anyone, led others to comprehend: *After Liberalism* (1995), *Utopistics: Or Historical Choices of the Twenty-First Century* (1998), and *Decline of American Power* (2003).[19] Those familiar with these writings understand very well that the epistemological meditations are part and parcel of a continuing and sustained reflection on political and economic history after the withering of the modern world-system.

I propose,[20] thus, to examine in close detail the general concepts of time and space as they appear in Wallerstein's writings. The purpose is twofold. The first is to put into renewed focus one of the most important but under-appreciated advances in social theory since the 1980s. The second is to describe and define aspects of Wallerstein's theory that might well be revised in order to take better account of the state of the global system since 1989–1991 and its sequelae (notably 2001–2003), which may reasonably be considered at least a prelude to a moment in what Wallerstein calls transformational TimeSpace.

WALLERSTEIN'S THEORY OF TIMESPACE

Wallerstein prefaces his theory of TimeSpace with a bold statement: "Time and space are the most obvious parameters of our existence."[21] Yet, in the various articles, lectures, and books in which he has commented on the subject,[22] Wallerstein maintains that the issue of time and space is an epistemological one, not an existential or even ontological one. Though slightly finicky, this is a distinction worth noting when attempting to examine the multiplicity of TimeSpaces within the broader theory of the structures of knowledge. In particular, epistemology bears directly on the exceptional importance Wallerstein assigns to the social sciences in the intellectual foundations of the modern world-system, initially after 1789 but markedly in the liberal geoculture formed after 1848.[23]

A historical account of time's relation to space is not, for Wallerstein, a question of how the experience of space and time may have changed but one of the means by which TimeSpace, the relation, is apprehended. In other words, space and time, though not universally or quasi-universally categorical in the Kantian sense, are above and beyond their articulations with human social histories, including cultures, sciences, and technologies. In this regard, Wallerstein is evidently and deeply critical of the nineteenth-century paradigms by which moderns have understood time and space. Still, I think, he retains at least a trace of the metaphysical assumptions he rejects in his unusual attachment to the primacy of knowledge as the medium through which time and space are translated.

By knowledge, Wallerstein does not, surely, intend a philosophy of mind; nor, at the other extreme, does he lapse (as well some might) into a historicist or (worse yet) a constructionist position. Still, his more sober third-way approach leaves unsettled the precise status of categorical TimeSpace—or, more accurately, TimeSpaces. The conceptual perturbations affect the ability of the analytic formulation to come to historical terms with the defining condition of his structural theory of historical time: transformational TimeSpace.[24] One measure of the tensions within Wallerstein's theory of time's relations to spaces is found in key passages in Wallerstein's earliest and most explicit philosophical presentation of the subject in the 1997 essay "SpaceTime as the Basis of Knowledge." On the one hand, he is exceptionally clear as to the limitations of any and all variants of a Kantian conception of metaphysical invariance—indeed, precisely such an attitude is at the heart of the dilemmas of nineteenth-century thinking, including the social sciences:

> Modern structures of knowledge have insisted that time and space are invariant exogenous factors of social reality within which everything we

do and say somehow fits. We are subjects acting within objective reality. We are humans, and time and space are external to us, part of our natural environment. We exist immanently, but time and space persist despite us. This belief in a radical disjuncture of humans and nature ... reflects the same binary, antinomic conceptualization of reality as the purported disjunctures between the particular and the universal, the idiographic and the nomothetic, philosophy and science—all part of the intellectual scaffolding of the modern world-system.[25]

On the other hand, in the same place where one comes upon his most systematic philosophical presentation of TimeSpace as such, Wallerstein is at pains to distinguish the prevailing modern concepts of TimeSpace as either episodic or eternal from structural TimeSpace as he defines it:

> Structural TimeSpace speaks to what we cannot change (the system in the short run) and what will surely change (the system in the long run), and why the system doesn't really change in the short run (cyclical rhythms) and why it in fact does change in the long run (the secular trends, leading far from equilibrium).[26]

So far so good, until he turns to the crucial and, for him, distinguishing instance of structural TimeSpace without which the concept would remain effectively, if not explicitly, invariant:

> This brings us to the last kind of TimeSpace we have neglected, what I call transformational TimeSpace. This is the brief, very rare, moment of fundamental change. It is moment of transition from one kind of historical system to another, from one mode of organizing social life to another. These moments do not come often. They come only when an historical system has exhausted its mechanisms of reequilibrating itself, has used up the efficacy of the cyclical rhythms, has gone sufficiently far from equilibrium that the oscillations have become wild and unpredictable. We enter then into the moment of which Prigogine speaks, the moment of bifurcation in which a new, but nonpredictable, order will emerge from the chaos into which the structure has acceded.[27]

In alluding, thus, to the "brief, very rare" occurrences of transformational TimeSpace as the decisive aspect that distinguishes his theory from those more embedded in the nineteenth-century paradigms, Wallerstein makes a leap that is comparable to the perplexing inadequacies of both Marx and Weber at a similar juncture.

As Marx could not account for his strong theory of transitions from one to another of the various historical modes of production he stipulated in *The German Ideology*, so Weber in his famous iron-cage lamentation at the end of *The Protestant Ethic* was unable to account for the future prospects of relief from the grinding effects of historical overrationalization save by the exceptional instance of a charismatic figure able to break the rationalizing mold. Both Marx and Weber, in effect, founded strong historical claims on the expectation of essentially ahistorical (or, better, pre- and posthistorical) variables. Wallerstein is well aware of these shortcomings of classic modern social thought. Indeed, it seems certain that, on these points, he would include both Marx and Weber in his indictment of nineteenth-century social science's reliance on a closet theory of eternal time. Yet, it is an open question whether Wallerstein's transformational TimeSpace escapes the hazards of the very double binds that limited his predecessors.

Still, it is right to pose a question of the limits of Wallerstein's idea of TimeSpace and to do so not on strict philosophical grounds but on the basis of problems in the way of any theory of history that attempts to transcend a theory of time and its desiderata that were themselves formulated within the terms of the nineteenth-century paradigm. Here, needless to say, Fernand Braudel again is the crucial reference for his thinking—one that when juxtaposed with Ilya Prigogine leads to a closing of the excluded middle of modernity's idea of historical time, as Wallerstein puts it.[28]

In the end, however, I would make the strong claim that the missing link to a more robust presentation of transformational TimeSpaces would be a theme to which Wallerstein pays relatively scant attention—namely, the technologies of the nineteenth century, which are closely linked to the scientific paradigms he so rightly attacks, yet which, as early as the 1780s, began to escape the trap of the episodic/eternal temporal binary. I suggest that the actual history of technological change in the modern era is both a strong instance of transformational TimeSpace and a history that in fact avoids, and in the end voids, episodic and eternal theories of historical time.

Wallerstein argues that space and time are human inventions rarely thought of as such. Even today, when the uncertainties of the TimeSpace relation have long been on the social theoretical table, their status as universal constants tends to be assumed.[29] This occurred, he says, after the rise of modern science over traditional philosophy as the dominant structure of (authoritative) knowledge in modernity. He claims that only two variants of TimeSpace were in fact given legitimacy—"episodic geopolitical timespace" and "eternal timespace,"[30] which make up two ends of the epistemological continuum. Episodic, geopolitical TimeSpace consists of the microevents that make up everyday life—"explanations of the immediate in time and space."[31]

It is episodic in the sense that it is embedded in a series of episodes, one event occurring after another, each in its own particular moment. Units of spatial differentiation, in this instance, are highly particular and equivalent to every other. "Every episodic moment," Wallerstein writes, "is equivalent to every other; hence no patterns which are trans-event can be discerned, because they cannot exist."[32] On the other hand, eternal TimeSpace purports to be the exact opposite. It maintains that laws hold across time and space, disavowing the particularity of contexts. As Wallerstein rightly points out, the major problem with this dichotomous approach to space and time is that most people do not live in social realities made up of two antonymous TimeSpaces. Inevitably, most people exist fluidly, migrating between at least two, if not more, TimeSpaces.

As in all things of his doing, Wallerstein's account of the TimeSpace divorce in modern culture is historical, which explains the prominence of a critique of the decisively modern conceptions in his own notion of the modern world-system. Modernity, he avows, necessarily involved the breaking down of the traditions of the church, which occurred with the rise of two intellectual movements: the Renaissance and the Reformation. These two movements had in common the de-deification of knowledge. Many social theorists have made this claim, including Anthony Giddens,[33] who has argued that modernity could very well be characterized as "posttraditional"—that is, based intellectually in a postreligious knowledge. But Wallerstein's point is quite unique in that he recognizes the methodological individualism that lay behind and came to the fore in the toppling of the church's dominion over the intellectual structures of Christendom. As he writes,

> Both [the Renaissance and the Reformation] involved the assertion that truth can be ascertained directly by human beings, in one case by insight into the natural laws of the universe, in the other by insight into the mysterious ways of God. But in both cases, truth was ascertained on the de facto authority of the one who had the insight, and in theory everyone might have such insight, or at least it was not an option that was linked to holding some office.[34]

Weber's famous argument as to the religious foundations of the individualism inherent in the protestantizing ethic is well-known. Wallerstein adds a deeper appreciation of the early effects of secularizing philosophy on, eventually, the geoculture of the modern era and the social sciences as they came to be in the nineteenth century.

This "revolt of the philosophers" against the theologians in the eighteenth and nineteenth centuries would turn in the twentieth into a revolt of the scientists against the philosophers, marked by a gradual but evident movement of philosophy and science away from each other. Analytic philosophies that sought to perfect the logic of science eventually faded away into a variety of un-ruly breaks, of which Ludwig Wittgenstein's *Philosophical Investigations* (1953; posthumous) is the *locus post classicus*. Thereafter, following Wittgenstein's lead, if not his example, language came to be not so much the pure, practical medium of truth as the primary surface of philosophical work—hence, Roland Barthes, Claude Lévi-Strauss, Jacques Lacan, Jürgen Habermas, Richard Rorty, Jacques Derrida, Michel Foucault, and many others. The transposition, however, was not caused by Wittgenstein (hardly); rather, it was a reaction to widespread uncertainties as to knowledge's ability to grasp the real historical events of the twentieth century that began in 1914 with what Wallerstein calls a thirty years war in Europe (1914–1945). This revolt against pure science, of which Theodor Adorno and Max Horkheimer and the Frankfurt tradition generally were the true originators, took an important, if not globally important, turn after the World Revolution of 1968 and its entailments. Thereupon arose a no less conspicuous divorce between the natural and human sciences. The challenges to pure social science, represented by, at the least, Habermas's *Knowledge and Human Interests* (1968) and, in another cultural disposition, the emergence of the French School after the important texts of Foucault and Derrida of 1966 and 1967,[35] constituted in the universities a riot of rethinking that, soon after, became the target for the now notorious culture wars. On all fronts, the ultimate outcome of the revolt against pure science rendered C. P. Snow's *Two Cultures* (1959) at once apt and passé—as a distinctively twentieth-century concern that the nineteenth was unable to resolve.

Another way still to define the issue—a way entirely consistent with Wallerstein's own philosophical positions—is that, from the point of view of the social sciences, the twentieth century, short though it was, became the century in which history as such intruded upon the calm of modernity's claim to a pure practical (hence philosophical) reason. The twentieth century was the most violent in human history. This is well agreed upon. The European diaspora's violence was executed under the cloak of its idealization of its own history as the history of humankind—what Wallerstein calls European universalism and its homologues: the ideologies of the self-evident superiority of the Western cultures and of the logically universal merits of liberal and neoliberal markets. In historical terms, Wallerstein predicts that the long period of uncertainty initiated by the World Revolution of 1968 reinforced the uncertainty that "the last and most powerful of European universal-isms—scientific universalism—is no longer unquestioned in its authority."[36]

Though Wallerstein engages the more philosophical question of essen-tialism at a distance, his critique of the limits of pan-European universalism clearly joins, however gingerly, the cultural Left's anti-essentialist attack on the grand narrative of modern man's evolution from the dark past of pure and abstract being into the philosophical movements spawned by the Renaissance and Reformation, of which the Enlightenment was the full, if not complete, blossoming. Though the axial virtues of these secularizing movements were, from the start, unstable, they were exposed in the events on either side of 1968 as an ambitious but fundamentally ridiculous ideology with at best a tenuous basis in actual history.

In effect, whether one speaks of political theories or philosophical epistemologies, modern universals of all kinds are in truth the most fungible of concepts—ideas that, while articulated in a variety of individualisms, fed off a philosophical idealism that drew its resources from classically platonic and neo-platonic theories of human rationality—of which René Descartes is as good as any a point of departure. This long tradition, exceptions and contestations here and there being noted, eventuated in the eighteenth and nineteenth centuries in a philosophical neoidealism that drew its energy, if not its logic, from Protestant religious ideas in the sixteenth century. Hence, in the common parody of Weber's ethic of disenchantment, Protestantism was it own gravedigger. Secular rationality, either in epistemology or political theory, was itself always half-baked, as are all varieties of idealism that require equally the philosophical death of the gods and the articulation of their functional equivalents in such forms as Descartes's cogito or Kant's moral imperative or, even, in the entailments of materialisms: Marx's socialist utopia and Freud's superego. Here, then, from still another angle, in the inner workings of modern philosophy and social science are the systematic instabilities that came to be known as liberalism.

*   *   *

The social and human sciences were marked and defined to a large extent by contradictions between their own classically modern positivisms and the empirical realities of unstable markets, scantily autonomous states, continuous (if intermittent) social revolutions, and other countervailing evidences that the modern paradigm of good events producing reliable progress was, if not bankrupt, at least overdrawn on a dwindling cash reserve. Recognition of these unthinkable uncertainties was, in many ways, most evident in the strains within and among the social sciences—that is, those disciplines too new, therefore, too distinctly modern, to take any definitive side within this drama between the old and new epistemological modes: the positivist and the hermeneutic.[37] For sociology, in particular, this methodological tension was relieved by the ascendancy of positivism, which favored the use of contemporaneous data—that is, data collected immediately by the researcher within a given period. The tension lay in the unacknowledged practical reality that all social and cultural data must be cooked over time such that, by the time their offerings are served, the structural claims they dish up refer to structures long since rotten if not outright dead. In terms of TimeSpace, data could only be properly referred to as existing within episodic, geopolitical TimeSpace, though with very unusual characteristics that also resembled eternal TimeSpace. Sociology and the other nomothetic disciplines, such as economics and political science, asserted the right to project the minutiae of their empirical findings, harvested from episodic, geopolitical TimeSpace (in respect to which they are called "findings") mapped onto an eternal TimeSpace phantasmagoria.

For anthropology and other idiographic social sciences, the same problem was turned on its head. In almost direct contrast, the preferred method was not closeness but distance. In other words, the researcher could minimize the observer effects of personal motivations when studying social things situated at an exotic remove. Thus, the anthropologist and historian studied spaces and times distal to their own, which figurative distancing guaranteed intellectual intimacy but emotional detachment. Yet, in terms of TimeSpace, the idiographic disciplines retrieved data within episodic, geopolitical TimeSpace, but like their nomothetic counterparts, they deployed a microcosmic methodology such that the detailed findings of a particular time and space were projected onto a movie-like screen where realities were projected into an illusion of universally pertinent laws of the social universe that even beggars outside the theater would reject were it not for their hunger.[38]

Wallerstein, mostly lucidly, identifies these methodological maneuvers within disciplinary social knowledge as a primary instance of Orientalism:

> Orientalism was the form of hypocrisy that vice had now to pay to virtue. For the heart of the Orientalist argument was that even if it were true that Oriental "civilizations" were as culturally rich and sophisticated as Western-Christian civilization, and therefore in some sense its peers, it remained the case that they had a small but crucial defect, the same in each of them. It was asserted that there was something in them that made then incapable of proceeding to "modernity." They have become frozen, suffering a sort of cultural lockjaw, which could be considered a cultural malady.[39]

Or, crudely put, at the heart of Orientalist faith is not so much the absence of reason as the lack of an indefinite but deep structural capacity for the apprehension (in both senses of the term) of the cultural meanings that distinguish the modern from its others. It hardly need be said that Wallerstein had to have drawn this distinction before he demonstrated the analytic range and fungibility of TimeSpace theory as it came into the mix of world-systems analysis. At the same time, in a point to which I will return, the same point that unsettles both the assurances associated with the modern world-system as *the* unit of historical (hence, global) analysis and the question of whether, upon the decline of the modern system, any other system will arise, from whichever global sector, if any, to reorganize global things in a manner that could be called a system of any kind.

The methodological sins of incongruence in the social sciences resulted in the polarization of the conceptions of TimeSpaces and the disavowal of at least three other TimeSpaces—cyclicoideologcal, structural, and transformational.[40]

Cyclicoideologcal TimeSpace, first, does not refer to the cyclical theories of history like those of Toynbee or Spengler. Rather, he means "cycles that occur within the functioning of particular historical systems and which are in effect the regulatory mechanisms of these systems."[41] To make the distinction, Wallerstein employs a figure from metabolic physiology. Homeostasis is, thus, put forth as the regulatory mechanism of historical social systems. As cellular biochemistry tends toward metabolic equilibrium, so, too, do social systems develop and maintain patterned cultural and ideological norms within certain spatial bounds. The concept, thus put, bears an apparent unfortunate comparison to Talcott Parsons's AGIL paradigm and, more fortuitously, to Niklas Luhmann's theory of the autopoiesis of social systems.[42] But, appearances aside, the difference is that Wallerstein does not intend a general theory of action systems. His idea of cyclicoideologcal TimeSpace is founded in a concern for historical change and stability—thus to answer the crucial question of how certain spatial parameters can have ideological markers. For example, the ability to refer to certain "stages" of capitalism (e.g., mercantile, industrial, and postindustrial) or even eras of modernity (e.g., early, late, and post) entails what Wallerstein calls "geocultural norms of historical systems." In other words, ideological spaces are limited by periods of time.[43] Wary of the limited explanatory potential of cyclicoideologcal TimeSpace, Wallerstein points to structural TimeSpace, which would curb the potential for regressing into the episodic, geopolitical TimeSpace.

Structural TimeSpace, he argues, is (in principle, if not always in reality) the key analytic in social sciences that aim to examine social continuity and change as they affect social interaction and conflict. Structural TimeSpace is, in a word, the space and time of social structures. As, again, Wallerstein says,

> Structural TimeSpace speaks to what we cannot change (the system in the short run) and what will surely change (the system in the long run), and why the system doesn't really change in the short run (the cyclical rhythms) and why it in fact does change in the long run (the secular trends, leading far from equilibrium).[44]

Yet, Wallerstein continues, structural TimeSpace, as traditionally conceived, falters before the same limitations that humble both eternal TimeSpace and episodic geopolitical TimeSpace. Eternal and episodic geopolitical TimeSpaces suffer from the fallacy of an abstract and static view of historical reality, neglecting what is surely Wallerstein's most important aspect of TimeSpace—the transformational.

Transformational TimeSpace, to repeat, is "the moment of transition from one kind of historical system to another, from one mode of organizing social life to another," which occurs when a historical system "has exhausted its mechanisms of reequilibrating itself, has used up the efficacy of the cyclical rhythms, has gone sufficiently far from equilibrium that the oscillations have become relatively wild and unpredictable."[45]

Here, precisely, is where the influence of Ilya Prigogine is pointed. Wallerstein describes an unpredictable new order emerging out of the chaos into which a historical system falls.[46] Where Prigogine had in mind thermodynamic systems—that is, changes in natural systems—Wallerstein's adaptation of complexity theory refers to the social historical "moment of bifurcation" in transformational TimeSpace. He writes,

> This moment of transformational change, or rather of the possibility of transformational change, has two vectors that are decisive. One is the political struggle between those who hold different, opposing value-systems. But the second is *the struggle within the world of knowledge, which determines whether we can clarify the historical alternatives that we face, make more lucid our choices, both criticize and empower those who are engaged in the political struggle (from which of course the world of knowledge is unable to dissociate itself).*[47]

The connection between politics and epistemology in Wallerstein's theory of TimeSpaces is clear. The struggle in the world of knowledge, as he characterizes it, is necessary to determine the historical significance of political action. In other words, an epistemological shift—or in Gaston Bachelard's original phrase, an "epistemological break"—would inform a new politics that would be more sensitive to the dynamism of transformational TimeSpace; hence, the salience of transformational TimeSpace to the present situation early in the 2000s.

THE LESSONS OF COMPLEXITY STUDIES
FOR THE MODERN WORLD-SYSTEM

The emphasis on transformational TimeSpace serves to lay the groundwork for what Wallerstein calls an "epistemological revolution" in social science.[48] One of his most acute ideas on epistemological revolutions is that transformational TimeSpace undermines both eternal TimeSpace and episodic, geopolitical TimeSpace because a crucial tenet of transformational TimeSpace is an inversion of the degree of importance attributed to certainty and stability. "Equilibria are temporary," says Wallerstein, "and all systems tend over time to move away from equilibria."[49] In terms of social science, this notion of complexity and far-from-equilibrated systems opens the possibility of studying social life without constructing a false notion of unchanging spatiotemporal stability, leaving open the possibility of reconsidering even the definition of society.

To be sure, Wallerstein's engagement with complexity studies, especially Prigogine's, is closely linked to his interest in geopolitics and geoculture in the framework of world-systems analysis. Wallerstein's ability to draw resource from advances in the natural sciences is so agile as potentially to mask the extent to which the borrowing is, in a way, absorbed into the basic tenets of world-systems analysis—absorbed, that is, without transforming the implicit theory of the modern world-system into a robust theory of historical complexities. And nowhere is the stolidity of the world-system in its historical aspect more analytically fixed than in respect to the spatial element in Wallerstein's TimeSpace.

The fundamental spatial principle of world-systems analysis remains the structural tensions between the core and the periphery. Though Wallerstein draws most significantly from Braudel's own spatialization of the three times of history, the infusion of Prigogine's complexity theory does not appreciably alter the analytic inclination of the core/periphery paradigm to be itself a representation of the dispersed spaces of modern TimeSpace. The core is the social space by which cultural, economic, and geopolitical power is articulated upon the periphery. To be sure, in this respect, one crosses the line from a general theory of TimeSpace to its analytic application to a temporal logic of modern capitalism's dependence on the ability of the core states to maintain the rank order—hence spatial fixedness—of the system as such. Both in historical fact and analytic design, the core serves as the stabilizing force of the modern world-system.

If we are to draw a parallel between the terminologies of complexity studies and world-systems analysis, it would be necessary to stipulate the successive cores as the equilibrating force of the modern world-system. Still, Wallerstein has recently made moves to argue the importance of liberal culture in the maintenance and functioning of the modern system. Liberal ideology maintains the "central position" of the geoculture of the world-system.[50] Liberalism (as well as its recent revisions) represents what, in opposition to the original tenets of systems theory, Gilbert Simondon refers to as the "metastability" of nonlinear systems, in which equilibrium is not necessary for the functioning of the system as a whole.[51] In point of fact, Wallerstein is making a point regarding the political ideology of liberalism that others have chosen to call neoliberalism, and to make it with a slightly different, more acute emphasis.[52]

In keeping with earlier arguments, Wallerstein identifies the liberal synthesis with the geoculture that emerged after 1848 and endured more or less intact until 1989–1991, when it fell headlong into the crisis that first broke in the World Revolution of 1968, then collapsed in the events of 2001–2003. Liberalism functions (or functioned) as a regulatory centrism that creates highly dynamic thresholds that stave off complete entropy while allowing the system to function. In the language of complexity studies, the liberal order maintains a center that is able to "create" chaos (or decentering), which in turn is able to create a new order. Hence, in the current moment of early-twenty-first-century uncertainties, Wallerstein's tendency to describe the crisis and instabilities of the modern world order assumes that a new system will in due (if hard to predict) course eventually reassert itself. "All systems are historic, and all history is systematic."[53]

Yet, even in his reckoning with culture—where he meant to respond to criticisms that his original scheme lacked a theory of culture[54]—Wallerstein's retains the basic spatial theory of the core/periphery. The idea of the multiplicity of TimeSpaces that emerged in the 1980s is one of the few serious considerations of the concept of nonlinear and equilibrium-indifferent systems in sociology. Nonetheless, in breaking down the nineteenth-century paradigms of time and space, Wallerstein, even in his championing of complexity studies, puts forth a normative theory that asserts that we must think of time and space differently. In the glossary appended to *World-Systems Analysis: An Introduction* (2004), the definitive succinct summary of his position, Wallerstein defines TimeSpace:

> The capitalization and running-together of the two terms reflects the view that for every kind of SOCIAL TIME, there exists a particular kind of social space. Thus, time and space should not be thought of as separate, measured separately, but as irrevocably linked into a limited number of combinations.[55]

The definition reflects, at the least, a detectable ambivalence instigated by the concept itself. If, indeed, TimeSpace owes the debt Wallerstein attributes to complexity theory, then it may not be enough simply to run the terms "time" and "space" together while also maintaining an evident correspondence theory in the form of "for every time there exists a particular kind of social space." One wonders whether in this irrevocable linking it is enough to stipulate a "limited number of combinations" as the principle of irregularities (if that is what, as I assume, is intended).

It is undoubtedly so that, say, medieval or feudal time, having been otherworldly, was a time that froze history under the glacial force of otherworldly space. In such worlds as these, the otherworldly effect is imposed on this world in respect to axial institutions, notably the throne and the church or their functional equivalents outside occidental cultures. Rome and Beijing, for two instances, are just so—the City of God and the City of Man (as Augustine put it) and the Temple of Heaven and the Forbidden City (as the Ming and Qing dynasties reconstructed the earlier Han center of China). In the former, local spires centered the settled locales by pointing to their transcending spaces. In the latter, still today China is politically and culturally centered in the space of its capital city, in a spatial form symbolizing the centrality of the party—this by locating Mao Zedong's tomb and the Great Hall of the People on the once-sacred square of dynastic China. By consequence, its still most prominent global city, Shanghai, is among the municipalities administered directly by the capital.

By contrast, modernizing theories of social space, being in principle this-worldly, were organized in respect to a linear theory of time consistent with a hierarchical principle of global space. Globally, the principle of axial space—whether traditional or modernizing—was, in effect, a variant of the cyclicoideologcal spatial forms that Wallerstein's world-systems analysis means to critique. There is little room for argument with Wallerstein's intent to distinguish the TimeSpaces of the world-system after the sixteenth century. Since the establishment of the Iberian cores, the peripheries were subjected to cores precisely because of the disjunctions between and among their times—disjunctions that rendered peripheries vulnerable to the avarice of the modern core states in their invention and imposition of a geoculture of so-called modern time as *the* time that corresponds to the dominating authority of the modern state, epitomized in the successive cores. This, we assume, is a notion taken from, among others, Frantz Fanon, whom Wallerstein acknowledges as an important, early influence on this thinking.[56]

It is unquestionably so that in the TimeSpaces of the modern world-system and its predecessor systems (or rival systems, as André Gunder Frank argued[57]) there was a "limited number of combinations." But I would suggest and will argue below, if a thorough going concept of TimeSpaces (plural) is to be applied to the analysis of the late or declining modern worlds, then, though the number of combinations of time and space may remain limited, a more robust complexity theory may be necessary—that is, one in which the relations of times to their spaces may be, for all intents and purposes, very much more arbitrary, fluid, and even complex to the point of chaos. Some might call this a limitation of Wallerstein's theory of TimeSpaces; more aptly, it should be seen as an entailment of the challenges of his analytic method with respect to the issue he has confronted, notably in the essays in and since *The Decline of American Power* (2003).

UNCERTAIN WORLDS

Prophet or not, Wallerstein is certain in his assessment that in the early decades of the twenty-first century and for time to come, the world-system has entered into decisively, and will remain in for time to come, a period of disequilibrium, bifurcated by the collapse of its own overreachings; hence, we must think of worlds (as before), but now think of them as undeniably uncertain. What will come after—whether a reequilibration of a version of the modern world-system or some other system of global magnitude—we cannot say. Here the prophecy comes to its point of indeterminacy. In his political writings since 2001, in particular, Wallerstein seems to be of the mind that we are left with an uncertain left politics. It is almost as if he is willing to grant that, whatever the worlds are or will become, the vestiges of the older liberal synthesis still hold the upper hand. This leaves the radical Left, such as it is, to push against the still dominant, if shaken, liberal powers.

The collapse of the liberal center is thus (and ironically) precisely the critical aspect of the current situation, mostly acutely since 2001–2003.[58] In this respect, the failure of the liberal synthesis is most telling in leftist or radical politics—particularly the now questionable status of antisystemic movements that, through much of the twentieth century, had been identifiable as socialist or nationalist. What is striking, however, is how systematic Wallerstein is in respect to the fates of socialist and nationalist antisystemic movements up to the beginning of the transformational time of global structures around 1968, and how, in reference to the thereafter, he seems to appeal increasingly to a loose concept of zones as a way of locating the instabilities of the global Left.

Though questions of the future prospects of the world-system appeared in general terms early in the 1980s (in, for example, the conclusion to *Historical Capitalism*[59]) and became quite explicit early in the 1990s (beginning with the truly prophetic essay that first appeared in *Theory and Society*[60]), the strongest statements were, quite naturally, in essays early in the 2000s, notably those collected in the concluding section of *The Decline of American Power* (2003).[61] Though Wallerstein offers a more succinct statement of the crises at the end of *World-Systems Analysis* (2004), the four essays at the end of *Decline* are, at once, the more fulsome statement of the crisis and of the dilemmas of politics in the period of uncertainty. The first ("The Left I: Theory and Praxis Once Again") is a focused reprise of ideas found in earlier texts (notably *After Liberalism*). But the two following are the more symptomatic ("The Left II: An Age of Transition" and "The Movements: What Does It Mean to Be Antisystemic Today?"). Here, Wallerstein takes stock of the effects of the crisis. As he put it elsewhere, and most succinctly, "The cultural shock of 1968 unhinged the automatic dominance of the liberal center which had prevailed in the world-system since the prior world revolution of 1848."[62] Politically the effect of 1968 was the blow dealt at least to the ideological foundations of the political array that, with ebbs and flows, had prevailed since 1848. Against the synthetic liberal center were set socialist and nationalist antisystemic movements that were (and, given Wallerstein's theory of bifurcation, that remain, to a degree) dispersed in zones against the liberal core: socialist to the east, nationalist to the south (where east and south are taken somewhat metaphorically or, better, orientationally).

When he turns to a discussion of the left political movements that may arise in and after the crisis, we find little more than a politics of possibilities:

1. Expand the spirit of Porto Alegre.
2. Use defensive electoral justice.
3. Push democracy unceasingly.
4. Make the liberal center fulfill its theoretical preferences.
5. Make antiracism the defining measure of democracy.
6. Move toward decommodification.
7. Remember always that we are living in the era of transition from our existing world-system to something different.[63]

One can hardly quibble with the virtue of the seven principles themselves. Yet, one can inquire into their nature—more general than systematic, more generic than strongly left, more abstract than direct to a possible analysis of the political spaces of political actions. Of course, it is evident that anyone trying to formulate a left politics for the crisis of the world-system will face the problem of a lack of structural foundation.

> I believe that a number of trends have today at last reached points where they threaten the basic functioning of the system.... Capitalism as a historical system is defined by the fact that it makes structurally central and primary the endless accumulation of capital. This means that the institutions which constitute its framework reward those who pursue the endless accumulation of capital and penalize those who don't.[64]

The critical threats after the 1990s are the three inexorable costs limiting capitalism's accumulative demands: the costs of labor, of input and infrastructure, and of taxation. These are the basic, if not exclusive, systematic factors that explain the crisis of the world-system. Wallerstein discusses them in a number of places where he has been quite clear, extensive, and analytic.[65]

The obvious problem with the new principles of left antisystemic politics is that when one is proposing politics meant to resist or transform (or even encourage the transformation of) a world-system that has been well structured over a half millennium, the loss of its structural salience (including the orderly capabilities of its almost two-centuries-old political ideologies), one is left with a lack. How are politics to be antisystemic when the system is, if not in ruins, at least in disarray? On a general level, Wallerstein proposes to manage this challenge by resorting to Prigogine's chaos theory, in particular the prospect of systemic bifurcation:

> Since the existing system can no longer function adequately within its defined parameters, ... a choice about the way out, about the future system (or systems) ... is inevitable. The process of bifurcation is chaotic, which means that every small action during this period [of crisis] is likely to have significant consequences ... [and] the system tends to oscillate wildly.... The modern world-system in which we are living, which is that of the capitalist world-economy, is currently in precisely such a crisis and has been for quite a while now [2004].[66]

Though the word "bifurcation" may to some degree imply a simple two-path breaking apart, the point made is actually stronger in its references to the chaotic state of the "system [that] tends to oscillate wildly." Still, the sentence immediately following is more in keeping with Wallerstein's conviction that systems always eventually return to homeostasis: "But eventually it leans in one direction."[67] And here, precisely, is where and when the issue of TimeSpace rubs up against the effects of a strong system claim on left politics.

The effect of conceiving a world-system as able to outrun a period of transformative TimeSpace puts left politics in a complicated bind. Where is the ground of action? What is the time of politics? What is the structured object of political movement or resistance? These are the basic questions of left politics in any time. They are, it would seem, all the more perplexing in a time of uncertainty.

Wallerstein's response is a strong and historically subtle diagnosis of the decline—a diagnosis that continues well after *Decline* (2003) in a series of essays and articles.[68] Yet, the overriding impression of the writings since 2003 is that the proposals for a left politics refer to largely ungrounded general principles like those (listed above) from "The Left II: An Age of Transition," of which the first is in many ways the most telling. "Expand the spirit of Porto Alegre" is a theme that appears in several places, most prominently as one of the three cleavages (or bifurcations?) in the post-1991 world-system outlined in the fourth of the essays in the political section of *Decline,* "Geopolitical Cleavages of the Twenty-First Century: What Future for the World?" The World Social Forum (WSF), associated by name with the site of its first meeting in January 2001 in Porto Alegre, Brazil, has indeed been a left- and social justice–based antisystemic movement. But when stacked up against the force of the neoliberal spirit of Davos (the World Economic Forum), the spirit of Porto Alegre is in effect heavy on spirit, light on groundwork. It remains to be seen whether the success of the antiglobalizing—hence antisystemic—worldwide Lefts will amount to much more than singular successes here and there, like their precursor movement against the World Trade Organization in 1999 in Seattle. But a close reading of the WSF's Charter of Principles adopted in 2001 reveals an organizing spirit that is antisystemic, to be sure, but also based on rather straightforward liberal principles of free discussion, rejection of state inference, open democratic procedures, and the like.[69]

There is room to quibble, even argue, with Wallerstein's political proposals for these uncertain times. But once it is agreed that the times—meaning the times of the real worlds of economic and social lives—are uncertain, then all quibbles are on the table. It is not, I think now (once having thought differently), that there is much left to contend with in the worlds as they are part of a weak (to be sure) but still powerful liberal system (however broken or bifurcated). Certainly, this uncertainty requires a politics that pushes, cajoles, attacks, and, where it might be for the common good, dismantles what remains of the liberal synthesis. Just as certain, what remains of the conservative politics in many worlds (and most acutely in the United States) is a kind of dumb certitude about old, old verities that have long since proven themselves bone weary to the point of death. And what remains at the other extreme of the radical traditions that survived 1848 is at best a liberal social democracy in Europe and a weak, episodic progressive movement in the United States. Neither of the three major alternatives—radical, right, and liberal—are enduringly viable except when from time to time, in differing degrees and by varying methods, one of them assumes a measure of (usually) shared power then to try as it might to assert or impose its version of a lost system.

What is to come in these uncertain worlds is what will come. The Left, by whatever name, cannot sit this one out, as too often in the past it has; nor can it continue to talk the old talk that no longer walks the hard lines. Everywhere the realities of uncertainty are apparent, for those who would see. Wallerstein has his view on these things. Where he goes far beyond the prophet is by his refusal to denounce the worlds as they are, thereby to warn the righteous to mend their ways. He makes his own ways, and, as in all things, his ways are sober and determined. It is up to others to show that there is a better way to right uncertain worlds like these.

NOTES

1. Immanuel Wallerstein, "America and the World: Today, Yesterday, and Tomorrow," *Theory and Society* 21 (1992): 1–28.

2. See, for a list of the best criticisms from various perspectives, Immanuel Wallerstein, *World-Systems Analysis: An Introduction* (Durham, NC: Duke University Press, 2004), 103; and Stanley Aronowitz, "A Metatheoretical Critique of Immanuel Wallerstein's *The Modern World-System*," *Theory and Society* 10 (1981): 503–20.

3. See, among others, the following by Immanuel Wallerstein: *Geopolitics and Geoculture: Essays on the Changing World-System* (Cambridge: Cambridge University Press and Maison de Sciences de l'Homme, 1991); *Unthinking Social Science: Limits of Nineteenth Century Paradigms* (Cambridge: Polity Press, 1991); *After Liberalism* (New York: The New Press, 1995); and *The Uncertainties of Knowledge* (Philadelphia: Temple University Press, 2004).

4. For an exemplary, if skeptical, summary of narrative in social science, see Charles Tilly, "Future Social Science," in *Roads from Past to Future* (Lanham, MD: Rowman & Littlefield, 1997), 17–33.

5. Joseph A. Schumpeter, *The Theory of Economic Development* (Cambridge, MA: Harvard University Press), 74.

6. W. W. Rostow, *The Stages of Economic Growth: A Non-Communist Manifesto* (Cambridge: Cambridge University Press, 1960), 51.

7. Rostow, *The Stages of Economic Growth*, 51–52; emphasis added.

8. Immanuel Wallerstein, *Historical Capitalism with Capitalist Civilization* (London: Verso, 1983), 17–18; emphasis added.

9. Ibid., 31.

10. Rostow, *The Stages of Economic Growth*, 11–12

11. Rankings are for 2011 according to the International Monetary Fund.

12. Wallerstein, *World-Systems Analysis: An Introduction*, 93.

13. Statements here and in the following paragraph are from the World Bank home page in 2010.

14. Giorgio Agamben, *Homo Sacer: Sovereign Power and Bare Life* (Stanford, CA: Stanford University Press, 1998).

15. Immanuel Wallerstein, "The Inventions of TimeSpace Realities: Towards an Understanding of Our Historical Systems," in *Unthinking Social Science: Limits of the Nineteenth Century Paradigms* (Cambridge: Polity Press, 1991); originally appeared in *Geography* 87, no. 9 (October 1988).

16. Immanuel Wallerstein, "SpaceTime as the Basis of Knowledge," keynote address at *Convergencia*, the World Congress of Convergence, Cartagena, Colombia, May 31 to June 5, 1997; subsequently published in Orlando Fals Borda, id., comp., *People's Participations: Challenges Ahead* (Bogota: Colciencias, 1998), 43–62. One notes the different usage of the key phrase: here, in the title, "SpaceTime," which later becomes "TimeSpace," which seems to have become the settled usage. As the idea took shape in the 1990s and since, "TimeSpaces" (plural) and an emendation that better reflects the salience of Prigogine's complexity theories, which are prominently about time's variance.

17. Immanuel Wallerstein, "Time and Duration: The Unexcluded Middle, or Reflections on Braudel and Prigogine," in *The Uncertainties of Knowledge* (Philadelphia: Temple University Press, 2004), ch. 5; originally published in *Thesis Eleven* 54, no. 1 (1998).

18. See the following by Immanuel Wallerstein: *Unthinking Social Science: Limits of Nineteenth Century Paradigms* (Cambridge: Polity Press, 1991); *The End of the World as We Know It: Social Science for the Twenty-First Century* (Minneapolis: University of Minnesota Press, 1999); *The Uncertainties of Knowledge* (Philadelphia: Temple University Press, 2004).

19. Immanuel Wallerstein, *After Liberalism* (New York: The New Press, 1995), *Utopistics: Or Historical Choices for the Twenty-First Century* (New York: The New Press, 1998), and *The Decline of American Power: The U.S. in a Chaotic World* (New York: The New Press, 2003).

20. I use "I" here in spite of the fact that a good bit of the following section is from Charles Lemert and Sam Han, "Whither the Time of World Structures after the Decline of Modern Space," *Review* 31, no. 4 (2009): 441–466. The use is with San Han's kind permission, as by prior arrangement with the editors of *Review*.

21. Immanuel Wallerstein, "SpaceTime as the Basis of Knowledge" (1997), 1 (here and hereafter reference is made to the online version at http://www2.binghamton.edu/fbc/archive/iwsptm.htm).

22. Notably Wallerstein's *Unthinking Social Science* (2001), *The End of the World as We Know It* (2001), and *The Uncertainties of Knowledge* (2004).

23. Wallerstein, *World-Systems Analysis,* ch. 4; compare with *The End of the World as We Know It,* especially part 3, and *The Uncertainties of Knowledge,* among other places.

24. Wallerstein has famously refrained from calling his conceptual scheme a theory. I admit to breaching this rule in part because locutions like "analytic formula" are awkward and in part because, at least when it comes to the specifics of TimeSpaces, the position is a theory—albeit a theory of the excluded middle as distinct from an operational theory of the middle range.

25. Wallerstein, "SpaceTime as the Basis of Knowledge," 2.

26. Ibid., 7.

27. Ibid., 8.

28. Wallerstein, "Time and Duration," 71–82.

29. Among the important examples of attempts to account for the uncertainties are the centrality of cultural geography and time-space to Anthony Giddens's structuration theory in *The Constitution of Society: An Outline of the Theory of Structuration* (Berkeley: University of California Press, 1984), ch. 3; Pierre Bourdieu's theory of social and symbolic spaces in *Practical Reason: On the Theory of Action* (Paris: Editions du Seuil, 1984; Cambridge: Polity Press, 1998), among other places; Manuel Castells's network theory in, inter alia, *The Rise of the Network Society* (Oxford: Blackwell Publishing, 1996); or David Harvey's critical geography in, among other places, *Spaces of Capital: Toward a Critical Geography* (London: Routledge, 2001), esp. part 2. Even these, probative though they are, do not go as far as Wallerstein in calling into question theories of time-space as fixed, if uncertain. Each, in the end, reverts to a quasi-invariance: in the renewal of structures in a necessary reflexivity (Giddens), the dispersion of practices in a field of action (Bourdieu), and the settled, if still to be formed, global information networks as

the site of capital accumulation (Castells) or of the production of space itself (Harvey). For a promising exception to this drift and a position that, like Wallerstein's (though from a much different point of view), avoids invariance in the theory of TimeSpace, see Zygmunt Bauman, *Liquid Modernity* (Cambridge: Polity Press, 2000), ch. 3.

30. Wallerstein, "SpaceTime as the Basis of Knowledge," 1–2.

31. Ibid., 2.

32. Ibid.

33. See Anthony Giddens, *Capitalism and Modern Social Theory* (Cambridge: Cambridge University Press, 1973); also Anthony Giddens, "Living in a Post-Traditional Society," in *Reflexive Modernization: Politics, Tradition and Aesthetics in the Modern Social Order,* ed. Ulrich Beck, Anthony Giddens, and Scott Lash (Palo Alto, CA: Stanford University Press, 1994).

34. Wallerstein, "SpaceTime as the Basis of Knowledge," 2.

35. Michel Foucault, *Order of Things* (New York: Random House, [1966] 1970); Jacques Derrida, *Of Grammatology* (Baltimore: Johns Hopkins University Press, [1967] 1974), and *Writing and Difference* (Chicago: University of Chicago Press, [1967] 1978).

36. Immanuel Wallerstein, *European Universalism: The Rhetoric of Power* (New York: The New Press, 2006), 70; here he also speaks about C. P. Snow's two cultures.

37. Wallerstein, "SpaceTime as the Basis of Knowledge," 3.

38. Though our interpretation may, at points, diverge from Wallerstein's, its debt to his should be plain—especially in a recent and remarkably succinct summary of the contradictions endemic to the social sciences; see Wallerstein, *European Universalism,* 61–69.

39. Ibid., 75.

40. Here, the reference is to Wallerstein, "SpaceTime as the Basis of Knowledge," 6–8.

41. Wallerstein, *European Universalism,* 5.

42. Talcott Parsons, "An Outline of the Social System," in *Theories of Society* (New York: The Free Press, 1961), 30–79; and Niklas Luhmann, "The Autopoiesis of Social Systems," in *Essays on Self-Reference* (New York: Columbia University Press, 1990). In both the homeostatic mechanism appears in many places. Also, in both association is made to cybernetics, notably in Luhmann's theory of the autopoiesis of social systems, which is based on the second-order cybernetics notion of autopoiesis as articulated by neurophysiologists Humberto Maturana and Fransisco Varela.

43. One open question is the precise status in this respect of Wallerstein's frequent references to Kondratieff A and B cycles. We take them at face value as a way of punctuating historical fluctuations in modern economies, yet note that they are vulnerable to a kind of cyclical interpretation.

44. Wallerstein, "SpaceTime as the Basis of Knowledge," 7.

45. Ibid., 7.

46. Ibid.; see also works by Ilya Prigogine and Isabelle Stengers, notably *Order Out of Chaos: Man's New Dialogue with Nature* (Millbrook, NY: Flamingo, 1985), and *The End of Certainty* (New York: The Free Press, 1997).

47. Wallerstein, "SpaceTime as the Basis of Knowledge," 7; emphasis added.

48. Ibid., 8.

49. Ibid.

50. Ibid.

51. See Gilbert Simondon, "The Genesis of the Individual," trans. M. Cohen and S. Kwinter, in *Incorporations,* ed. Jonathan Crary and Sanford Kwinter (New York: Zone, 1992), 297–319.

52. Among many works on the subject, see David Harvey, *A Brief History of Neoliberalism* (Oxford: Oxford University Press, 2005), and Aihwa Ong, *Neoliberalism as Exception: Mutations in Citizenship and Sovereignty* (Durham, NC: Duke University Press, 2006).

53. Wallerstein, *European Universalism,* 83. Recently, Brian Massumi has interestingly attempted to work out a similar problematic, arguing that under the Bush administration, the dominant *dispositif* of politics was that of the "affective fact." He describes the post-9/11 ontology of threat within the logic of what he calls "radical neoconservatism": "If we feel a threat, such that there was a threat, then there always will have been a threat. Threat is once and for all, in the nonlinear time of its own causing." Whereas Wallerstein identifies liberalism as having this function of "creating chaos," Massumi suggests it is that of the affective transmission of terrorist "threat" that allows for the future-oriented creation of "chaos"—or in this scenario, terrorism. See Brian Massumi, "The Future Birth of Affective Fact: The Political Ontology of Threat," in *Conference Proceedings: Genealogies of Biopolitics,* October 2005, at http://browse.reticular.info/text/collected/massumi.pdf (accessed May 1, 2012).

54. For example, in his estimation, the best criticism was Stanley Aronowtiz, "A Metatheoretical Critique of Immanuel Wallerstein's *The Modern World-System,*" *Theory and Society* 10 (1981): 503–20.

55. Wallerstein, *World-Systems Analysis,* 98.

56. Immanuel Wallerstein, "The Itinerary of World-Systems Analysis, or How to Resist Becoming a Theory," in *The Uncertainties of Knowledge* (Philadelphia: Temple University Press, 2004), 85–86. This essay is reproduced as chapter 5 of the present volume.

57. See Andre Gunder Frank, *ReOrient: Global Economy in an Asian Age* (Berkeley: University of California Press, 1998), among other sources.

58. Wallerstein has quite a few discussions of the periodization of the decline of the liberal center since 1945, which we take not as inconsistency so much as an attempt to come to terms with historical evidence as it unfolds (if that is the right figure of speech). Thus, in respect to 2001 to 2003, see Immanuel Wallerstein, "The Curve of American Power," *New Left Review* 40 (July–August 2006), and "Precipitate Decline: The Advent of Multipolarity," *Harvard International Review* 29 (2007).

59. Immanuel Wallerstein, *Historical Capitalism with Capitalist Civilization* (London: Verso, 1983), 95–112.

60. Wallerstein, "America and the World," 1–28.

61. Wallerstein, *The Decline of American Power,* 219–26; but also see "The Modern World-System in Crisis: Bifurcation, Chaos, and Choices," ch. 5 in *World-Systems Analysis,* 76–90, in which the Prigogine effect is more apparent.

62. Ibid., 85.

63. "The Left II," in Wallerstein, *The Decline of American Power,* 252–58; compare with "Geopolitical Cleavages," the fourth of the essays.

64. Wallerstein, "The Left II," 225.

65. Among others, see Wallerstein's *After Liberalism* (1995) and *Utopistics* (1998); for more extensive treatment, see his *The Decline of American Power* (2003), as mentioned; for more succinct treatment, see his *World-Systems Analysis* (2004); see passingly his *European Universalism* (2006), 53–58, and even (as he himself says in ibid., 54n) the four volumes of *The Modern World-System* (1974–2011), where the discussion of the history of system spells out, at the least, the potential for crisis. Important to note, as Wallerstein states in the preface to *The Modern World-System IV: Centrist Liberalism Triumphant, 1789–1914* (Berkeley: University of California Press, 2011), two further volumes are planned.

66. Wallerstein, *World-Systems Analysis,* 76–77.

67. Ibid., 77.

68. Wallerstein, "Precipitate Decline," 54–59, and "The Curve of American Power," 1–20.

69. See " World Social Forum Charter of Principles," Fórum Social Mundial, June 8, 2002, http://www.forumsocialmundial.org.br/main.php?id_menu=4&cd_language=2.

Chapter Four

The Itinerary of World-Systems Analysis; or, How to Resist Becoming a Theory

Immanuel Wallerstein

The term theory tends to evoke for most people the concept of a set of interconnected ideas that are coherent, rigorous, and clear, and from which one may derive explanations of empirical reality. The term theory however also denotes the end of a process of generalization and therefore of closure, even if only provisional. In the construction of adequate or plausible explanations of complex phenomena, proclaiming that one has arrived at a theory often imposes premature closure on scientific activity, and therefore can be counterproductive. The more complex the reality, the more this tends to be true. What I believe it is often better to do in such cases is to explore empirical reality using spectacles that are informed by theoretical hunches but not bound by them. It is because I believe this is eminently the case in the explanation of historical systems, which are large-scale and long-term, that I have long resisted the appellation of world-systems *theory* for the kind of work I do, insisting that I was engaged instead in world-systems *analysis*. This is thus the story of the itinerary and growth of a non-theory, which I call world-systems analysis.

J. Berger and M. Zelditch, Jr., eds., *New Directions in Contemporary Sociological Theory*, Lanham, MD: Rowman & Littlefield, 2002. Reprinted in Wallerstein, *The Uncertainties of Knowledge* (Philadelphia: Temple University Press, 2004).

The story begins for me in the 1950s when I entered the graduate program in sociology at Columbia University. My principal empirical interest was contemporary politics, in the United States and in the world. Columbia sociology at the time was considered to be the center of structural-functional analysis, and the department was particularly proud of pursuing research that combined the theorizing of Robert K. Merton with the methodological approaches of Paul F. Lazarsfeld. What is less often noticed is that Columbia was also the center of a major new subfield of sociology, political sociology.[1] At the time, its faculty (and visitors) included S. Martin Lipset, Daniel Bell, and Johan Galtung, all of whom were prominently associated with political sociology, plus Robert S, Lynd, C. Wright Mills, Herbert Hyman, Ralf Dahrendorf, Daniel Lerner, as well as Lazarsfeld, all of whom in fact did political sociology under other rubrics.

Political sociology was a thriving and growing field. One of the very first research committees of the newly founded International Sociological Association was the one in political sociology. The Social Science Research Council sponsored a multiyear, multivolume project by its Committee on Comparative Polities. I considered it obvious that I would consider myself a political sociologist.[2]

I did have one peculiarity, however. I did not believe the Cold War between the Western "free world" and the Soviet "Communist world" was the primary political struggle of the post-1945 arena. Rather, I considered the main conflict to be that the industrialized nations and what came to be called the Third World,[3] also known as the struggle of core vs. periphery, or later still North-South. Because of this belief, I decided to make the study of contemporary social change in Africa my main scholarly pursuit.[4] The 1950s was a period in which the Western world took its first serious look on what was happening outside its own redoubt. In 1955, the Bandoeng conference of Asian and African independent states was the moment of self-assertion by the non-Western world, the moment in which they laid claim to full participation in world politics. And 1960 was the Year of Africa, the year in which sixteen different states became independent; the year also of the Congo crisis, which led to massive United Nations involvement in its civil war, a civil war that was bedeviled by much outside interference.

The year 1960 was also the year in which I came to know Frantz Fanon, an author I had long been reading, and whose theorizing had a substantial influence on my own work. Fanon was a Martinican and a psychiatrist, who went in this latter capacity to Algeria, where he became a militant of the Algerian Front de Liberation Nationale. His first book, *Black Skin, White Masks* (first published in French in 1952), is about the psychic impact on Blacks of White dominance. It has been widely revived and republished in the 1990s, and is considered highly relevant to the discussions on identity that have become so prevalent. But at the time, it was his fourth and last book, *The Wretched of the Earth* (published in French in 1961 just before his very premature death from leukemia) and prefaced by Jean-Paul Sartre, which made him world-famous. The book became in a sense the manifesto of the world's national liberation movements, as well as of the Black Power movement in the United States.

In the best tradition of both Freud and Marx, Fanon sought to demonstrate that what on the surface was seemingly irrational, notably the use of violence by these movements, was beneath the surface highly rational. The book was therefore not merely a polemic and a call to action but a reflective work of social science, insisting on a careful analysis of the social basis of rationality. I wrote a number of articles at the time, seeking to explain and defend Fanon's work,[5] and I returned to the issue in my discussion of Freud and rationality in my presidential address to the International Sociological Association in 1998 (Wallerstein 1999c, 9–12).

The 1960s was a period of cascading independences in Africa. It was also a period of the first post-independence difficulties—not only the Congo crisis but the beginnings of military coups in a large number of states. Since I was lecturing on and writing about the contemporary scene, I was called upon to explain these multiple new happenings. I came to feel that I was chasing headlines, and that this was not the proper role of a social scientist. During the time that I was doing the fieldwork on the movement for African unity in 1965, I decided to try out a new approach to these issues by expanding the space scope and the time scope of my analyses. I gave three versions of a first cut at this approach at three African universities—Legon in Accra, Ghana; Ibadan in Nigeria; and Dar es Salaam in Tanzania.

The interested reception led me to try two things when I returned to Columbia. I created a new course that embodied this expanded scope into the analysis and I found considerable student response to this approach. At the same time, Terence Hopkins and I were asked by the department to give a course on the methodology of "comparative analysis," which we turned into a critique of "the comparative study of national societies." We wrote jointly an article assessing past modes of doing such work (Hopkins and Wallerstein 1967).

At the same time, we undertook a big content analysis project, seeking to extract systematically the propositions to be found in the by then innumerable articles purporting to be comparative in method. We enlisted some twenty graduate students as our readers (in a dozen languages) who were asked to fill in a schedule about each article that we had devised. We never published this gigantic content analysis because we discovered that an extremely large proportion of articles that were "comparative" according to their title compared one somewhat "exotic" country with one the author knew well, since he came from that country (most often the United States). Unfortunately, too many authors compared the data they collected in the exotic country with the remembered or imagined (but not empirically examined) reality of their own. Something, we thought, was very wrong.

About this time, I discovered some wonderful articles by Marian Malowist while roaming through *Africana Bulletin,* an obscure source, since it was the journal of Polish Africanists. Malowist was an economic historian of the fourteenth to seventeenth centuries. He wrote primarily about Eastern Europe, but he wandered afield to write both about colonial expansion and about the gold trade in the fourteenth to fifteenth centuries between the west coast of Africa and North Africa (Malowist 1964, 1966). The articles had two merits in terms of my further development. They led me to Malowist's other writings. And in the first article, Malowist introduced me to Fernand Braudel's great work on *The Mediterranean.*[6]

It was at this point that my dissatisfactions with the comparative study of national societies combined with my discovery via Braudel of the sixteenth-century world inspired a bad idea which serendipitously turned my work around, and toward world-systems analysis. Since I, along with multiple others, had been describing African and other postcolonial states as "new nations," I said to myself that must mean that there are "old nations." And old nations must at one time have been new nations. So I decided to investigate how old nations (essentially Western Europe) had behaved when they were new nations, that is, in the sixteenth century. This was a bad idea, as it was based on premises of modernization theory, which I was to reject so strongly later.[7] Western European states in the sixteenth century were in no way parallel to Third World states in the twentieth century.

Fortunately, I was reading both Braudel and Malowist.[8] What I discovered in Braudel was two concepts that have been central to my work ever since: the concept of the world-economy and the concept of the *longue durée.* What I discovered in Malowist (and then of course in other Polish and Hungarian authors) was the role of Eastern Europe as an emergent periphery of the European world-economy in the sixteenth century. I should elaborate on the three discoveries.

What Braudel did in *The Mediterranean* was to raise the issue of the unit of analysis. He insisted that the Mediterranean world was a "world-economy." He got this term from its use in the 1920s by a German geographer, Fritz Rörig, who spoke of *Weltwirtschaft.* Braudel translated this term not as *économie mondiale* but as *économie-monde.* As both he and I were to make explicit many years later, this distinction was crucial: between *économie mondiale* meaning the "economy *of the* world" and *économie-monde* meaning an "economy *that is a* world" (see Braudel 1984, esp. 21–24). The difference was first of all conceptual. In the latter formulation, the world is not a reified entity that is there, and within which an economy is constructed; rather, the economic relationships are defining the boundaries of the social world. The second difference was geographic. In the first usage, "world" equals the globe; in the second usage, "world" means only a large geographic space (within which many states are located), which however can be, and usually is, less extensive than the globe (but also can encompass the entire globe).

I faced one problem immediately. The Romance languages permit making this distinction easily, by using an adjectival noun in place of a true adjective (that is, *économie-monde* as opposed to *économie mondiale*). German doesn't permit the distinction at all orthographically, because one can only use the adjectival noun and it is attached to the noun it is modifying to form a single word. This is why Rörig's usage, which could only be understood contextually, never really received notice. English as a language is in between. I could translate Braudel's term by inserting a hyphen (thus: "world-economy" instead of "world economy"), the hyphen turning the adjective into an adjectival noun and indicating the indissolubility of the two words, which represent thereby a single concept.[9]

I then took Braudel's concept of the "world-economy" and combined it with Polanyi's notion that there were three modes of economic behavior, which Polanyi had called reciprocity, redistribution, and exchange (see Polanyi 1957, 1967, and finally a very clear version, 1977). I decided that reciprocity referred to what I called minisystems (that is, small systems that were not world-systems), and that redistribution and exchange referred to what I called the two varieties of world-systems: world-empires, and world-economies.[10] I then argued that the modern world-system was a capitalist world-economy, that capitalism could only exist within the framework of a world-economy, and that a world-economy could only operate on capitalist principles. I make this case throughout my writings. The earliest (and most widely read) version is Wallerstein 1974b, reprinted in 1979a.

I faced a second problem in orthographies. Both Braudel and I believed that world-economies were organic structures that had lives—beginnings and ends. Therefore, there had to have been multiple world-economies (and of course multiple world-empires) in the history of humankind. Thus I became careful to speak not of world-system analysis but of world-system*s* analysis. This may seem obvious, except that it would become the cornerstone of a fierce attack by André Gunder Frank in the 1990s, when he argued that there had been only one world system ever and that it had been covering the Euroasiatic ecumene for twenty-five hundred years at least and the entire world for the last five hundred years (hence no need for either a hyphen or a plural). Obviously, different criteria were being used to define the boundaries of a system. Along with these different criteria came the assertion that the concept of capitalism was irrelevant to the discussion (it either having always existed or never).[11]

If the appropriate unit of analysis of the modern world is that of a world-system, and if there had been multiple world-systems in human history, then Braudel's concept of multiple social temporalities became immediately central. Braudel had built *The Mediterranean* (1949) around an elementary architecture. He would tell the story three times in terms of three temporalities, the short term, the middle term, and the long term. It was only later, however, that he explicitly theorized this fundamental decision in a famous article published in 1958, entitled "History and the Social Sciences: The *longue durée*" (Braudel 1958).[12]

In this article, Braudel speaks not of three temporalities, as we might expect, but rather of four, adding the *"very* long term." He has conceptual names for the four. The short term is *histoire événementielle,* the middle term is *histoire conjoncturelle,* and the long term is *histoire structurelle.* About the very long term he says, "If it exists, it must be the time of the sages" (ibid:76). There are problems with the translation of each of these terms,[13] but the crucial issue to discuss is epistemological. Braudel zeroed in on the fact that, in the last 150 years, the social sciences had seen a split between nomothetic and idiographic modes of knowing, the so-called *Methodenstreit.* Braudel identified this as the split between those who looked only at the eternal truths of social reality (the very long term) and those who thought that everything was particular and therefore nonreplicable (the short term). Braudel wished to assert that the crucial social temporalities were in fact the other two, and first of all that of the *longue durée*—which harbored those structural constraints that have three characteristics: they are not always immediately visible, they are very long-lasting, and very slow to change, but they are *not* eternal.

The most immediate impact on me of this Braudelian imperative—about the priorities scholars should give different social temporalities—was in the conception of how I would write *The Modern World-System.* It became not the search for the eternal truths of comparative organizational analysis, which was the norm in post-1945 sociology (including in political sociology), but rather the story of a singular phenomenon, the modern world-system, informed by a mode of explanation I was calling world-systems analysis. Braudel called this *histoire pensée,* which may best be translated as "analytic history." Braudel's insistence on multiple social times would also lead me later to larger epistemological concerns as well.

What Malowist (and then the larger group of East European historians) did for me was to give sudden flesh to the concept of periphery, as had been initially adumbrated by the Latin American scholars grouped around Raúl Prebisch in the Economic Commission for Latin America (ECLA). The term "second feudalism" to describe what took place in Europe "east of the Elbe" in the sixteenth to eighteenth centuries had long been commonplace. What had not been commonplace, perhaps still isn't, is to see that the "second" feudalism was fundamentally different from the "first" feudalism, and that sharing a common descriptor has done a great disservice to analytic thought.

In the "first" feudalism, the manorial units produced largely for their own consumption and perhaps for that of surrounding small zones. In the so-called "second feudalism," the estates were producing for sale in distant markets. The view that such units were part and parcel of the emerging capitalist world-economy became one of the fundamental themes of my book, and of world-systems analysis. Furthermore, the view that the so-called second feudalism was a feature of a capitalist system had important implications for the prior theorizing, both by Marxists and by liberals, about the nature of capitalism. For a long time, capitalism had been defined in terms of an imagery drawn from the history of nineteenth-century western Europe, of wage-workers in factories (often newly proletarianized and not "owning the means of production") receiving wages (which was their entire income) from an employer who was seeking profits in the market. So strong was this imagery that most analysts refused to categorize as capitalist any enterprise organized in any other mode of labor compensation. Hence, it followed that most of the world could not be considered to be capitalist, or rather was said not *yet* to be capitalist.

Rejecting this nineteenth-century view was a crucial step in the development of world-systems analysis. The classic liberal-Marxist view was based on a theory of stages of development that occurred in parallel ways in units of analysis called states (or societies or social formations). It missed what seemed to us the obvious fact that capitalism in fact operated as a system in which there were *multiple* modes of compensating labor, ranging from wage-labor, which was very widely used in the richer, more central zones, to various forms of coerced labor very widely used in the poorer, more peripheral zones (and many other varieties in between). If one did one's analysis state by state, as was the classical method, it would be observed that different countries had different modes of compensating labor, and analysts could (and did) draw from this the conclusion that one day the poorer zones might replicate the structure of the richer zones. What world-systems analysis suggested was that this differential pattern across the world-economy was exactly what permitted capitalists to pursue the endless accumulation of capital and *was* what in fact made the richer zones richer.[14] It was therefore a defining structural element of the system, not one that was transitional or archaic.

Did I theorize this insight? In a way, yes, but diffidently, although I was sure I was on the right track. When I completed *The Modern World-System*,

I realized that it was replete with analytic statements, and that there was a whole series of architectonic devices, but that they were nowhere systematically laid out. I worried less about the legitimacy of the exercise than about the potential confusion of the reader. So I added a final chapter, which I called a "Theoretical Reprise." This, plus the "Rise and Demise" article (which was largely a critique of the theorizing of others plus an attempt to show how changing a few premises increased the plausibility of the results), constituted my initial theorizing statements in world-systems analysis.

It wasn't enough for my critics. Many reviewers, even some friendly ones,[15] chided me for insufficiently explicit theorizing—I believe the term is "disprovable hypotheses"—and argued that without it my effort was at most interesting narrative.[16] I was also chided for excessively long footnotes, "winding around the page." To me the long footnotes reflected a deliberate strategy of building my analysis around scholarly discussions on empirical issues, attempting to show how recasting the issues (theorizing?) inserted clarity into what had become for most people murky debates.[17]

I should note that not all the criticism was about the absence of theorizing. There were also important debates about empirical issues. Was Russia really an "external arena" in the sixteenth century, as I asserted, or was it rather a "peripheral zone" just like Poland (see Nolte 1982)? How could I have ignored the Ottoman Empire in the analysis of Charles V and his difficulties in constructing a world-empire? Was the Ottoman Empire really "external" to the European world-economy?[18] While I was ready to defend myself on my empirical choices, such criticisms constantly raised definitional (and therefore theoretical) problems. They forced me to refine my position in order to defend it.

There were two kinds of fundamental theoretical attacks. One came from a Marxist stance, arguing that I had grossly understated the fundamental importance of the class struggle and misdefined capitalism. This was the Robert Brenner critique, suggesting that my view had a "market" bias (sometimes called "circulationism") rather than being a properly "class-based" view of capitalism.[19] In his article, Brenner had attacked not only me but Paul Sweezy and André Gunder Frank as well. And the three of us decided that we would not write either a joint reply or separate replies to the article, which was widely read and discussed at the time. I decided to take another path in response to Brenner, whose views struck a resonant note among many persons.

At the same time, a second fundamental critique came from what might be called the Otto Hintze camp. Both Theda Skocpol and Aristide Zolberg launched polemics arguing that world-systems analysis puts into a single arena political and economic phenomena, and that analytically they were separate arenas, operating on separate and sometime contradictory premises.[20] Of course, they were right about what I had done, but I did not think this was an error. Rather I considered it a theoretical virtue. This pair of articles also was widely read.

My substantive answer to both theoretical critiques is to be found in Volume II of *The Modern World-System*, which bore the subtitle *Mercantilism and the Consolidation of the World-Economy, 1600–1750* (Wallerstein 1980). I sought to show in it that, contra a Brenner version of Marxism, there were not multiple forms of capitalism—mercantile, industrial, financial—but rather that these referred to alternate ways for capitalists to make profits, which were better or worse for particular capitalists according to conjunctural shifts in the operations of the world-economy. Furthermore, I argued that the itinerary of Dutch hegemony incarnated a necessary sequence. It was made possible by first achieving supremacy (in terms of efficiency) in productive activities, which led to supremacy in commercial activities, which then led to supremacy in the financial arena; and that the decline of the Dutch followed the same sequence. As for the supposed separate logics of the market and the state, I sought to show that, on the contrary, a singular logic operated in the world-system as a whole and in all of its parts—the core zones, the periphery, and the semiperiphery (whether rising or declining).[21]

What I was also trying to do, as a matter of tactics, became clear to me. Each volume and each chapter of the succeeding volumes was moving forward in time, discussing new empirical issues, and raising further elements of an architectonic scheme. One cannot discuss everything at once. And how all the pieces fit together becomes clear (or clearer) only as one works through the complex empirical data. Furthermore, I had decided on a tactic of overlapping time segments. The second volume starts in 1600, whereas the first ended in 1640, and the third starts in the 1730s, whereas the second ended in 1750. And so it will continue to be the case in further volumes. In addition, the chapters within the books had each their own chronological limits, sometimes violating those of the overall book. This is because I came to believe firmly that chronological limits, always difficult to set, are a function of the problem being discussed. The same event belongs in two different chronological limits, depending on the issue. Writing a complex story requires an intelligently flexible schema.

By now I was also writing a large series of articles, published all over the place. If one wishes in an article (talk) both to argue the case for world-systems analysis and to discuss a specific issue, one has to balance the presentation between fundamental premises and particular discussion. I tried to make each important article say at least something worth saying that had not been said before by me. But I had of course also to repeat much of what I had already said, or the audience/readers might not have been able to follow my reasoning.

Grouping these articles together in collections had the virtue not merely of making them more available, but of elaborating the theoretical skein.

In the early 1980s, I was asked to give a series of lectures at the University of Hawaii. At the same time, a French publisher asked me to do a short book on "capitalism." I replied that I would write such a book, provided I could call it "*historical* capitalism." The adjective was crucial to me, since I wanted to argue that there was no point in defining in our heads what capitalism is and then looking around to see if it was there. Rather, I suggested we should look at how this system actually worked. Furthermore, I wanted to argue that there has only ever been *one* capitalist system, since the only valid unit of analysis was the world-system, and only one world-economy survived long enough to institutionalize a capitalist system. This is of course the same issue as that discussed above in my rejection of wage-labor as the defining feature of a capitalist system. Is the system a *world-system* or are there as many capitalist systems as there are states?

So I gave the lectures at Hawaii on "historical capitalism" and revised them into a short book. Despite its title, the book has very little empirical/historical data in it. It is a series of analytic statements, assertions about how the system has historically worked, and why. Twelve years later, I was asked to give another series of lectures at the Chinese University of Hong Kong, and I used that occasion to make an overall assessment of the capitalist world-system over its history. I called these lectures "Capitalist Civilization," and there now exists a book in print which puts the two sets of lectures together (Wallerstein 1995a). This book is the closest effort I have ever made to what might pass as systematic theorizing. It is not possible here to summarize the book, but it is the only place in which I tried to cover the whole range of issues I had discussed in other books and essays, and I did try to show how the various parts of the whole fit together.

In 1976, I went to Binghamton University to join my collaborator, Terence Hopkins. We established the Fernand Braudel Center for the Study of Economies, Historical Systems, and Civilizations (FBC),[22] of which I have been the director ever since. There are three things to note about the center: its name, its mode of operation, and its substantive activities.

The use of Braudel's name was intended to indicate our commitment to the study of the *longue durée*, that is, of long-term, large-scale social change. But the rest of the name was taken from a modification of the subtitle of the name of the journal, *Annales*. Its subtitle (at the time) was ESC, standing for "economies, societies, and civilizations," all in plural form. We changed, however, "societies" to "historical systems." This was a deliberate theoretical stance. The term *society*—fundamental to general sociological orientations (Merton 1957, 81–89)—seemed to us to have led social science in a seriously mistaken direction. In practice, the boundaries of the term *society* have been determined by the adjective placed before it. In the modern world, these adjectives are virtually always the names of states—Dutch society, Brazilian society, and so forth. So the term required that the unit of analysis be state-structured, thereby extending present-day states into their (presumed) historical past. German society was to be seen as the society of the "Germanic peoples" over perhaps two thousand years, although the state itself came into existence only in 1871, and then only in boundaries which were contested and were to change several times thereafter.[23] We insisted instead on the term *historical system,* by which we meant an entity that was simultaneously systemic (with boundaries and mechanisms or rules of functioning) and historical (since it began at some point, evolved over time, and eventually came into crisis and ceased to exist). The term *historical system* involved for us a more precise specification of the concept of the *longue durée.*

The mode of operation of the FBC was somewhat unusual. It involved an organizational shift that reflected a further theoretical stance. Almost all organized research has been done in one of two ways. One mode is the research program of one individual (or sometimes several), either alone or using assistants who are hierarchically subordinate and whose intellectual function is to carry out assigned tasks. Using assistants is simply the expanded version of the functioning of the isolated scholar. The second is the collaborative format, in which several (even very many) scholars (or research institutes) work together (perhaps under the leadership of one person) on a common problem. The outcome is typically a work of many chapters, individually authored, to which someone writes an introduction attempting to show how they fit together.

The FBC sought to institutionalize not collaborative research but collective, unitary research. The mode was to bring together a potential group around a common concern "coordinated" by one or several persons. These groups are called Research Working Groups (RWGs). Each group spends a considerable amount of time defining the research problem and developing a research strategy, at which point the group assigns to its members research tasks. Assignment makes it different from the collaborative project. The assignment process is collective and not hierarchical. Researchers report back to the group regularly, which criticizes their work and sends them out with new group-defined tasks. The results of such work are thus not collections of individual papers but an integrated book written by many hands designed to be read as a monograph.[24] As should be immediately obvious, this approach is the concrete application of the stance advocated in this paper toward theorizing—the avoidance of premature closure.

In addition, it was combined with the assumption that addressing complex intellectual problems requires multiple hands and multiple skills.

More than that, these problems require the intrusion of multiple founts of social knowledge, drawn from the multiple social biographies of the participants. It should be noted that typically such RWGs at the Fernand Braudel Center had researchers coming from across the globe and knowing a multiplicity of languages, a crucial element in accumulating multiple kinds of knowledge, including those that are buried in the unconscious psyches of the researchers.

As for the substantive activities, the RWGs have over the years engaged in research on a wide series of major areas which the logic of world-systems analysis suggested needed exploring. And exploration is the key word. Each of the topics was big. Each had enormous problems of locating, in effect creating, appropriate data to utilize. Each resulted in a small step forward in the specification of the integrated theoretical architecture we hoped to build. None contained carefully delineated disprovable hypotheses. Rather each contained somewhat novel conceptualization and the utilization of incomplete and inadequate data (but the best we have presently at our disposition, or at least so we believed), And each sought to rewrite the received canons of presumed theoretical knowledge.

Not every group succeeded even that far. Some research projects had to be abandoned. But those carried through to completion and thereupon published included: the relationship of cyclical rhythms and secular trends of the world-system; the functioning of transnational commodity chains; hegemony and rivalry in the interstate system; regionality and the semiperiphery; incorporation of the external arena and consequent peripheralization; patterns of antisystemic movements; creating and transforming households; the tension between racism-sexism and universalism; the historical origins and development of social science; the trajectory of the world-system, 1945–2025; the origins of the two cultures and challenges to the epistemology; and currently, a massive project on what others call globalization but which we perceive as "crisis, stability, or transformation?"[25] Each project typically required three to ten years of collective work.

The FBC, like other research structures, constantly sought funds to permit its operation, and therefore submitted projects to multiple foundations. We discovered that when we applied to the National Science Foundation or even to the National Endowment for the Humanities, we typically received outside evaluations that were evenly balanced between enthusiasm and panning. Few reviewers seemed neutral. Sometimes we got the money and sometimes we didn't. But the panning would always center on methodological questions, on the degree to which the research mode we suggested was insufficiently positivist and therefore in the view of some reviewers insufficiently scientific. We realized some twenty years ago that if one wished to reconstruct the way the analysis of the contemporary world was done, it was insufficient to present data, or even to present data undergirded by a solid theoretical explanation. We had to tackle the question of how one knows what one purports to know, or more properly the appropriate epistemology for social science.

In the 1980s, a second challenge to our work raised its head, coming from that broad current some call cultural studies and others postmodernism or post–other things. For these critics, it was not that we had too few disprovable hypotheses, but that we had far too many. World-systems analysis was said to be just one more "grand narrative," to be cast into the dustbin however recently it had been constructed. We may have had the illusion that we were challenging the status quo of world social science; for these critics we incarnated that status quo. We were said to have committed the fatal sin of ignoring culture.[26]

I turned my attention to these issues, as did the Fernand Braudel Center. I could argue that this was just a matter of our unfolding agenda (one can't do everything at the same time), but no doubt it speeds up the pace of one's agenda when one has the fire beneath one's feet. I suppose it was therefore fortunate, but then there are really no accidents in intellectual history, that it was at this time that I discovered Ilya Prigogine. I heard him speak at a conference in 1981 (not having even known his name before that) and was amazed to hear someone formulate so clearly what I had long been feeling in a confused fashion. And to find that this someone was a Nobel Prize in chemistry was, to say the least, astonishing, or at least so it was to me at that time.

Prigogine is a chemist by training. The historic relationship of chemists to physicists is one in which the physicists reproached the chemists for being insufficiently Newtonian, that is, for being in fact insufficiently positivist. Chemists were constantly describing phenomena in ways, such as the second law of thermodynamics, that seemed to contradict the premises of classical dynamics, for example, by seeming to deny time-reversibility. Physicists argued that these descriptions/laws must be considered interim formulations, essentially the result of incomplete knowledge, and that eventually what the chemists were analyzing would come to be described in more purely Newtonian terms. Prigogine received his Nobel Prize in 1977 for his work on "dissipative processes" but more generally in fact for being a leader in the analysis of the physics of nonequilibrium processes, central to the emerging large field of "complexity studies." What is more, as he has continued his work, Prigogine has gotten bolder. He is no longer merely saying that nonequilibrium processes exist *as well as* equilibrium processes. He is now saying quite clearly that equilibrium processes are a very special, an *unusual* case, of physical reality, and this can be demonstrated in the heartland of classical physics itself, dynamical systems.[27]

I shall not review the details of his arguments here.[28] What became central for my own analysis, and in my opinion for social science as a whole, are two interrelated elements of the Prigogine construct. The first is the fundamental indeterminacy of all reality—physical and therefore social. One should be clear what one means by indeterminacy. It is *not* the position that order and explanation do not exist. Prigogine believes that reality exists in a mode of "deterministic chaos." That is, he takes the position that order always exists *for a while*, but then inevitably undoes itself when its curves reach points of "bifurcation" (that is, points where there are two equally valid solutions for the equations), and that the choice actually made in a bifurcation *intrinsically* cannot be determined in advance. It is not a matter of our incomplete knowledge but of the *impossibility* of foreknowledge.

I have since argued that Prigogine's position is the call for an "unexcluded middle" (determined order and inexplicable chaos) and is, in this regard, absolutely parallel to that of Braudel, who also rejects the two extremes presented as the exclusive antinomies of particularism and eternal universals, insists on orders (structural time) that inevitably undo themselves and come to an end (Wallerstein 1998b). Prigogine's position had two consequences for world-systems analysis: one was psychologico-political, and the second was intellectual.

The psychologico-political one is not to be underestimated. Nomothetic social science is based on the absolute legitimacy of the Newtonian verities, as a model and a constraint. To have a physical scientist challenge these verities in a plausible way, and to see this challenge become a central part of a serious and substantial knowledge movement within the physical sciences itself undermines the intimidating effect so pervasive within the social sciences of arguments put forward by those who hold on to outmoded scientific methodologies (for example, methodological individualism) when the physicist progenitors of these methodologies are in the process of rethinking them, or rather (as I have insisted) *unthinking* them, that is, of removing them from our internalized and now subconscious assumptions.[29]

The intellectual consequence is nonetheless still more important. Prigogine's work has immediate implications for how one does world-systems analysis, and indeed how one does any kind of social science. It enables one to place precise referents to the concept of the "normal" development of a structure, when the laws of that structure hold and when processes tend to return to equilibrium (what we call the "cyclical rhythms" of the world-system), and to distinguish this period of "normal" development (the development taking the form of "secular trends") from the moments of structural crisis. The moments of structural crisis are those in which the system has moved "far from equilibrium" and is approaching the bifurcation. At that point, one can only predict that the existing system cannot continue to exist, but not which fork it will take. On the other hand, precisely because at a bifurcation the swings of the curve are more violent, every input has more significant impact, the opposite of what happens during "normal" periods, when large inputs result in small amounts of change.

We were now able to take this as a model of transformation of the most complex of all systems, social systems. We could argue, with both Braudel and Prigogine, that such systems have lives—beginnings, normal development, and terminal crises. We could argue that, in terminal crises, the impact of social action was much greater than in periods of normal development. We could call this the period in which "free will" prevails.[30] And we could then apply this to an analysis of the modern world-system. Thus, in the collective work of the Fernand Braudel Center, we argued, on the basis of an analysis of six vectors of the world-system between 1945 and 1990, that the world-system was in structural crisis and was facing a bifurcation (Hopkins and Wallerstein 1996).[31]

The second contribution of Prigogme was to insist that time reversibility was absurd—absurd not only where it seemed obviously absurd, as in heat processes or social processes, but in every aspect of physical reality. He adopted the forgotten slogan of Arthur Eddington, "the arrow of time," and argued the case that even atoms were determined by an arrow of time, not to speak of the universe as a whole. Here, too, he joined forces with Braudel, and here too it was crucial that this theme was coming from a physical scientist. Of course, it added plausibility to our insistence that social systems were *historical* systems, and that no analysis, at any level, can omit taking into account the arrow of time.[31]

We had been thrust into the maelstrom of epistemological debates, which in the end are philosophical as well as scientific questions. These issues moved to the center of world-systems analysis. What we could contribute is to understand the evolution of these debates as a process of the modern world-system, as an integral reflection of its geoculture. I discussed these issues in *Unthinking Social Science.* And in 1993, with a grant from the Gulbenkian Foundation, we set about convening an international commission to study the historical evolution of the social sciences and to look into its possible restructuring.

Constructing the commission was a key part of the task. We decided to keep it small, in order that it be workable—hence ten persons. We decided we wanted persons from different disciplines in the social sciences. We decided we also wanted to have some physical scientists, and some persons from the humanities. We ended with quotas of 6–2–2. We also decided we wanted persons from all over the world (all five continents), and from different linguistic traditions (we managed four). With a ten-person limit, we couldn't include everything, but we came close. We also wanted persons who had shown prior interest in the large epistemological issues.[33]

The committee's report, *Open the Social Sciences*,[34] contains four chapters. The first is on the historical construction of the social sciences from the eighteenth century to 1945 (Wallerstein et al. 1996). The second deals with three major debates since 1945: the validity of the distinctions among the social sciences; the degree to which the heritage is parochial; and the reality and validity of the distinction between the "two cultures." The third chapter asks, What kind of social science shall we now build? and discusses four issues: humans and nature; the state as an analytic building block; the universal and the particular; and objectivity. The final chapter is a conclusion on restructuring the social sciences.

Aside from the contribution the report tried to make to the understanding of the historical construction and current intellectual dilemmas of the social sciences, it also pointed (albeit in a minor way) to the historical construction of the more enveloping schema, the "two cultures." It seemed to us the next step for world-systems analysis to take was to understand how the very categories of knowledge had come into existence, what role such categories played in the operations of the world-system, and how they shaped the emergence of world-systems analysis itself. Here I can only report on a work in progress at the FBC, which has taken as its object of study just that: the reasons why the distinction between "philosophy" and "science" became so central to modern thought in the eighteenth century, for it is easy to show that before then most thinkers thought the two concepts not only were not antagonistic but overlapped (or were even virtually identical). We are also studying why a series of challenges emerged in multiple fields to this distinction in the post-1945 and especially the post-1970 period. We are trying to tie these challenges to the structural crisis of the world-system.[35]

In the Giddens-Turner (1987) volume, I wrote an article on "world-systems analysis," calling for a debate about the paradigm. It opens with the sentences: "'World-systems analysis' is not a theory about the world, or about a part of it. It is a protest against the ways in which social scientific activity was structured for all of us at its inception in the middle of the nineteenth century."[36] In 1989, I gave a talk on "World-Systems Analysis: The Second Phase" (Wallerstein 1990, 1999a).[37] In that article, I outlined a number of tasks unfinished. I said that the key issue, and "the hardest nut to crack" was how to overcome the distinction of three social arenas: the economic, the political, and the sociocultural. I pointed out that even world-systems analysts, even I myself, although we proclaimed loudly the spuriousness of separating the three arenas that are so closely interlinked, nonetheless continued to use the language of the three arenas and seemed unable to escape it. And in a millennium symposium of the *British Journal of Sociology* in 2000, I called for sociologists to move forward to the construction of a new and reunified discipline I call "historical social science" (Wallerstein 2000b).

I continue to believe that world-systems analysis is primarily a protest against the ways in which social science is done, including in theorizing. I continue to believe that we must somehow find modes of description that dismiss the very idea of the separation of the three arenas of social action. I continue to believe that the historic categorizations of the disciplines of the social sciences make no intellectual sense anymore. But if we continue to protest, it is because we remain a minority. And if we cannot solve the "key" theoretical conundrum, perhaps we deserve to be. For without solving it, it is hard to convince many of the irrelevance of our consecrated disciplinary categories.

Hence I continue to believe that we are in an uphill battle, but also that this battle is part and parcel of the systemic transformation through which we are living and which will continue for some time yet. Consequently, I continue to believe that it is very worth trying to do what we are doing. But we must be open to many voices and many critics if we are to go further. And that is the reason I continue to believe it is premature to think of what we are doing as a theory.

NOTES

1. For a very brief statement of the cultural importance of this subfield, see Wallerstein (1995b).

2. My M.A. thesis in 1954 was titled "McCarthyism and the Conservative." My PhD dissertation in 1959 was titled "The Role of Voluntary Associations in the Nationalist Movements in Ghana and the Ivory Coast." It was later published as *The Road to Independence: Ghana and the Ivory Coast* (Wallerstein 1964). At the first ISA meeting that I attended in Stresa, Italy, in 1959, I spent my time at the meetings of the Committee on Political Sociology. Later, I attended one of the conferences of the SSRC Committee in Frascati, Italy, in 1964 and contributed a paper to the volume resulting from the conference (see Wallerstein 1966).

3. See my look backward as of 2000 in Wallerstein (2000a).

4. My first two books, aside from the published dissertation, were *Africa: The Politics of Independence* (Wallerstein 1961) and *Africa: The Politics of Unity* (Wallerstein 1965). In 1973 to 1974, I was elected president of the African Studies Association.

5. See my entries on Fanon (Wallerstein 1968, 1970, 1979b).

6. *La Méditerranée et le monde méditerranéen à l'epoque de Philippe II* was first published in 1949, with a revised edition in two volumes in 1966 (Braudel [1949] 1966). Its English translation, based on the revised version, *The Mediterranean and the Mediterranean World in the Age of Philip II*, did not appear until 1972 (Braudel 1972).

7. My "manifesto" is found in Wallerstein (1976). Delivered in 1975, it appeared originally in *The Uses of Controversy in Sociology* and was reprinted in Wallerstein (1979a).

8. I acknowledge my debt to both of them in Wallerstein (1974a).

9. I discuss the issue of the hyphen in Wallerstein (1991b).

10. Note the hyphen in all of these formulations. "World empire" (and *Weltreich*) is a term that others have used before me. I felt, however, that since none of these structures was global, in English the hyphen was required by the same grammatical logic that made it requisite in the case of world-economy.

11. By now Frank has published these arguments in many texts. See especially the early version, Frank (1990), and the mature version, Frank (1999). For my critique of *ReOrient*, see Wallerstein (1999b). The same issue of *Review* also contains critical reviews of Frank by Samir Amin and Giovanni Arrighi.

12. Republished in Braudel (1969), this has appeared in English in at least four different versions. The reader must beware of the most accessible translation, that found in *On History* (Braudel 1980), since it is inaccurate at points crucial for this discussion.

13. I discuss how best to translate them into English in Wallerstein (1991b).

14. This view is argued in many of my writings. See in particular part 1 of Wallerstein (1979a).

15. See, for example, Hechter (1975, 221), who tempers his praise with a critique of shortcomings, two of which revolve around theorizing. "[T]here is no theory to account for the triumph of the European world-economy in the sixteenth century.... There is a certain lack of conceptual precision which mars the analysis."

16. See the marvelous discussion of the criticism that Wallerstein has "only one case" in Wulbert (1975).

17. One of the few persons to remark favorably upon this technique, and to explicate clearly the strategy, is Franco Moretti (2000, 6–57): "Writing about comparative social history, Marc Bloch once coined a lovely 'slogan,' as he himself called it: 'years of analysis for a day of synthesis'; and if you read Braudel or Wallerstein you immediately see what Bloch had in mind. The text which is strictly Wallerstein's, his 'day of synthesis,' occupies one third of a page, one fourth, maybe half; the rest are quotations (fourteen hundred, in the first volume of *The Modern World-System*). Years of analysis; other people's analysis, which Wallerstein's page synthesizes into a system."

18. "Is there good reason for considering Poland part of the periphery within Europe's world-economy and regarding the Ottoman Empire as part of an external arena?" (Lane 1976, 528).

19. "Thus the correct counterposition cannot be production for the market versus production for use, but the class system of production based on free wage labour (capitalism) versus pre-capitalist class systems" (Brenner 1977, 50).

20. Theda Skocpol (1977, 1079) suggests, like Brenner, who acknowledges seeing her article before publication, that I have ignored the "basic Marxist insight that the social relations of production and surplus appropriation are the sociological key to the functioning and development of any economic system." However, her more fundamental critique has to do with the relation of the economic and political arenas: "[The] model is based on a two-step reduction: first, a reduction of socioeconomic structure to determination by world market opportunities and technological production possibilities;

and second, a reduction of state structures and policies to determination by dominant class interests" (ibid., 1078–79). Aristide Zolberg (1981), in his critique of my work, specifically recommends Hintze as a more "fruitful avenue for theoretical reflection." He says that Hintze "remains one of the very few scholars who identify the interactions between endogenous processes of various kinds and exogenous *political* processes as a *problématique* for the analysis of European political development." Note the italicization of "political." For Zolberg, as for Skocpol, as indeed for Brenner, I am too "economistic."

21. Core-periphery as an antinomy to be applied to the analysis of the world-economy was first made famous by Raúl Prebisch and his associates in the UN Economic Commission of Latin America in the 1950s, essentially to replace the then dominant antinomy of industrialized and agricultural nations. Prebisch was implicitly using a world-systems perspective by insisting that what went on in the two sets of countries was a function of their interrelations more than of social structures internal to each set of countries. The Prebisch framework was further developed, particularly in its political implications, by what came to be known in the 1960s as dependency theory. In my book *The Modern World-System* I (Wallerstein 1974a), I insisted on adding a third category, the semi-periphery, which I claimed was not merely "in between" the other two but played a crucial role in making the system work. What the semiperiphery is, and how exactly it can be defined, has been a contentious issue ever since. An early attempt by me to spell this out may be found in Wallerstein (1979a, 95–118).

22. See the website http://fbc.binghamton.edu.

23. See my discussion of this issue, precisely using the case of Germany to make a general theoretical point, in "Societal Development, or Development of the World-System?" (Wallerstein 1986). This was an address to the Deutsche Soziologentag and was published first in *International Sociology* and then republished in *Unthinking Social Science* (Wallerstein 1991a).

24. I have discussed a bit of this organizational history and philosophy in "Pedagogy and Scholarship" (Wallerstein 1998a).

25. The story from 1976 to 1991 can be found in a pamphlet, *Report on an Intellectual Project: The Fernand Braudel Center, 1976–1991*. It is now out of print but can be found on the Internet at binghamton.edu/fbc/about-fbc/intellectual-report.html. The annual story since then can be found in the newsletters of the FBC, as well as on the Internet at http://www2.binghamton.edu/fbc/scholarly-acitvities/newsletters.html.

26. The bulk of the article attacks the uses of "systems theory" for its nomothetic bias and then draws this inference: "Ideologies of legitimation, questions of cultural domination, etc. take on little or no importance.... Wallerstein sees no need to account for the specific development of hegemonic bourgeois democratic ideologies which are already in the process of formation in the period of capitalism's early rise" (Aronowitz 1981, 516).

27. "[O]ur position is that classical mechanics is incomplete, because it does not include irreversible processes associated with an increase in entropy. To include these processes in its formulation, we must incorporate instability and nonintegrability. Integrable systems are the exception. Starting with the three-body problem, most dynamical systems are nonintegrable.... We therefore obtain a probabilistic formulation of dynamics by means of which we can resolve the conflict between time-reversible dynamics and the time-oriented view of thermodynamics" (Prigogine 1997, 108).

28. The latest and clearest version is to be found in *The End of Certainty*. It should be noted that even here, the issues of orthography intrude themselves. "Certainty," in the English edition, is singular. But the French original is entitled *La fin des certitudes*, and there "certainty" is plural. I believe the publishers made a serious error in the translation of the title.

29. On the importance of "unthinking" as opposed to "rethinking," see the introduction, "Why Unthink?" to *Unthinking Social Science: The Limits of Nineteenth-Century Paradigms* (Wallerstein 1991a, 1–4 and passim).

30. I placed the discussion of "free will" within a fifth social time not dealt with by Braudel. I called it "transformational time" and suggested that this was the *kairos* discussed by Paul Tillich (1948, esp. 32–51). *Kairos* means "the right time," and Tillich says, "All great changes in history are accompanied by a strong consciousness of a kairos at hand" (ibid., 155). See "The Invention of TimeSpace Realities: Towards an Understanding of Our Historical Systems," in *Unthinking Social Science* (Wallerstein 1991a, 146–47), where I specifically tied the concept of transformational time to the discussion by Prigogine of the consequences of "cascading bifurcations."

31. The six vectors are the interstate system, world production, the world labor force, world human welfare, the social cohesion of the states, and structures of knowledge. These six vectors are then summed up in two chapters that I wrote, titled "The Global Picture, 1945–1990" and "The Global Possibilities, 1990–2025."

32. The importance of the time dimension in the redirecting of sociological theorizing is at the heart of my ISA presidential address (Wallerstein 1999c).

33. The final list of the commission was Immanuel Wallerstein, chair, sociology, United States; Calestous Juma, science and technology studies, Kenya; Evelyn Fox Keller, physics, United States; Jürgen Kocka, history, Germany; Dominique Lecourt, philosophy, France; V. Y. Mudimbe, Romance languages, Congo; Kinhide Mushakoji, political science, Japan; Ilya Prigogine, chemistry, Belgium; Peter J. Taylor, geography, United Kingdom; Michel-Rolph Trouillot, anthropology, Haiti. Given the academic and geographic mobility of scholars, the disciplines listed are those of their doctorates and the countries those of their identification (via birth or nationality).

34. As of 2002, the report existed in twenty-five editions in twenty-two languages. Others are in process.

35. See a first treatment of this last issue in Richard Lee, "Structures of Knowledge" (1996).

36. The article is reprinted in *Unthinking Social Science* (Wallerstein 1991a). The quote is found on p. 237.

37. It was published in *Review* and reprinted in *The End of the World as We Know It: Social Science for the Twenty-First Century* (Wallerstein 1990, 1999a).

REFERENCES

Aronowitz, Stanley. 1981. "A Metatheoretical Critique of Immanuel Wallerstein's *The Modern World-System." Theory and Society* 10:503–20.

Braudel, Fernand. [1949] 1966. *La Méditerranée et le monde méditerranéen à l'epoque de Philippe II*. Paris: Armand Colin.

———. 1958. "Histoire et sciences sociales: La longue durée." *Annales E.S.C.* (October–December): 125–53. Reprinted in *Écrits sur l'histoire.* Paris: Flammarion, 1969.

———. 1969. *Écrits sur l'histoire.* Paris: Flammarion.

———. 1972. *The Mediterranean and the Mediterranean World in the Age of Philip II.* New York: Harper and Row.

———. 1980. *On History.* Chicago: University of Chicago Press.

———. 1984. *Civilization and Capitalism, 15th–18th Century.* Vol. 3: *The Perspective of the World.* New York: Harper and Row.

Brenner, Robert. 1977. "The Origins of Capitalist Development: A Critique of Neo-Smithian Marxism." *New Left Review* 104:25–92.

Frank, André Gunder. 1990. "A Theoretical Introduction to 5,000 Years of World System History." *Review* 13:155–248.

———. 1998. *ReOrient: Global Economy in the Asian Age.* Berkeley: University of California Press.

Giddens, Anthony, and Jonathan Turner, eds. 1987. *Social Theory Today.* Cambridge: Polity Press.

Hechter, Michael. 1975. "Essay Review." *Contemporary Sociology* 4:217–22.

Hopkins, Terence K., and Immanuel Wallerstein. 1967. "The Comparative Study of National Societies." *Social Science Information* 6:25–58.

———, coordinators. 1996. *The Age of Transition: Trajectory of the World-System 1945–2025.* London: Zed Press.

Lane, Frederic. 1976. "Economic Growth in Wallerstein's Social System." *Comparative Studies in Society and History* 18:517–32.

Lee, Richard. 1996. "Structures of Knowledge." In *The Age of Transition,* coordinated by Terence K. Hopkins and Immanuel Wallerstein, 178–206. London: Zed Press.

Malowist, Marian. 1964. "Les aspects sociaux de la première phase de l'expansion coloniale." *Africana Bulletin* 1:11–40.

———. 1966. "Le commerce d'or et d'esclaves au Soudan occidental." *Africana Bulletin* 4:49–93.

Merton, Robert K. 1957. "The Bearing of Sociological Theory on Empirical Research." In *Social Theory and Social Structure,* 85–101. Rev. enl. ed. Glencoe, IL: The Free Press.

Moretti, Franco. 2000. "Conjectures on World Literature." *New Left Review* 1:54–68.

Nolte, H. H. 1982. "The Position of Eastern Europe in the International System in the Early Modern Times." *Review* 6:25–84.

Polanyi, Karl. 1957. *The Great Transformation.* Boston: Beacon Press.

———. 1967. "The Economy of Instituted Process." In *Trade and Market in the Early Empires,* edited by Karl Polanyi et al., 243–70. Glencoe, IL: The Free Press.

———. 1977. "Forms of Integration and Supporting Structures." In *The Livelihood of Man,* edited by Harry W. Pearson, 35–43. New York: Academic Press.

Prigogine, Ilya. 1997. *The End of Certainty: Time, Chaos, and the New Laws of Nature.* New York: The Free Press.

Skocpol, Theda. 1977. "Wallerstein's World Capitalist System: A Theoretical and Historical Critique." *American Journal of Sociology* 82:1075–90.

Tillich, Paul. 1948. *The Protestant Era.* Chicago: University of Chicago Press.

Wallerstein, Immanuel. 1961. *Africa: The Politics of Independence.* New York: Random House.

———. 1964. *The Road to Independence: Ghana and the Ivory Coast.* Paris: Mouton.

———. 1965. *Africa: The Politics of Unity.* New York: Random House.

———. 1966. "The Decline of the Party in Single-Party African States." In *Political Parties and Political Development,* edited by Joseph LaPalombara and Myron Weiner, 201–14. Princeton: Princeton University Press.

———. 1968. "Frantz Fanon." *International Encyclopedia of the Social Sciences.* Vol. 5:326–27.

———. 1970. "Frantz Fanon: Reason and Violence." *Berkeley Journal of Sociology* 15:222–31.

———. 1974a. *The Modern World-System.* Vol. 1: *Capitalist Agriculture and the Origins of the European World-Economy in the Sixteenth Century.* New York: Academic Press.

———. 1974b. "The Rise and Demise of the World-Capitalist System: Concepts for Comparative Analysis." *Comparative Studies in Society and History* 16:387–415. Reprinted in I. Wallerstein, *The Capitalist World-Economy.* Cambridge: Cambridge University Press and Maison des Sciences de l'Homme, 1979.

———. 1976. "Modernization: Requiescat in Pace." In *The Uses of Controversy in Sociology,* edited by L. Coser and O. Larsen, 131–35. New York: The Free Press. Reprinted in I. Wallerstein, *The Capitalist World-Economy.* Cambridge: Cambridge University Press.

———. 1979a. *The Capitalist World-Economy.* Cambridge: Cambridge University Press.

———. 1979b. "Fanon and the Revolutionary Class." In *The Capitalist World-Economy,* 250–68. Cambridge: Cambridge University Press.

———. 1980. *The Modern World-System.* Vol. 2: *Mercantilism and the Consolidation of the European World-Economy, 1600–1750.* New York: Academic Press.

———. 1986. "Societal Development or Development of the World-System?" *International Sociology* 1:3–17. Reprinted in Immanuel Wallerstein, *Unthinking Social Science: The Limits of Nineteenth-Century Paradigms.* Cambridge: Polity, 1991.

———. 1988. "The Invention of TimeSpace Realities: Towards an Understanding of Our Historical Systems." *Geography* 73:289–97. Reprinted in Immanuel Wallerstein, *Unthinking Social Science: The Limits of Nineteenth-Century Paradigms.* Cambridge: Polity, 1991.

———. 1990. "World-Systems Analysis: The Second Phase." *Review* 13:287–93. Reprinted in Immanuel Wallerstein. *The End of the World as We Know It: Social Science for the Twenty-First Century.* Minneapolis: University of Minnesota Press, 1999.

———. 1991a. *Unthinking Social Science: The Limits of Nineteenth-Century Paradigms.* Cambridge: Polity.

———. 1991b. "World System Versus World-Systems: A Critique." *Critique of Anthropology* 11:189–94.

———. 1995a. *Historical Capitalism, with Capitalist Civilization.* London: Verso.

———. 1995b. "The Significance of Political Sociology." In *Encounter with Erik Allardt,* edited by R. Alapuro et al., 27–28. Helsinki: Yliopistopaino.

———. 1998a. "Pedagogy and Scholarship." In *Mentoring, Methods, and Movements: Colloquium in Honor of Terence K. Hopkins by His Former Students,* edited by I. Wallerstein, 47–52. Binghamton, NY: Fernand Braudel Center.

———. 1998b. "Time and Duration: The Unexcluded Middle, or Reflections on Braudel and Prigogine." *Thesis Eleven* 10:79–87.

———. 1999a. *The End of the World as We Know It: Social Science for the Twenty-First Century.* Minneapolis: University of Minnesota Press.

———. 1999b. "Frank Proves the European Miracle." *Review* 22:355–71.

———. 1999c. "The Heritage of Sociology, the Promise of Social Science." *Current Sociology* 47:1–37.

———. 2000a. "C'était quoi le tiers-monde?" *Le monde diplomatique* (August):18–19.

———. 2000b. "From Sociology to Historical Social Science: Prospects and Obstacles." *British Journal of Sociology* 51:25–35.

Wallerstein, Immanuel, et al. 1996. *Open the Social Sciences: Report of the Gulbenkian Commission on the Restructuring of the Social Sciences.* Stanford, CA: Stanford University Press.

Wulbert, Roland. 1975. "Had by the Positive Integer." *American Sociologist* 10:243.

Zolberg, Aristide. 1981. "The Origins of the Modern World System: A Missing Link." *World Politics* 33:253–81.

Index

About the Authors

Immanuel Wallerstein is Senior Research Scholar in the Department of Sociology, Yale University.

Charles Lemert, a distinguished sociologist, is currently Senior Fellow, Center for Comparative Research at Yale University.

Carlos Antonio Aguirre Rojas is a distinguished social scientist and researcher at the National Autonomous University of Mexico.

Lightning Source UK Ltd.
Milton Keynes UK

9 781594 519796